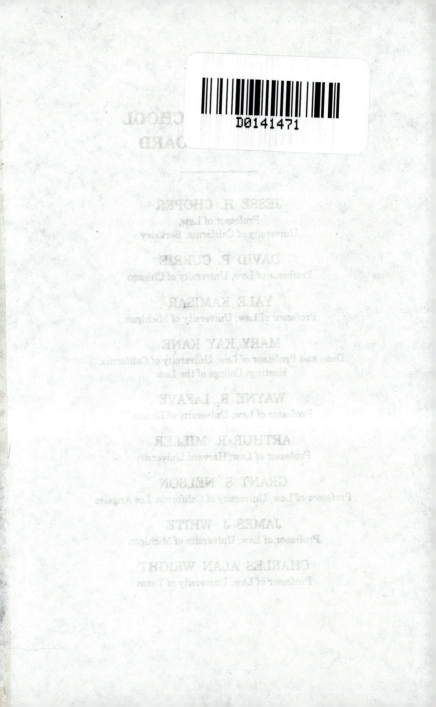

WEST'S LAW SCHOOL
ADVISORY BOARD

JESSE H. CHOPER
Professor of Law,
University of California, Berkeley

DAVID P. CURRIE
Professor of Law, University of Chicago

YALE KAMISAR
Professor of Law, University of Michigan

MARY KAY KANE
Dean and Professor of Law, University of California,
Hastings College of the Law

WAYNE R. LaFAVE
Professor of Law, University of Illinois

ARTHUR R. MILLER
Professor of Law, Harvard University

GRANT S. NELSON
Professor of Law, University of California, Los Angeles

JAMES J. WHITE
Professor of Law, University of Michigan

CHARLES ALAN WRIGHT
Professor of Law, University of Texas

HOW TO STUDY LAW AND TAKE LAW EXAMS

IN A NUTSHELL

By

ANN M. BURKHART
Associate Professor of Law
University of Minnesota Law School

ROBERT A. STEIN
Executive Director
American Bar Association
Formerly Dean and William S. Pattee Professor of Law
University of Minnesota Law School

WEST GROUP

Bancroft-Whitney • Clark Boardman Callaghan
Lawyers Cooperative Publishing • WESTLAW® • West Publishing

For Customer Assistance Call 1-800-328-4880

1996

Nutshell Series, In a Nutshell, the Nutshell Logo and the WP symbol are registered trademarks of West Publishing Co. Registered in the U.S. Patent and Trademark Office.

COPYRIGHT © 1996 By WEST PUBLISHING CO.

610 Opperman Drive
P.O. Box 64526
St. Paul, MN 55164–0526
1–800–328–9352

All rights reserved
Printed in the United States of America

ISBN 0–314–06596–2

TEXT IS PRINTED ON 10% POST
CONSUMER RECYCLED PAPER

To Ruth Vendley Neumann,
whose love of life and love of writing
have been an inspiration

AMB

To Robert Martin Routh, Sarah Elizabeth Routh,
Amanda Stein Conrad, Christopher Stein Conrad,
and Matthew James O'Boyle, who give me great con-
fidence in the future

RAS

*

PREFACE

This book has two purposes. The first is to answer the many questions you have about law school as you begin your studies. Both authors have taught thousands of law students and know the kinds of questions they have. What is a hornbook? What is a tort? Should I join a study group? Should I work during the first year of law school? These and many other mysteries will be explained.

The book's second purpose is to help you maximize your law school experience. The book offers concrete and practical advice on preparing for law school before the academic year begins and for your first-year classes and examinations. Because exams are so important, the book includes questions that were given in actual first-year law school classes and model answers prepared by professors. In many law schools, the professors do not make their answers available to students, so this book gives you a valuable insight into exam grading, as well as an opportunity to practice your exam-taking skills. The book also acquaints you with the law library and with all the other aspects of your first year in law school. With this information, you can get off to a strong start.

Many people have made important contributions to this book. We are grateful to our colleagues, Professors Barry C. Feld, Richard S. Frase, Philip P. Frickey, John H. Matheson, C. Robert Morris, and Eileen A. Scallen, for generously permitting us to publish their examination questions and answers. We are also grateful to three outstanding reference librarians at the University of Minnesota Law Library, George R. Jackson, Suzanne Thorpe, and Julia Wentz, for reviewing drafts and for researching innumerable questions. Special thanks are due to Suzanne for her suggestions for the reading list in Chapter 2. We have been very ably assisted in the preparation of the book by three research assistants, Nancy L. Moersch, William J. Otteson, and Brian J. Schoenborn. Our secretaries, Beverly Curd, Amy Eggert, and Andrea Sheets, have suffered through draft after draft with unflagging patience and professionalism. Finally, the Partners in Excellence Fund at the University of Minnesota Law School generously provided summer research grants to Professor Burkhart, which greatly facilitated work on the book.

In 1971, Professor Stanley V. Kinyon of the University of Minnesota Law School published a book on law study and law examinations, which has helped a generation of law students in their studies. We hope this book will provide the same help to the next generation of law students.

AMB
RAS

OUTLINE

OUTLINE

OUTLINE

OUTLINE

HOW TO STUDY LAW AND TAKE LAW EXAMS

IN A NUTSHELL

*

CHAPTER 1
INTRODUCTION

Hello!

First of all, congratulations on your decision to study law. It will prepare you for a wonderful profession that will challenge you intellectually and will provide you an opportunity to benefit humankind. As a lawyer, you will be able to help people deal with some of the most important events in their lives, such as the death of a family member, adoption of a child, buying a home or business, and defending a criminal charge. Furthermore, law study is excellent training for an enormous variety of fulfilling career choices in addition to the practice of law.

We have written this book in as practical a manner as possible to answer all the questions you might have about the study of law and the writing of law exams. Both authors have taught thousands of law students, and we have learned from them the kinds of questions beginning law students frequently have. We have included in this book all the practical advice we could to maximize your success, to ease your anxieties, and to remove the mystery about the study of law.

1

You are about to embark on a most exciting adventure. You will be entering law school with a very talented group of high achievers and will study under the direction of very bright and knowledgeable professors who will challenge you to do the best work that you can. The study itself is intellectually demanding and will stretch you so that you will grow intellectually. Because the study of law is different from other educational experiences, students sometimes have difficulty understanding how to do it and may not do as well as they had hoped as a result. In this book, we will help you understand it more quickly so that you can get off to a good start.

Our purpose in writing this book is not only to make your law school experience as successful as possible, but also to make it enjoyable. Although it will be intellectually demanding, there is no reason why it should not also be a stimulating and enjoyable experience. We have observed that law students usually experience what they expect in their legal education. If you begin with an expectation of a long, grueling time of anxiety, you probably will find law school to be an unhappy experience. On the other hand, if you look forward to law school as one of the most exciting adventures of your life, you will find that to be true.

Long after lawyers have graduated from law school, they talk about their law school experiences. The friendships made in law school will be some of your closest friendships for the rest of your life. In addition to your classes, law school offers opportunities for intellectual and personal growth through speakers, student organizations, and public interest activities. This demonstrates a very important point. Law school is not just a time of preparation for the rest of your life, it is also one of the high points of your life. Make a commitment to do it as well as you can and to enjoy yourself while doing so.

Our book will guide you throughout the first year of law school as you begin to study law and to take law examinations. In the next chapter, we will begin by reviewing some preparations you should make before you begin the study of law. The months after you have been admitted to law school but before you begin your studies can be used to great advantage.

Chapter 3 is an overview of the American legal system, which you will find helpful in orienting you to your law studies. It is a brief description of the roots and evolution of our legal system and its modern structure. Because our legal system builds on the past, it is important to know the history of the law. You will find it to be helpful to reread this chapter from time to time during your first year.

If you are like most law students, you are unlikely to know which area of the law you want to practice. Therefore, in Chapter 4, we identify the various kinds of work done by lawyers. It will be helpful for you to have in mind the many ways in which lawyers use their legal training as you decide what you wish to do with your legal education.

This will help illuminate the purpose and content of your legal education.

In Chapter 5, we discuss the nature of the study of law. It is a different form of education than you have experienced previously. This chapter will give you an overview of the legal educational process and will help you to understand the purpose of your class discussions and readings.

Chapter 6 will describe the first-year curriculum. Most American law schools have similar first-year educational objectives, although the specific courses may vary somewhat. We have described eight of the most common first-year courses so that you have some idea of what to expect when you begin these classes.

Chapter 7 will guide you through the law library. In the study and practice of law, you will use information intensively. Therefore, you must know what kind of information is available and in what format. You also must become adept at finding these materials in the library and through an electronic research system.

Much of what you learn during the first year of law school will be learned in the classroom. In Chapter 8, we discuss the ways in which you can best prepare for class. In Chapter 9, we discuss the classroom experience. These chapters will enable you to be as well prepared as possible and to maximize the benefits of class discussions.

A great deal of law school learning also occurs outside the classroom, and we discuss that subject in Chapter 10. The chapter describes how to organize the materials you have learned in preparation for the final exam in the course. In that process, you will find it helpful to use various study aids in addition to the materials assigned for your classroom discussion, and that is the next chapter. Chapter 11 describes the different types of study aids and the best ways to use them.

In Chapter 12, we turn to the important subject of exam taking. Law school exams are designed to evaluate your ability to analyze issues presented in the exam question and to describe how they should be resolved. Just as legal analysis is a learned skill, successful exam writing also relies on acquired skills. In this chapter, we will help you develop these skills as quickly and completely as possible.

During your first year of law school, you will have an opportunity to participate in many extracurricular activities. These are the subject of Chapter 13. The chapter also offers valuable advice for balancing the many demands on your time during your first year of law school. In Chapter 14, we introduce you to the challenges and opportunities you will have during your second and third years of law school.

In the last section of the book, we have included a number of examination questions and model answers. These questions are taken from actual law school examinations and show the amount of exam time that was allocated to answer each question. The answers were written by law professors. These samples will acquaint you with the types of questions you will encounter in your own examinations and the kind of answers your professor would like to see you write. These questions provide an opportunity for you to practice your skills of analysis, writing, and time management.

We have made every effort to make this book as helpful to you as possible as you begin your law studies. If there are subjects we have not discussed in this book that you feel would have been of value, please let us know by writing to us at West Publishing Company. We will be pleased to consider your suggestions for future editions of this book.

Good luck on your exciting new adventure.

CHAPTER 2

PREPARING TO ENTER LAW SCHOOL

The time period covered by this chapter begins when you have received notice of your admission to law school and have responded that you will attend. It may be early in the calendar year, and classes will not begin until late summer. The weeks and months before you begin your actual law studies can be used to prepare for your law school experience.

A. READINGS

Reading about the law and the study of law can be helpful to you. This book is intended to be a guide for you, and we hope you will read it in its entirety before you begin your law studies and then reread relevant portions of it throughout your first year. In addition, there are a number of other interesting books about the law and the study of law that you would find helpful.

In addition to books about the law, you might wish to read some books that will introduce you to legal history and legal philosophy. You might find biographies of famous lawyers and judges or accounts of celebrated cases to be interesting. Newspaper reading also is important in order to become knowledgeable about current legal issues and controversies, pending legislation, and recent judicial decisions.

It would not be especially helpful for you to read legal treatises or otherwise try to learn the substance of the law during this time. You do not know what topics your professors will cover, and legal education is not about memorizing legal doctrine. Instead, use your time before law school begins to read for pleasure and for background information. Once school begins, you will have little time for reading other than for your classes.

Here is a list of some books and articles we recommend, although you can find numerous other writings by browsing in the library or a bookstore:

1. NONFICTION

Albert T. Blaustein, The American Lawyer: A Summary of the Survey of the Legal Profession (University of Chicago Press, 1954)

Catherine Drucker Bowen, The Lion and the Throne: The Life and Times of Sir Edward Coke (Little Brown, 1957)

Benjamin N. Cardozo, Selected Writings (Fallon, 1947)

James G. Cozzens, The Just and the Unjust (Harcourt Brace, 1942)

Charles P. Curtis, It's Your Law (Harvard University Press, 1954)

Michael D. Davis, Thurgood Marshall: Warrior at the Bar, Rebel on the Bench (Carol Pub. Group, 1992)

Mary Ann Glendon, A Nation Under Lawyers: How the Crisis in the Legal Profession is Transforming American Society (Farrar, Strauss, & Giroux, 1994)

Learned Hand, The Spirit of Liberty: Papers and Addresses (University of Chicago Press, 3d ed., 1977)

Oliver Wendell Holmes, The Common Law (Little Brown, 1923)

John F. Kennedy, Profiles in Courage (Harper, 1956)

Herbert M. Kritzer, The Justice Broker: Lawyers and Ordinary Litigation (Oxford University Press, 1990)

Anthony Lewis, Gideon's Trumpet (Random House, 1964)

Karl N. Llewellyn, The Bramble Bush: Our Law and its Study (Oceana, 1951)

Dudley Cammett Lunt, The Road to the Law (McGraw Hill, 1932)

Alpheus T. Mason, Brandeis: A Free Man's Life (Viking, 1946)

Roscoe Pound, The Spirit of the Common Law (Marshall Jones, 1921)

Robert Stevens, Legal Education in America from the 1850s to the 1980s (University of North Carolina Press, 1983)

Irving Stone, Clarence Darrow for the Defense (Doubleday, 1941)

2. FICTION

Louis Auchincloss, Powers of Attorney (Houghton Mifflin, 1963)

Charles Dickens, Bleak House (Dent, 1972)

Harper Lee, To Kill a Mockingbird (Lippincott, 1960)

Arthur Train, Tutt and Mr. Tutt (Scribner's, 1924)

B. VISIT YOUR LAW SCHOOL

If at all possible, visit your law school sometime before you arrive to begin your law studies. While there, it would be instructive for you to visit one or more law classes if school is in session. Usually, the admissions office is able to work out class attendance arrangements at least on certain days of the week. Explore the campus and discover what university and law school resources are available, such as medical clinics, athletic facilities, and bookstores.

In addition, you should visit the law school admissions office to get the information you will need for registration for the upcoming school year. If your law school has assigned you a faculty advisor, this would be a good time to meet with that faculty member and introduce yourself. Talk with current students about their recommendations regarding housing, restaurants, and any other questions you may have.

You also might find it helpful to browse through the law library and learn where the various materials and departments are located. You should check out the various reading rooms, tables, and carrels to identify a quiet study space where you can study after you begin law school. You also can acquaint yourself with the circulation policies, library hours, and computer and copying facilities.

C. OTHER PREPARATIONS

Other ways in which you can prepare before law classes begin include visiting a courthouse and observing a trial and talking with lawyers and judges about their work. You also can ask for their tips about the study of law. This is a good time to wind up all of your current commitments so that you will not be distracted by them after you start law school.

Most of all, during the months before you begin your law studies, you should rest up and prepare yourself physically and mentally for an intensive experience. Take time to pursue activities you enjoy—see a movie, read some books, and spend time with family and friends. Establish an exercise and recreation routine that you can continue after starting law school.

D. ARRIVING AT LAW SCHOOL

If you are traveling to another city for your law studies, you should plan on arriving some days in advance of the date for registration. You will need time to find a place to live and to make all the other necessary living arrangements. Your law school may have dormitory rooms available for first-year law students, or you may decide to live in private housing. In either case, you should look for a place close to your law school that is quiet and does not have a lot of distractions. You will be spending a great deal of time in your law library reading materials, oftentimes late into the evening, and so you should minimize the commuting time between home and law school.

If it is possible, take your spouse or partner with you to visit the law school, classes, and campus, to provide that person with a better understanding of what your life as a law student will be like. If you have children or other people for whom you provide care, work out a system for caring for them before school begins. After school starts, there will be enormous demands on your time.

Check the postings on the course board at your law school to determine the books you will need for your courses. Sometimes, that list is available in your law school bookstore. In purchasing your books, be sure to get the correct edition of the casebook, which may be available in used condition, as well as information about any book supplements. If you buy used books, try to find relatively unmarked ones so that you will have enough space to make your own annotations.

Many of your professors will post a reading assignment for the first class. You should identify the place in your school where class assignments are posted and look for your assignments in the days before classes begin. You should read all of the material that will be discussed in the first meeting of each of your classes in order to get off to a good start in your studies.

E. COMPUTERS

One final subject: should you purchase a computer? As a member of the information age, you probably have developed computer literacy by now. You will find a computer to be very helpful in your legal research and writing. It will help you organize your class notes and prepare a course outline. You can use it to type your writing assignments. Your law school may provide you access to online legal research services, so that you can do legal research from your home. Subject to your law school's exam policies, a computer also can be very helpful to you in writing your exam answers under the strict time limitations that apply.

If at all possible, we recommend that you purchase a computer if you do not already have one. If you need to learn how to use it, that would be an excellent use of your time during the weeks before the start of law school. If you do not purchase a computer, find out whether your school makes computers available to students. If so, start learning how to use those computers. You also should investigate the software that is available for briefing cases, creating course outlines, and organizing class notes and research.

CHAPTER 3

THE AMERICAN LEGAL SYSTEM

The law progresses by building on its past. Therefore, to understand the modern American legal system, you must understand its historical background. In your first year of law school, you may be asked to read decisions of seventeenth and eighteenth century courts that include foreign phrases, such as *Nemo est haeres viventis* ("the living have no heirs"), and discussions of archaic actions, such as detinue and trover. While a good legal dictionary is the best tool for solving such mysteries, an appreciation of the American legal system's origins will help you understand how the practice of law evolved to its present form. Therefore, this chapter provides an overview of American legal history, beginning with its roots in England, and of the current American legal system.

A. ENGLISH ROOTS: THE BEGINNINGS OF THE COMMON LAW

The American legal system is a direct descendant of the English system, primarily because many of the original colonists came from England. The

15

legal system they brought with them had evolved over several centuries. It originated in 1066, when William the Conqueror took the throne of England by force. William, who was from the Normandy region of France, claimed all the land of England for his own and imposed a feudal system. In this system, the king retained ownership of all land but granted the right to use large tracts to lords who swore an oath of homage to him and who agreed to provide him with certain services, such as military service.

An important consequence of William claiming ownership of all English land was that a single system of laws could be applied to the entire country. Before William's invasion of England, government was highly decentralized. The basic unit of government was the shire (county), and local courts resolved most disputes between the common people. Local laws and procedures varied widely throughout the country. Although the conquered Anglo–Saxon king and his council had the power to control the local courts, they primarily administered justice for the upper class.

When William took the throne, he agreed that he would not alter the existing laws, and, in fact, the law governing relations between the people was not significantly changed during the next century. However, the methods by which the law was administered were changed. William created a royal council, of which he was the head. Its members were lords to whom he had given land and religious leaders who held church lands. Although the local courts still decided disputes between ordinary citizens, the king increasingly exercised his authority over the courts. Lords were authorized to preside over the courts, and disputes could be removed from the local courts. The king now also appointed the shire sheriffs, which gave him greater control over the shires.

Perhaps the most important development, however, was the creation of the royal courts. After the Conquest, the king's council heard cases involving the upper class, as had its Anglo–Saxon predecessors. Unlike its predecessors, however, the king's council also began to exercise jurisdiction over cases that traditionally had been heard in the local courts. Over time, the royal case load became so large that the king's council could not decide each case. Therefore, to handle the cases, administrative systems were developed that evolved into a variety of royal courts.

To initiate an action in a royal court, the petitioner had to obtain a writ from the chancellor, who was one of the king's chief ministers. The writ set forth the petitioner's allegations and ordered the alleged wrongdoer to either give the requested relief or contest the claim in court. Over time, the types and styles of writs became standardized. If a petitioner's case did not come within one of the existing writs, the chancellor originally could create a new writ for the action. Later, however, that power was substantially curtailed. Thereafter, although a petitioner whose grievance did not fit within an existing writ could petition the king for relief, he would intervene only in exceptional cases.

The body of law applied in cases before the royal courts was called the common law, and the first three royal courts—Common Pleas, Exchequer, and King's Bench—were called common-law courts. The key feature of the common law system is that the law is created by judicial decisions in actual cases. Although law also is created by legislatures, legislation is rather piecemeal in common law jurisdictions. In contrast, the civil law system, which exists throughout continental Europe, Latin America, and in many other countries, is based on legislatively adopted codes that are designed to be comprehensive statements of the law. When a civil law court decides a case, it looks for the relevant code provision and applies it.

In developing the law on a case-by-case basis, common-law courts generally use one of two approaches. When considering an issue that has not been decided previously, a judge derives the applicable legal principle from society's customs and norms. People are far more likely to feel that they have been treated fairly and to support a legal system if it comports with their notions of justice. Sensitive to the charge that they were deciding cases based merely on their personal opinions, however, common-law judges described their decision-making as a process of discovering the law, not of making it.

On the other hand, when considering an issue that has been decided in an earlier case, the doctrine of *stare decisis* ("stand by the decision") requires a judge to apply the law stated in that decision. As early as the thirteenth century, records were kept of judicial decisions and of arguments made on behalf of the parties. During this early period in the common law, the records were sketchy, and previous decisions were treated as simply providing guidance. Over time, however, the doctrine has evolved to require a judge to apply the law stated in an earlier opinion if it was rendered by an equal or superior court in the same jurisdiction. The only exception to *stare decisis* is when conditions have changed so much that applying the law in the previous decision would cause an unjust result.

The common-law courts developed the doctrine of *stare decisis* to create certainty and stability in the law, and the doctrine had that effect. As the law became more standardized, however, it also became unworkably rigid. The judges of the common-law courts strictly applied established procedures, doctrines, and remedies even when they produced unjust results. For example, despite the complexities of the writ system, the common-law courts frequently ruled against a petitioner if the wrong writ had been used or did not contain the precise words required for the writ. The common-law courts also would apply a rule of law to decide a case even if the rule caused a patently unfair result because of the unique facts of the case. Even if a court ruled in the petitioner's favor, the court would grant only money remedies or remedies concerning land. It would not grant an injunction to prohibit future wrongdoing.

Because the king had retained power to administer justice even after creation of the common-law courts, citizens began petitioning him and his council for relief from the court's rigidity. The citizen petitions routinely were delegated to the chancellor, especially as they increased dramatically in number. Eventually, people began petitioning the chancellor directly. By the late fifteenth century, the judicial system created by the chancellor to handle these petitions developed into an established court, Chancery. The chancellor remained at its head.

Chancery attracted a great number of petitions because it was not bound by the common-law court's rigid rules of procedure and law. For example, Chancery could hear a case even if it did not fit within an existing writ, could conduct hearings without a jury when one would be required in a common-law court, and could grant injunctions. Most important, however, Chancery was free to examine the particular facts of a case to determine the most equitable result, regardless of what the outcome would have been by applying the rules of law developed by the common-law courts. For this reason, Chancery was designated a court of equity, and the common-law courts were designated courts of law.

Because Chancery felt free to ignore the rules of the courts of law, two separate bodies of law and procedure developed. In fact, on the petition of a party who lost before a court of law, Chancery might overturn the result reached by that court. Chancery characterized its actions as buttressing, not circumventing, the courts of law by providing relief that otherwise would be unavailable. The judges of the courts of law were understandably skeptical, and the centuries during which this dual court system existed often were marked by a power struggle between them. In the nineteenth century, the courts were merged.

The American colonies and states followed a similar evolutionary path. Many of them established a dual judicial system of law and of equity, but these courts now have been merged with limited exceptions. However, the distinctions between them are still relevant. For example, the right to a jury trial in a civil case extends only to cases that were triable in courts of law. Thus, to decide whether a jury trial can be granted, a present-day court must determine whether the suit historically would have been brought in a court of law or in the court of equity. Similarly, if a litigant requests both a legal remedy (monetary damages) and an equitable remedy (injunctive relief), the jury will decide the legal issues and grant any money damages, and a judge will determine if equitable relief is warranted. Courts still also must deal occasionally with conflicting legal and equitable precedents and actions.

In addition to the dual court system, the American legal system has been influenced in many other important ways by the English system. The colonists adopted both the common-law system of judicially-created law and the doctrine of *stare decisis*. In the absence of a body of American judicial decisions, the colonial and early state courts relied on English judicial decisions to a greater or lesser degree. Over time, however, as the body of American decisions grew, American judges began to rely on those cases. Today, American courts infrequently cite English precedents.

The American adversarial system also is a direct descendant of the English system. In American trials, as in English trials, each party presents the merits of its case before a judge who acts as an impartial referee, rather than as an inquisitor. In many cases, the parties have a right to trial before a jury of their peers. The jury system also is an English tradition.

Although heavily influenced by the English legal system, the American system did not become a carbon copy. Colonial judges created a more simplified court system and eliminated many technicalities of the writ system. Early American judges also rejected those aspects of the common law that were inconsistent with American society. For example, most colonial courts rejected the English legal principle of primogeniture, by which the oldest son inherits all the family property to the exclusion of his siblings. Nevertheless, many of the most important aspects of the modern American system can be traced directly to the English.

B. OTHER INFLUENCES ON THE AMERICAN LEGAL SYSTEM

Just as the differences between America and England caused their common-law systems to develop differently, each state's legal system reflects its unique features, such as its history and geography. For example, the water laws of the arid western states differ dramatically from those of states where water usually is plentiful. One of the most influential circumstances in the development of a state's legal system has been the traditions of its inhabitants. As the United States grew beyond the original thirteen colonies, it extended into areas settled by people from countries that followed the civil law system, rather than the common-law system. For example, the western states' legal systems have been influenced by the Spanish civil law tradition.

The most notable example of the civil law influence in America is the State of Louisiana. During most of the eighteenth century, the land that became Louisiana was controlled first by the French and then by the Spanish. During their periods of control, each of these civil law countries imposed their laws. Shortly after Spain transferred the land back to France, the United States acquired it as part of the Louisiana Purchase in 1803. Although the American government pressed Louisiana to adopt the common-law system, it refused to do so.

In 1808, the Louisiana legislature adopted a civil law digest, which was the basis for the Louisiana Civil Code. The digest was based on French, Spanish, and Roman sources. Although the Louisiana legal system has incorporated some elements of the common-law system, it has remained an island of civil law in the United States as a result of its early French and Spanish inhabitants.

Although the colonies' and states' legal systems were substantially influenced by their European settlers' traditions, they were largely uninfluenced by the cultures of the country's original inhabitants, the Native Americans. In an 1823 opinion, *Johnson v. McIntosh*, the United States Supreme Court characterized the European settlers as conquerors of this country. The Court held that, as conquerors, they were entitled to impose their legal system on the country without regard for pre-existing rights in land or otherwise. Although Native American traditions still play an important role within Native communities, a specialized body of federal law has developed with respect to many other aspects of Native American life. In addition, Native Americans have brought suits in state and federal courts to enforce treaty, religious, and other rights.

C. THE MODERN AMERICAN
LEGAL SYSTEM

The judicially-created common law, rich in history and tradition, is an important part of the American legal structure. Law also is made by the other two branches of government, the legislative and executive branches, and they have played important roles in the development of the American legal system. As described below, each branch of government has unique powers and methods for exercising them. Together, they constitute a system of checks and balances and separation of powers, in which power is distributed among the three branches in such a way that they can check each other's actions. In this way, the country's founders sought to prevent tyrannical rule by any one branch.

1. JUDICIAL BRANCH

The federal government, the District of Columbia, and each state has its own court system. The main federal court system has three different levels of courts: district courts, courts of appeals, and the United States Supreme Court. These are called the Article III courts because they were created pursuant to Article III of the U.S. Constitution. Judges on Article III courts have lifetime appointments, barring misconduct. In addition to these courts of general jurisdiction, a few specialized federal courts exist, such as the bankruptcy courts and tax courts. Federal court judges are appointed by the president, subject to Senate confirmation.

Except for the specialized federal courts, the district courts are the trial courts of the federal system. Litigants first bring their disputes to the district court and present their witnesses and other evidence. The person who brings the lawsuit is the "plaintiff," and the person against whom it is brought is the "defendant." In many cases, the litigants can request that the trial be conducted before a jury. Most cases are heard by one district court judge, though a few types of cases are heard by a panel of three judges.

If a litigant is dissatisfied with the decision at the district court level, the decision can be appealed to the federal court of appeals. There are thirteen circuit courts of appeals. The Courts of Appeals for the First through Eleventh Circuits and for the District of Columbia Circuit each hears appeals from district courts in a particular geographic area that is called a "circuit." For example, as shown on the map, the Court of Appeals for the Second Circuit hears appeals from the federal district courts in Connecticut, New York, and Vermont. The Court of Appeals for the Federal Circuit, on the other hand, hears appeals from a few specialized courts, such as the Court of International Trade, or from federal district courts on certain specialized issues, such as patent law issues.

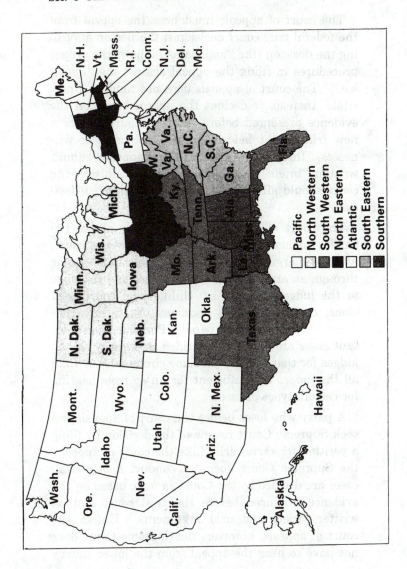

The court of appeals must hear the appeal from the federal trial court decision if the person appealing the decision (the "appellant") follows the proper procedures in filing the appeal against the "appellee." The court of appeals does not conduct a new trial. Instead, it decides the appeal based on the evidence presented before the trial court. Since a new trial is not held, there are no juries or witnesses. Instead, the appellant and appellee submit written "briefs" to the court that explain why the court should affirm or reverse the trial court decision.

The court of appeals also frequently allows the parties to make oral arguments before the court. At an oral argument, each party, either in person or through an attorney, presents its case and responds to the judges' questions. Unlike trial court decisions, court of appeals decisions usually are rendered by a three-judge panel. Particularly important cases are heard and decided en banc by all the judges for that circuit. In some circuits, fewer than all the judges are sufficient for an en banc hearing for certain types of cases.

A party who loses before the court of appeals can seek Supreme Court review of the decision by filing a petition for certiorari. Like the court of appeals, the Supreme Court does not conduct a new trial; cases are decided by the Court en banc based on the evidence produced before the trial court and on written briefs and oral arguments. Unlike the court of appeals, however, the Supreme Court does not have to hear the appeal from the lower court's decision. The Supreme Court will grant certiorari only if at least four of the Court's nine justices vote to grant certiorari. The Supreme Court receives thousands of petitions for certiorari each year and grants only a relatively small number. During the 1994 Term, for example, it received 8,100 petitions and granted only 136, which is less than 2%.

Usually, the Court will grant certiorari only if the case raises a particularly important issue or an issue about which courts of appeal have rendered conflicting decisions. Contrary to popular belief, the Court's denial of certiorari does not necessarily mean that the Court agrees with the lower court's decision. By denying certiorari, the Court simply has decided not to decide. In your civil procedure course, you will learn about more specialized avenues for having a case heard by the United States Supreme Court, such as the right to appeal from a court of appeals decision and the right to a trial before the Supreme Court. You also will study the division of authority ("jurisdiction") between the federal courts and the state courts.

Each state has its own system of courts, most of which are organized like the federal system with district courts (called "trial courts," "circuit courts," or "superior courts" in some jurisdictions), an intermediate appellate court, and a state supreme court. In a few states, the names of the appellate courts are reversed. For example, in New York the trial and intermediate appellate courts are called the "Supreme Court," and the highest court is the "Court of Appeals." Some states do not have an intermediate appellate court, so that a disappointed litigant has only one opportunity to reverse the trial court decision. Many states also have specialized courts for matters such as family law, small claims, or juvenile crimes. The states have different methods for selecting state court judges. In some states, judges are elected; in other states, they are appointed by the governor or legislature or are chosen under a merit plan.

2. LEGISLATIVE BRANCH

Like courts, legislatures play an important role in creating law. Legislative and judicial lawmaking differ in crucial respects, however. Courts make law on a case-by-case basis. The court determines the legality of events that already have occurred, and the court's holding binds only the parties to the case. Laws enacted by a legislature, on the other hand, usually apply only to future actions and to all people within the legislature's jurisdiction. When judicially-created common law and legislatively-enacted law conflict, the latter normally prevails unless it violates the United States Constitution. A state law also is invalid if it violates the state constitution.

At the federal level, legislative power is vested in the United States Congress. Congress is bicameral, meaning that it consists of two chambers, the Senate and the House of Representatives. The Senate has 100 members. Each state elects two senators, each of whom serves a six-year term. The House of

Representatives, on the other hand, has 435 members (sometimes called "congressmen" and "congresswomen"), each of whom is elected for a two-year term. The number of representatives from each state is determined by the state's population. Congress also includes non-voting members from the District of Columbia, Guam, American Samoa, and the Virgin Islands.

Enacting a federal law normally requires several steps. First, a member of Congress must introduce the proposed law (the "bill"). Occasionally, a bill has sponsors in both chambers of Congress and is introduced in both at the same time. When the bill is introduced, it is assigned a number that shows where it was introduced and how many bills had been introduced before it during that session of Congress. For example, the tenth bill introduced in the Senate during a congressional session would be "S. 10," and the fifteenth bill introduced in the House of Representatives would be "H.R. 15." A bill introduced in both chambers would be given two numbers, one for each chamber.

After being introduced, the presiding officer of the chamber in which it was introduced assigns ("refers") it to the committee in that chamber that has jurisdiction over the bill's subject matter. The committee chair then decides whether to put the bill on the committee's agenda. If it is not put on the agenda, it may go no further in the legislative process. If it is included, however, the committee chair normally refers the bill to a more specialized subcommittee. The subcommittee gathers informa-

tion concerning the bill, such as reports from affected agencies, and may hold public hearings. Based
on the information it has received and on its deliberations, the subcommittee can amend the bill. It
then gives the full committee a written report concerning the bill, which includes the subcommittee's
recommendation for committee action on the bill.
If the subcommittee wants to kill the bill for the
legislative session, it will give an unfavorable review
or will not act on it.

If the subcommittee's report is favorable, the
committee will consider the bill. Like the subcommittee, the committee can hold public hearings and
can amend the bill. The committee then determines whether to submit the bill to the congressional chamber of which it is a part. If the committee
decides that the bill should not be considered further, it can give an unfavorable recommendation or,
more simply, fail to act on the bill or table it, which
normally will kill it for the legislative session. If
the committee supports the bill, the committee will
forward it with a favorable recommendation and a
written report that may include an analysis of the
bill and a description of the information that was
gathered during the committee's deliberations and
of any dissenting opinions. If the bill comes within
the jurisdiction of more than one committee, the bill
then must be referred to the other committee(s),
where the same process begins again.

After committee review is completed, the bill and
the committee's recommendation are forwarded to
the congressional chamber in which the bill was

introduced. If the committee recommends the bill, the chamber's leaders decide whether the bill will be considered by the entire chamber. In the House, the Rules Committee also is instrumental in determining whether a bill will reach the House floor. If a bill is sent to the floor, the members of that chamber debate its merits and vote on whether to adopt it. The bill can be amended again on the floor. If the bill passes, it is sent to the other chamber of Congress, where the whole process begins again.

The congressional chamber to which the bill now has been sent and its committees and subcommittees can amend the bill. Therefore, the bill passed by one congressional chamber may differ in language and in substance from the bill passed by the other chamber. If the differences are insignificant, the other chamber simply may accept them. More substantial differences, however, normally will be referred to a conference committee, which includes senators and representatives as members. The committee will attempt to negotiate compromises. If the compromises are accepted by a majority of the committee members from each chamber, the committee issues a report concerning its recommended compromises. Both congressional chambers must approve the report. If they do not, the conflicting bills may be referred back to the committee.

When the Senate and the House have agreed on the terms of the bill, it is sent to the president. Even after all the levels of review and compromise, the bill still may not become law. The president can veto the bill, which will kill it unless Congress overrides the veto by a two-thirds vote in each chamber. If Congress is not in session for ten days after sending the bill to the president, the president's failure to sign the bill (a "pocket veto") also kills it. On the other hand, the bill will become law if the president either signs it or, if Congress is in session, fails to veto it within ten days.

Although the structures and procedures of state legislatures vary, they generally are similar to the U.S. Congress. In every state except Nebraska, the legislature has two chambers. The Nebraska legislature has one chamber ("unicameral"). State legislatures often refer bills to legislative committees. In many states, all the members of a chamber sit as a committee of the whole to consider a bill, rather than referring it to a committee composed of fewer chamber members.

Cities and other smaller political subdivisions often also have a legislature, such as a city council or village board. These legislative bodies normally are unicameral. The committee structure, if any, normally is much less elaborate than at the state or federal level. The laws enacted by these legislatures often are called "ordinances" and are valid only if consistent with the local charter and with state and federal law. Thus, a person can be subject to three or more sets of laws—federal, state, and local—and must comply with each.

3. EXECUTIVE BRANCH

The executive branch is responsible for administering the law. The president, who is the chief executive officer of the United States, occasionally discharges this responsibility by personally creating new law. The president has a few tools to use for this purpose, including an executive order and an executive agreement. An executive order interprets or implements a federal law. An executive agreement, on the other hand, is used in dealings with other countries. Both have the full force of law.

The enormous number and complexity of the laws that must be administered by the executive branch, however, necessitate a more extensive and specialized method of administration. Therefore, a wide variety of activities now are administered by government agencies, such as the Food and Drug Administration, Environmental Protection Agency, and Veterans Administration. Agencies can exercise only those powers that have been delegated to them. Any action an agency takes beyond the scope of its delegated authority is invalid. Interestingly, even though an agency's power is wholly dependent on this delegation of authority, an agency can exercise powers that are unavailable to the legislature, executive, and judiciary. While these three branches of government can exercise only one type of power because of the separation of powers concept, agencies generally can exercise both legislative and judicial powers.

Agencies exercise their legislative power by promulgating regulations. Regulations set standards, such as pollution control standards, and otherwise govern conduct. Like other types of legislation, regulations usually are not focused on particular individuals, but rather are designed to regulate all conduct within the agency's area of authority. Before promulgating binding regulations, an agency normally conducts hearings, publishes proposed regulations for public comment, and responds to the comments. Regulations have the full force of law, though a court can invalidate them if they exceed the scope of the agency's authority or the Constitution.

An agency often also is charged with responsibility for applying its regulations to individuals. In this way, the agency is acting in a quasi-judicial capacity. The agency may adjudicate whether someone has violated a regulation and may impose a fine or other penalty. The agency also might be required to determine whether an individual has satisfied the regulatory standards to obtain a license or other type of government benefit. In exercising these functions, the agency can conduct a hearing, take evidence, and issue a decision.

State executive branches are similar to the federal model, though they differ in some ways. The chief executive officer in state government is the governor. At the local level, the title varies, but "mayor" is commonly used. As is true at the federal level, a great deal of the executive branch's responsibilities are discharged by administrative agencies. State agencies often are similar in form and in function to their federal counterparts.

CHAPTER 4

WHAT DO LAWYERS DO?

Most students entering law school have not yet decided what they would like to do after graduation. Those students who do have a career plan often change their minds after starting their law studies. You should not worry if you are not now ready to make this choice.

As you begin your law study, however, it will be helpful for you to think about what lawyers actually do with their legal training. This will enable you to have various career choices in mind as you consider various subjects in law school and make course selections.

A. GENERALIST TRAINING

One of the most attractive characteristics of law study is that it is useful training for a wide variety of career paths. Indeed, a law degree might be viewed as the ultimate generalist degree. In addition to providing the professional training necessary to be admitted to the practice of law, it also is training in critical thinking and analysis, which are valuable skills for many other occupations, such as business management and elective and appointive government office. Law training also creates

37

knowledge and expertise about process, which is why the lawyer in a group often is the one who is appointed to chair the group, lead the discussion, or write the group's report. These process skills also are important in a wide variety of occupations.

B. THE PRACTICE OF LAW

Most law school graduates do enter the practice of law and do so in a law firm setting. The firm may be very large—up to several hundred attorneys with offices in many cities and countries—or very small—as small as a solo practice. While the large (over 100 lawyers) or medium (25 to 100 lawyers) sized law firm is often the firm setting about which people think, more than half the lawyers who practice law in the United States practice in a solo practice or in a small firm of five or fewer attorneys. The firm size is often significant in determining how many resources are available to assist the lawyer's legal practice. However, many solo or small firm practitioners have access to the types of resources associated with a large firm, such as a large law library, computerized accounting and billing, and other support services, through consortiums of small firms or through electronic online services.

Most law firms are organized as a partnership or as a professional corporation that is equivalent to a partnership. Partnerships are likely to have at least two categories of lawyers in them: partners, who are the owners and share in the profit or loss of the business; and associates, who are salaried employees working for the partnership. There are several variations of these categories, such as non-equity partners and associates who receive bonus distributions of partnership profits. Most typically, a young lawyer initially will be employed by a law firm as an associate and may be promoted to partnership after working for the firm for a number of years. For professional corporations, the categories are similar, but the owners are called shareholders.

Another common category of lawyers working in a law firm is identified by the designation as "of counsel." This title might refer to any one of several relationships. Frequently, it designates a former partner who has retired from the partnership but who still practices with the firm. The term also might refer to a lawyer associated with the firm on a part-time basis or for a particular case. For example, law professors who provide consulting advice to a law firm often are designated as being "of counsel" to the firm.

C. SPECIALIZATION

The complexities of legal practice and a desire to provide a very high quality of legal representation cause many lawyers to specialize in a particular area of law. Generally, the largest law firms have the most specific specializations. Occasionally, however, a solo or small firm practitioner may decide to specialize in a very specific subject and depend on referrals from other law firms as a source of clients. This may be referred to as a "boutique" law firm.

Even if a lawyer specializes in one area, the lawyer must remain generally knowledgeable about other areas of the law. In this way, the lawyer can provide expert services within the area of specialty and can recognize other problems that a client may have that should be referred to another lawyer. Being a lawyer requires a lifetime commitment to continuing professional education, both in the area of specialization and in broad legal developments. This lifetime learning is called continuing legal education.

The number of specialties continues to grow as new fields of practice emerge each year. Oftentimes, an area becomes a specialty area because of the enactment of new legislation. For example, since Congress enacted the Employees Retirement Income Security Act (ERISA) in 1974, it has become a significant specialty area.

The following is a list of many of the specialty areas that you might wish to pursue in your legal practice:

Administrative Law
Admiralty and Maritime Law
Adoption Law
Advertising and Marketing Law
Agency and Partnership Law
Agricultural Law
Animal Law
Antitrust and Trade Regulation Law
Appellate Advocacy
Arbitration
Art Law
Aviation Law
Banking Law
Bankruptcy Law
Biomedical Ethics Law
Biotechnology Law
Business Law
Civil Litigation
Civil Rights Law
Class Action Litigation

Collections Law
Commercial Transactions Law
Commodities Trading Law
Common Carrier Law
Communications Law
Complex Litigation
Computers and Software Law
Constitutional Law
Construction Law
Consumer Protection Law
Contracts Law
Co-op Law
Corporate Finance Law
Corporate Law
Criminal Defense
Criminal Prosecution
Debtor and Creditor Law
Defamation and Libel
Disabilities Law
Discrimination Law
Divorce Law
Domestic Abuse Law
Education Law
Elder Law
Election Law
Employee Benefits Law
Employment Law
Energy Law
Entertainment Law
Environmental Law
Equipment Finance and Leasing Law
Estate Planning
Evidence Law
Family Law
Fidelity and Surety Law
Franchise Law
Gaming Law
Government Contracts Law
Government Relations
Guardianship Law
Health Care Law
Historic Preservation Law
Hospital Law
Human Rights Law
Immigration

Import/Export Law
Insurance Law
Intellectual Property Law
International Law
Investment Banking
Juvenile Law
Labor Law
Land Use Law
Legal Ethics Law
Litigation
Media Law
Mergers and Acquisitions Law
Military Law
Municipal Law
Native American Law
Natural Resources Law
Negligence and Personal Injury Law
Non–Profits and Tax Exempt Organizations Law
Occupational Safety and Health Law
Oil, Gas, and Mining Law
Patents and Trademark Law
Pension Law
Prisoners Rights Law
Probate Law
Product Liability Law
Professional Liability Law
Public Utilities Law
Public Finance Law
Publishing Law
Real Estate Conveyancing and Finance Law
Religion Law
Securities Law
Sexual Harassment Law
Social Security Law
Space Law
Sports Law
Taxation Law
Technology and Science Law
Telecommunications Law
Tort Law
Transportation Law
Utilities Law

Venture Capital Law
White Collar Crime Law
Worker's Compensation Law

There are other practice specialties in addition to subject matter specialties. For example, you might decide to be a specialist in alternative dispute resolution (ADR), in which you would assist parties to resolve a dispute without resorting to a traditional law suit. Or you might decide to practice public interest law—by working for a legal aid office that provides legal assistance to low income clients or by working for a public interest group, such as an environmental law organization or a prisoners rights group.

This brief review shows that you have an enormous number of choices about what kind of law you will practice. In addition, you will have to decide where to practice. You might choose to practice in a small town, a large city, or overseas in the foreign office of an American law firm. You may not be fully prepared to make these choices based upon the information you learn in law school. Studying a subject in law school may not give you a real feel for the practice of law in that area.

You should use your summer employment experiences after your first and second years of law school to examine these choices. Explore different sized firms, different geographic areas, different subject matter specialities, and any other alternatives you are considering so that you will have the maximum information available to make career practice decisions by the time you graduate.

D. CORPORATE LAW OFFICE

Many lawyers practice law within a corporation, bank, or other business as part of an in-house legal department. In the past several years, many in-house law offices have grown in size as corporations have developed more expertise in handling work that formerly was referred to outside law firms. As in a firm, an in-house law department may include many specialty areas, such as litigation, tax, international transactions, government regulation, securities law, and intellectual property law.

E. GOVERNMENT

Another major practice option for lawyers is working for the government. This can be at any level—from the federal government, to the state government, to city and county governments.

At the federal level, many attorneys work for the United States Justice Department or for one of the many federal executive agencies. Within these offices, there may be many areas of specialization. Many other attorneys work for Congressional committees or for the federal court system.

In fact, a large number of attorneys work for courts at all levels of government. These positions include working as a law clerk for a specific judge or as a staff attorney for the entire court. Indeed, a highly prized career opportunity for a recent law school graduate is serving as a law clerk for a judge for a year or two before beginning a permanent position with a law firm or other employer.

At the state level, the State Attorney General's Office is usually the largest employer of attorneys. In addition, many state agencies employ attorneys to handle the agency's work. As at the federal level, the state legislative and judicial branches of government also employ a large number of attorneys.

Another large employer of attorneys are city and county governments who employ attorneys to work in the civil and criminal justice systems. Many attorneys work in the city or county attorney's office handling civil matters, such as land use disputes and litigation. Other attorneys are employed in the district attorney's office prosecuting criminal defendants or in the public defender's office defending criminal defendants.

There are also a large number of attorneys working as military attorneys in both civil law matters and the military justice area. This will frequently, but not always, require the attorney to become a member of the Judge Advocate General's Corps of the military service for which the work is done.

F. LAW–RELATED INSTITUTIONS

Another career choice for attorneys is to work in a law-related institution. For example, law schools hire lawyers to be faculty members and to serve in administrative positions in the school. To become a faculty member, you do not need an advanced law degree beyond the J.D. degree, but you can enhance your chances for such a position by serving as an editor of one of your law school's journals and as a law clerk for a judge. In addition, many other academic departments in higher education appoint lawyers to their faculty—usually to teach law-related subjects, such as business law in the business school or education law in the college of education. A number of other law-related institutions, such as bar associations, law research institutes, and legal publishers, employ a large number of attorneys. They are employed to do legal research, to edit journals, to direct staff work, and to provide management leadership for these organizations.

G. BUSINESS CAREER

It was noted earlier that law is a generalist degree and that it is excellent training for many careers other than the practice of law. Many law graduates use their legal training to enter the business world and pursue a management career even though a law degree is not a prerequisite. Oftentimes, the successful corporate manager holds both a law degree and an MBA. Indeed, the CEOs of many large corporations in the United States have an educational background that includes a law degree. Investment banker, registered securities representative, and insurance underwriter are other business careers commonly pursued by holders of a law degree. The training in critical thinking and analysis, which is at the core of legal education, is of proven value for success in the business world.

The accounting profession attracts many persons with a law degree. Many persons holding both an accounting degree and a law degree go on to become certified public accountants and practice as an accountant, rather than a lawyer.

H. OTHER CAREER PATHS

The number of other careers pursued by persons with a law degree is almost as broad as the number of careers. Law trained persons successfully use their training in a wide variety of occupations from elective and appointive government positions, to the clergy, hospital administration, architecture, and athletic coaching and administration. The skill of critical thinking and analysis learned in law school is a valuable skill that is useful in virtually every avenue of human endeavor.

As a reflection of the value of law study to many different careers, many law schools offer joint degree programs in which a student can obtain both a law degree and a degree in another discipline in less time than would be required to pursue the degrees separately. Some examples of these joint degree programs include:

Law and Business Administration (JD/MBA);

Law and Economics (JD/MA or PhD);

Law and International Relations (JD/MA or PhD);

Law and Journalism (JD/MA);

Law and Medicine (JD/MD);

Law and Public Health (JD/MPH); and

Law and Public Policy (JD/MPP).

I. PRO BONO COMMITMENT

Whatever your career choice or practice specialty, we hope you will recognize your obligation as a member of the legal profession to do "pro bono" (literally, "for the good") legal services without compensation. As a lawyer, you will have an obligation to improve the administration of justice in this country. This obligation may be discharged by providing legal services without fee to those who cannot afford to pay for those services and by working to broaden access to justice for groups that have historically been excluded.

We hope you begin to do pro bono legal services while you are a law student and continue it throughout your career. Pro bono service is one of the characteristics that distinguishes law as a profession.

CHAPTER 5

THE STUDY OF LAW

This entire book is intended to be a practical guide to assist you as you begin the study of law. It will be helpful, however, to take a few pages in this chapter to provide a brief overview of the objectives of the study of law. In this way, you will have a better understanding of the ultimate purpose of legal education before you get caught up in the daily preparation for your classes.

A. THINKING LIKE A LAWYER

The late U.S. Supreme Court Justice Felix Frankfurter, who had been a law professor, once said that the object of law school in the United States was not so much to teach law as to teach "lawyering." By "lawyering," Justice Frankfurter was referring to learning the critical analytical process that has become known as "thinking like a lawyer."

"Thinking like a lawyer" is developing a critical analytic skill that has proven to be very successful in problem-solving—whether it is a legal problem or any other kind of problem. As your class begins its law studies together, you represent a group of highly intelligent individuals who have been given the opportunity to study law from among many thousands of applicants. In your approach to problem-solving, you are not much different from any other group of very intelligent people that might be gathered together. As a result of your law studies over the next several months, however, you will change very significantly as you develop the unique skills and techniques for legal problem-solving referred to by the phrase "thinking like a lawyer." Because this skill or technique is so successful in problem-solving, lawyers tend to be very successful in many fields of endeavor.

Your approach to problem-solving will begin to change very early in your first semester. The class discussion will change noticeably as you and your classmates develop this skill. In addition, you will acquire a legal vocabulary, an awareness of policies underlying legal principles, an understanding of the importance of process, and a sensitivity to professional and ethical norms. It is a very exciting development for your faculty to observe. For this reason, faculty love to teach first-year courses and experience the excitement of this change in the class.

B. SOCRATIC METHOD

The pedagogical approach used in most first-year courses is known as the "Socratic method." It involves teaching by asking questions. The questions are asked by the professor of the whole class, but individual students respond. The whole class participates vicariously, however, by mentally framing their own answers to the questions. The professor will encourage this vicarious response by asking other students whether they agree with the answer of the responding student and by asking other students to critique the answers previously given.

This pedagogical approach was initially used by Dean Christopher Columbus Langdell when he was appointed the first Dean of the Harvard Law School about 125 years ago. Dean Langdell found that he could teach large numbers of students in a lecture hall effectively with this technique. Because the approach worked so well, it has been continued in law schools ever since, particularly in first-year courses. In fact, the Socratic method has been so effective in teaching large classes of students, it has enabled law schools to provide high quality instruction without the lower student-teacher ratio that is more common in other graduate studies.

C. CASE METHOD

In your first-year classes, you primarily will study judicial opinions in appellate cases. This is referred to as the case method of instruction, and your course books will be called casebooks.

The case method of instruction involves a process of reasoning from the specific facts of a case to a general principle established by that case. Then, your professor will ask the class to apply that general principle to other sets of specific facts to determine whether the general principle has been identified precisely. In the process, your professor will ask the class to consider many hypothetical fact situations testing the scope of the general principle. The principle that is identified represents a precedent that will be controlling in future cases.

This method of law development is known as the common law, in which prior judicial decisions form the basis of determining how future cases will be decided. The factual patterns of the prior case and the subsequent cases may be extremely different, but the principle established in the prior case may control the decision in the different factual setting of the subsequent cases.

In engaging in case method analysis, you should be very conscious of the facts of the case. It will be necessary to distinguish relevant facts from those that are irrelevant to the decision in the case. Your professor will ask you many questions to ascertain whether a particular fact is or is not relevant.

Determining the scope of the principle of a case is critically important to predicting the result of future cases. When your professor asks a series of questions about the breadth of a principle established by a case, you may find yourself led far out on a limb as the professor changes the facts ever-so-slightly with each question. You then may find the limb abruptly sawed off, as your professor points out that you have asserted a principle that would produce an unwise or even ridiculous result on some set of facts. You should not take this criticism personally, because it is not intended to be. Instead, it is part of the process by which you will learn to think critically about the exact scope of a legal principle established by a case.

D. OTHER LAW SCHOOL INSTRUCTION

Law school instruction has improved enormously in recent years. You will have more clinical educational programs, more skills training courses, more seminars, more interdisciplinary courses, and more international study opportunities than law students had even a few years ago. But the Socratic method of instruction, combined with the case method of analysis, continues to be the dominant pedagogical approach used in the first year of law school.

CHAPTER 6

FIRST–YEAR CURRICULUM

The first year of law school is designed to introduce law students to the analytical skills discussed in the prior chapter, which are referred to as "thinking like a lawyer." This is typically done in several broad conceptual courses that form the foundation for many of the advanced courses that may be taken in the second and third years of law school. In most law schools, all your first-year courses will be required. Even in law schools that permit an elective course in the first year, you probably will be limited to only one elective course. All the students in your required first-year courses will be first-year students like yourself (referred to as 1Ls in many law schools).

A. FIRST–YEAR COURSES

At most law schools, the first-year curriculum includes courses in the following broad conceptual subjects: civil procedure, constitutional law, contracts, criminal law, property, and torts. In some schools, criminal procedure or legislation may be added to that list, and one or more of the subjects may be moved to a later year. In addition, many law schools include an introduction to law course that covers a variety of subjects to introduce students to the legal process.

The specific content of each of the broad substantive courses varies depending on the casebook used and the specific subjects in which the professor is most interested and knowledgeable. For example, a course in property law might or might not include a unit on the law concerning possession of wild animals to introduce students to the concepts of possession and ownership. The course may or may not include historical materials on the different estates in land to give students a conceptual grounding in the concepts of ownership in our modern property law. Today, most property courses include a variety of topics relating to housing issues, such as landlord and tenant law, federal housing regulation, and zoning. Most first-year property courses also will introduce students to the basics of modern real property conveyancing and financing law. The emphasis in the course will vary greatly, however, depending on the professor and on the casebook used.

Recognizing that the specific first-year course content will vary from professor to professor, the following are topics that may be covered in the most common first-year courses. Because of time constraints, it is unlikely that any one course would cover all of the topics identified for that course.

1. CIVIL PROCEDURE

Civil Procedure ("Civ Pro") provides an overview of the civil litigation system and the procedural requirements of filing and maintaining civil lawsuits (or, in popular lawyerly parlance, "actions"). The course usually centers upon the study of the Federal Rules of Civil Procedure, which many state courts have adopted as well. Note that the course is devoted to *civil* litigation, not criminal prosecution, which is dealt with in other courses. Common civil procedure topics include:

Jurisdiction. Does a particular court have the power to issue binding judgments over a particular matter? This will depend on the type of claim, the parties (or property) involved, and the constitutional or statutory power of the court hearing the case. Federal and state courts operate under different rules and look at different factors in determining whether jurisdiction in a given case is proper.

Choice of law. Depending on the subject of the lawsuit and the location of the pertinent parties and occurrences, courts often must decide a case based on the applicable substantive law of another jurisdiction. That is, a court in New York may find itself looking at the rulings of a court in Oregon to decide the proper outcome of a case. Many civil procedure courses address how a court should determine the appropriate law to apply.

Pleadings, claims, and defenses. All jurisdictions have procedural rules governing the filing of lawsuits, responding to lawsuits, filing countersuits, and the like. Civil procedure covers these rules.

Discovery. Discovery is the fact-finding process that the parties to a lawsuit go through before a case goes to trial. Many procedural rules govern how adversaries may obtain information from one another to prepare for trial. This may include scheduling expert examinations, taking depositions, and developing and responding to interrogatories.

Motions. The rules of civil procedure allow for lawyers to make motions of many kinds, such as motions to dismiss a case for some procedural flaw (such as improper jurisdiction), motions to strike language from the record, motions to dismiss based upon an insufficient claim, and summary judgment motions. For a motion to be successful, it must satisfy certain criteria specific to that motion.

Res judicata and collateral estoppel. As a law student, you cannot avoid learning a bit of Latin to impress (or disgust) your friends, and civil procedure is no exception. The law of claim preclusion (*res judicata*) and issue preclusion (collateral estoppel) considers what effect prior decisions have on current lawsuits. For instance, if a court finds in one trial that Charlie Truckdriver was negligent when he collided with Dawn Driver, does it follow that he was negligent with respect to Patty Passenger, who was riding with

Dawn at the time? The issues become infinitely more complex than this, but you get the idea.

2. CONSTITUTIONAL LAW

Constitutional Law ("Con Law") provides an introduction to the United States Constitution and its delegation of rights and obligations among the states, citizens, and branches of federal government. Because of the doctrine of judicial review, the Supreme Court of the United States has long been the final arbiter on the meaning and interpretation of the Constitution. As a result, the course focuses primarily on the Constitution and the Supreme Court cases interpreting it. Common topics include:

Judicial review. Nowhere in the Constitution itself does it say who has the last word on constitutional issues. In the important constitutional case of *Marbury v. Madison,* the Supreme Court established that "it is emphatically the province and duty of the judicial department to say what the law is." The Constitutional Law course examines the desirability, scope, and effect of this decision and its implications for our system of government.

Procedural aspects of constitutional litigation. As with any lawsuit, constitutional claims must be included in an actual case or controversy between adverse parties. The parties must have legal "standing" to assert a claim, the claim must be "ripe" (actually existing and not merely anticipatory), and the claim cannot be "moot" (no longer an issue because of subsequent events).

Government structure. Federalism, intergovernmental relations, and separation of powers issues often arise in conflicts between states, between a state and the federal government, or between branches of the federal government. How such claims are resolved is a matter for Supreme Court consideration.

Individual rights and limitations on government power. To what extent does the Constitution protect the rights of the citizens? The bulk of most Constitutional Law courses focuses on this issue as it applies to economic and property claims, equality under the law, personal liberties, and freedom of speech and of religion.

3. CONTRACTS

The Contracts course covers the law of contract and promissory obligation under the common law rules of the various states. In some courses, the Uniform Commercial Code article on sales law is also covered. Topics in the Contracts course typically include:

Formation of contracts. At what point does a contract possess the legal authority to bind the parties to it? The Contracts course looks at the concepts of offer, acceptance, consideration, and revocation. Few law students have survived law school without paying homage to the various permutations of the dreaded "mailbox rule."

Legal validity and construction. A good contract will sufficiently define and delineate the rights and obligations of the parties to it. As such, examples of well-drafted contracts rarely find their way into Contracts casebooks. Moreover, the law has developed rules governing the interpretation of contracts when something does go wrong. These rules and doctrines include parol evidence, mistake, unconscionability, and changed circumstances.

Material breach vs. substantial performance. One party to a contract may sue another party to the contract if the other party has breached the contract. Much of contract law concerns how courts should determine when a breach occurs and when a contract has been satisfactorily performed.

Remedies. If one party breaches a contract, what is the other party's remedy? The course looks at the issues of damages and court-ordered performance.

4. CRIMINAL LAW

Criminal Law ("Crim Law") courses focus on the nature of the criminal justice system in modern America. Topics include:

Purposes and functions of the criminal process. How does the criminal justice system work? Who are the parties involved and what is the extent of their powers?

Justification of punishment. Why do we punish criminals? This is a question that most lay people take for granted, but a solid understanding of the criminal law cannot leave the question unanswered. Types of punishment and issues of sentencing also are addressed.

Establishment of guilt. Two of the most significant concepts in criminal law are the presumption of innocence and the "beyond a reasonable doubt" burden of proof. Most Criminal Law courses spend time considering the rationale and effect of these concepts.

Defining criminal conduct. What are the statutory requirements for establishing the commission of various crimes? Two important concepts, *actus reus* (a "bad act") and *mens rea* (a "vicious will"), are considered. Many courses apply these concepts through the study of the Model Penal Code, often with respect to specific crimes such as rape and homicide.

5. CRIMINAL PROCEDURE

The Criminal Procedure ("Crim Pro") course addresses the procedural aspects of the investigation and adjudication of criminal violations. Most Criminal Procedure courses focus on the Supreme Court's interpretation of the fourth, fifth, and sixth amendments to the Constitution:

Fourth amendment. The fourth amendment prohibits unreasonable searches and seizures and requires authorities to have probable cause to obtain a search warrant. In examining whether these requirements have been satisfied, courts look to various doctrines and legal tests. If the amendment is violated, the seized evidence can be withheld from the jury under the "exclusionary rule."

Fifth amendment. The fifth amendment is a laundry list of criminal procedural requirements. It requires a grand jury indictment in many cases, prohibits the suffering of double jeopardy (multiple punishments for the same offense), grants a privilege against self-incrimination, and prohibits the government from depriving an individual of "due process."

Sixth Amendment. The sixth amendment includes such rights as the right to a speedy and public trial by an impartial jury, the right to be informed of the nature of the accusation, the right to confront witnesses, and the right to assistance of legal counsel.

6. LEGISLATION

While many first-year courses focus on common law (i.e., judge-made law), most aspects of modern life are now regulated by statutes passed by the Congress and the various state legislatures. Like a contract, statutes often require judicial interpretation to inform their meaning in a particular case. The Legislation course looks at the role of legislation and the legislative process in American law, the relationship between legislation and the common law, and the formulation of legislative policy. The course mainly focuses on methods of statutory interpretation and implementation.

7. PROPERTY

The Property course covers the law's protection of possession and ownership of real and personal property. Much of American property law is derived from the English system, which evolved over hundreds of years. Topics include:

Role of sovereign in defining property rights. Who determines legal ownership of property? To what extent may property rights be created and diminished, and by whom? These threshold questions are often addressed at the outset in Property courses.

The estate concept. Common usage of the term "estate" conjures up notions of deceased relatives. In legal parlance, "estate" has a much broader meaning and refers to the right, title, and interest a person holds in a given piece of property. The nature of one's estate in property depends on the nature of its acquisition, its limitations, and other factors.

Landlord-tenant law. At last, a legal concept with which most law students are intimately familiar—or so you thought. Landlord-tenant law concerns the legal relation between the lessor (landlord) and lessee (tenant) of real estate. The relationship is a contractual one and must satisfy certain requirements. Many property cases examine the extent to which legislatures have increased the rights of tenants in the interest of fair housing.

Future interests. If a person holds a future interest in property, that person does not have the right to possess and enjoy that property yet but may in the future. There are many varieties of future interests, each offering an assortment of characteristics, requirements, and consequences. You will learn them all.

Rule Against Perpetuities. The Rule Against Perpetuities (affectionately referred to as "RAP") is the source of much confusion and befuddlement for many law students. It is actually part of the law of future interests and works to limit the power of a deceased owner to control the use of property at points too remote in the future.

Concurrent estates. When two or more people have the right to possess the same piece of property, many issues arise. What happens if one of them dies? May the interest be willed to another against the wishes of the survivor? May the interest be sold? What is the value of each interest individually? The law has established several forms of concurrent ownership, each of which results in different answers to these and other questions. Many Property courses consider concurrent ownership issues in the context of the marital relationship.

Real property conveyancing and financing. Most Property courses provide an introduction to the basic principles of conveyancing and financing real property.

8. TORTS

What is a tort? The Torts course examines various types of wrongs that violate the legal rights of another and for which damages (usually, money) can be obtained. Tort law is almost entirely common law-based, so the course will examine the evolution of tort law through numerous case opinions. Torts come in many varieties, including:

Intentional torts. The intentional torts are battery, assault, false imprisonment, infliction of mental distress, trespass to land, trespass to chattels, and conversion. For each of these torts, certain elements must be proved. Conversely, each of these torts allows for certain privileges and defenses.

Negligence. Even unintentional but harmful actions may result in liability. Like intentional torts, the law of negligence requires the establishment of certain elements. Defense of a negligence claim requires the establishment of certain privileges and defenses.

Additional topics often covered include imputed negligence, strict liability, products liability, nuisance, defamation, and privacy.

B. LEGAL RESEARCH AND LEGAL WRITING

In addition to the substantive courses, in most law schools the first-year curriculum includes a course on legal research and legal writing. The legal research portion of the course introduces students to the materials and services available in the law library and teaches the research methods for using them, including electronic research. As a specialized body of knowledge, the law has its own publications and reference systems. As a result, you will be learning a method of research different from any you have used before. Strong research skills are essential to your success in law school and in the practice of law. Chapter 7 of this book gives you an overview of the legal resource materials and research methods.

The legal writing portion of the course teaches the techniques for writing legal documents, such as memoranda and legal advocacy briefs. Just as legal research is different from other types of research, legal writing is different from many other forms of writing. Although briefs and other legal documents may be written in forceful and stirring language, most legal writing is a form of technical writing. The key emphases are on preciseness and conciseness. For example, in some other forms of writing, such as in a creative writing course, varying the words that are used to describe the same object or event is highly desired. In legal writing, however, using two different words to describe the same object or event creates potential confusion as the reader tries to determine whether a difference in meaning was intended by using the different words. Therefore, you must learn to master the unique rules of legal writing.

C. FIRST–YEAR SECTIONS

Most law schools divide the first-year class into several sections of students. You will be assigned to a section and will take all your first-year courses with that section, either alone or in conjunction with other first-year sections. Because you will be spending so much time with the other students in your section and will get to know them through your class discussions and study groups, some of your closest friends throughout law school will be classmates in your first-year section. Indeed, many lifelong friendships result from students being in the same section in the first year of law school.

D. GRADING

The system of grading varies considerably from law school to law school, so it is difficult to be specific about what you will experience. A few generalizations can be made, however.

In most first-year law school courses, your grade will be based primarily, if not exclusively, on your final examination answer. Some professors will give some weight to your class participation or to a mid-term exam that might be given. You should ask your professor to clarify the basis for your final grade in the course.

Law schools want to ensure that grading is impartial. As result, most, if not all, law schools use a blind system of grading so that a professor will not know the identity of the student when giving a grade to an exam answer. You will be given an exam number to write on your examination blue book, and that number will be used to assign the grade to you. The professor normally will be told the students' identities and grades after the grades have been made available to the students.

In some law schools, records are not kept for grades that are given in the first semester of the first year. The purpose of such a policy is to give all the students some time to learn the skills of critical analysis and of writing law exams before their permanent law school academic record is established. Before the school year begins, you should investigate your school's policy.

E. A REMINDER

You continually should keep in mind that the primary objective of the first year of law school is to learn the skill of legal analysis—of "thinking like a lawyer." This skill is learned by studying judicial opinions in several broad conceptual courses in the first-year curriculum. In addition to developing the critical analytical skills, you will be expected to learn fundamental principles in these substantive areas. These broad principles will be foundational for much of the rest of your law school courses.

CHAPTER 7

FINDING YOUR WAY AROUND THE LAW LIBRARY

Whoever first described the common law as the "unwritten law" had never seen a modern law library. The average American law library collection consists of thousands of books, periodicals, and other reference materials. These materials include decisions by trial courts, intermediate appellate courts, and courts of final appeal in the state and federal court systems; laws enacted by cities, counties, states, and the federal government; regulations promulgated by local, state, and federal agencies; treatises and other writings by legal scholars; legal journals and digests; and laws and judicial decisions from countries around the world. Knowing how to make your way through this maze is an essential skill for law school and for the practice of law. In fact, a lawyer has an ethical obligation to research the law to provide competent representation for a client.

Legal research is the core of an attorney's practice because of our system of law. The common law system is built on past decisions by courts and by laws enacted by legislatures. Therefore, to determine the state of the law on an issue, you must research at least the judicial precedents and legislative enactments on that issue. Your school's law library will contain many, if not all, the tools you will need for your research. This chapter will describe the most important of these tools.

A. CASE LAW

As described in Chapter 3, our system of common law is heavily dependent on previously decided cases. Therefore, most of the reading in your law school courses, especially during the first year, will center on the judicial opinions in your casebooks. In addition to these opinions, you will want to read the opinions in other cases to learn more about the subjects you are studying and to perform legal research. To find these cases in the law library, you will use a "case citation." Citations guide you to the exact location of an individual case among the hundreds of thousands that have been published.

Judicial decisions are published in books called "reporters." Many reporters also include a "syllabus" and "headnote" at the beginning of each case, which summarize the decision and the statements of law in the opinion, respectively. Reporters also include an index to the opinions published in that volume and may include a subject index.

Reporters are published at the federal, state, and regional levels. Decisions of the federal courts are published in several different series of reporters, each of which includes opinions for a particular court level. The Federal Supplement (F.Supp.) contains decisions of the federal district courts. Decisions of the federal courts of appeal are published in the Federal Reporter (F., F.2d, or F.3d). Decisions of the United States Supreme Court are published in three different reporters, each of which contains all the United States Supreme Court decisions: United States Reports (U.S.), United States Supreme Court Reports, Lawyers' Edition (L.Ed. or L.Ed.2d), and Supreme Court Reporter (S.Ct.). The Supreme Court reporter that you use is a matter of personal preference, although the preferred citation is to United States Reports. In fact, many courts require that Supreme Court case citations be to United States Reports because it is published by the federal government (the "official" reporter). In addition to these reporters, reporters are published for some of the specialized federal courts, such as the Reports of the United States Tax Court (T.C.) and the Bankruptcy Reporter (B.R.).

At the state level, cases often are published in more than one series of reporters. Most states publish their own reporters, which include only decisions by that state's courts. In some states, decisions by the intermediate appellate court and by the highest appellate court are published in the same reporter. In other states, they are published in separate reporters. For example, Massachusetts publishes both Massachusetts Appeals Court Reports, which includes decisions of the Massachusetts Court of Appeals, and Massachusetts Reports, which includes decisions of the Supreme Judicial Court of Massachusetts. Some states also publish reporters for more specialized courts. Most states do not publish trial court opinions because they are so numerous and have limited precedential value.

Some states publish their own official case reporters. In many states, however, cases are published only in the "unofficial" West National Reporter System. This System divides the United States into seven geographic regions and publishes a separate reporter series for each: Atlantic (A. or A.2d), North Eastern (N.E. or N.E.2d), North Western (N.W. or N.W.2d), Pacific (P. or P.2d), South Eastern (S.E. or S.E.2d), South Western (S.W. or S.W.2d), and Southern (So. or So.2d). For example, the Southern Reporter includes state court decisions from Alabama, Florida, Louisiana, and Mississippi. The geographic coverage of each reporter is shown on the map on page 72.

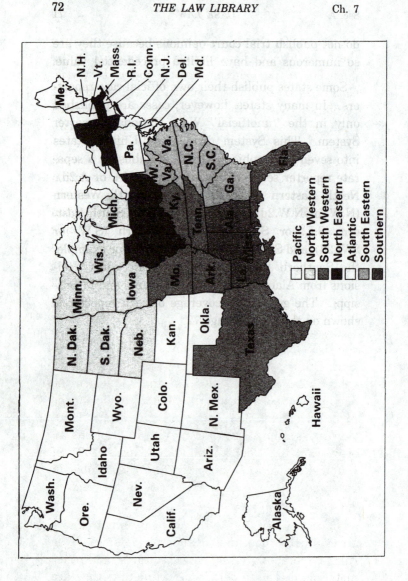

Citations (or "cites") to the reporters always take the same form. For example, the citation to the published opinion in the case *Garratt v. Dailey* is: *Garratt v. Dailey*, 46 Wash.2d 197, 279 P.2d 1091 (1955). Two separate citations are given ("parallel citations") because this opinion is published in two different reporters—the State of Washington reporter and the Pacific regional reporter. Between the two numbers in each citation is the abbreviation for the reporter system in which the case is published. *Garratt v. Dailey* is found in the Washington Reports, Second Series (Wash.2d) and in the Pacific Reporter, Second Series (P.2d). The "2d" shows that when the number of volumes in the series became too large, the publisher began numbering the new volumes from number 1 again. As you can see, each of the reporter systems in which *Garratt v. Dailey* is published was in its second series. Once you have located the appropriate reporter series in your library, the number preceding the reporter abbreviation in the cite is the volume in which the opinion is published, and the number following the reporter abbreviation is the page number. Thus, *Garratt v. Dailey* begins on page 197 of volume 46 of Washington Reports 2d and on page 1091 of volume 279 of Pacific Reporter 2d. The number in parentheses at the end of the cite is the year in which the case was decided.

An accurate citation is the only easy way to locate a case in the thousands of reporter volumes. The rules for properly citing cases, statutes, and other materials are quite detailed. Fortunately, they are contained in A Uniform System of Citation, known to lawyers and law students as The Bluebook. If you have not done so already, you should purchase this inexpensive book and keep it within easy reach.

Obviously, judicial decisions cannot be published immediately in the bound reporters. Instead, courts in most states first disseminate decisions to subscribers and to certain government document depositories in the form of individual "slip opinions." After a sufficient number of slip opinions has accumulated, they are published together in volumes called "advance sheets." The advance sheets are organized in the same manner as the reporters but are published in paperback form. When a sufficient number of advance sheets has accumulated, they are published as the next volume of the hardbound reporter series.

The United States Law Week, which is published by The Bureau of National Affairs in Washington, D.C., is a good source for recent U.S. Supreme Court decisions. Law Week is published weekly and prints U.S. Supreme Court decisions in their entirety, as well as excerpts from cases of general interest from other federal and state courts. Law Week generally is second only to slip opinions in the speed with which it publishes opinions. It also reports on the status of cases on the U.S. Supreme Court's docket, judicial and executive nominations and confirmations, and other items of national interest. Your school's law library should have a Law Week subscription.

B. CASE DIGESTS

Knowing how to find cases from their citations is only the beginning of legal research in the library. Often, you will want to find cases about a certain issue but do not have any citations. In that situation, you can use the case digests. Digests are a subject-matter index to the case reporters and help you locate cases involving a specific issue. Digests are arranged alphabetically by legal topic. For each topic, the digest includes a listing of each case in which a court has addressed that topic and a brief description of the court's opinion.

The West Publishing Company key number digest system is the most widely used. West publishes state digests, regional digests, federal digests, and comprehensive digests.

1. STATE DIGESTS

West publishes a separate digest for the judicial decisions in each state, except Delaware, Nevada, and Utah, and for the District of Columbia. Cases from North and South Dakota are combined in one digest, as are cases from Virginia and West Virginia. The digests include all the appellate court decisions for that jurisdiction's courts and all the federal court decisions for cases arising in or appealed from that jurisdiction.

2. REGIONAL DIGESTS

West also publishes a separate digest for each of the Atlantic, North Western, Pacific, and South Eastern Reporters. West digests exist for the North Eastern Reporter for cases until 1972, for the South Western Reporter for cases until 1958, and for the Southern Reporter for cases until 1988. For more recent decisions in these three regions, you can use the relevant state digest or the American Digest System, which is described below. The regional digests include only state court decisions.

3. FEDERAL DIGESTS

The West federal digests include opinions from all the federal courts and are divided into five time periods. West's Federal Digest includes cases from before 1939; Modern Federal Practice includes cases from 1939 to 1960; West's Federal Practice Digest 2d includes cases from 1961 to 1974; and West's Federal Practice Digests 3d and 4th include cases from 1975 to date. West also publishes a digest that includes only United States Supreme Court decisions—the U.S. Supreme Court Digest—and digests for certain specialized federal courts, such as the Bankruptcy Digest for bankruptcy court decisions.

4. COMPREHENSIVE DIGESTS

Finally, West publishes the American Digest System, which includes digest entries for the cases in

West's state, regional, and federal digests. The American Digest System is divided chronologically into three parts: (1) the Century Digest, which includes digests of cases decided from 1658 to 1896, (2) the First through Tenth Decennial Digests, which include digests of cases in five-year or ten-year intervals from 1897 to 1991, and (3) West's General Digest, Eighth Series, which includes digests of cases from 1991 to the present. Although the American Digest System is bulky and can be time-consuming to use, it provides a good overview of the case law in all jurisdictions. This overview is particularly valuable to determine trends in the law and to research issues that have not been decided in your jurisdiction. Digests are updated at least annually by "pocket parts," which are inserted into the back of each volume. Therefore, when using a digest, always check the pocket part to ensure that you have the most recent information.

A primary reason for the widespread use of the West digests is their use of the West "key number system." West has categorized the law into groups of topics and subtopics. Each topic has an individual "key number," which consists of a general topic name, such as "Libel," and a number for each subtopic within that topic name. You can find the key number for the issue you are researching by referring to the Descriptive Word Index, which usually is located at the beginning of each digest system. The same key numbers are used in all West publications, including digests (except the Century

Digest) and case reporters, to form a uniform and comprehensive system of legal reference.

For a better understanding of the West digest system, try working through the following research problem. Assume that you represent a client in Iowa who wants to know if her child can be subjected to corporal punishment in a public grade school. You would begin your research by looking for the relevant key number in the Descriptive Word Index for the Iowa Digest or for the North Western Digest, which is the region in which Iowa is located. Search for the narrowest applicable topic, which in this case is "Corporal Punishment." Skimming through the entries under "Corporal Punishment," you will find "PUPILS of public schools. Schools 176." Next, you should check the pocket part of the Descriptive Word Index for any more recent entries. Finding none, you now know that the key number you should research is "Schools 176." You should locate the topic "Schools" in the Iowa or North Western Digest and then locate subtopic 176 under "Schools." Under this key number, you will find the citation for an Iowa decision from 1961. The digest entry also includes the citation for any published decision rendered by a court to which the case subsequently was appealed. You then should check the pocket part for any more recent cases. To ensure that the 1961 decision is on point, you should use the case citation to locate the case and then read it to determine what effect, if any, that decision will have on your case.

C. LEGISLATION AND CONSTITUTIONS

In addition to case law, legislation and constitutions are the primary sources of law in our legal system. Unlike case law, which is fact specific, legislation and constitutions normally address issues at a more generalized level. They govern classes of activities, rather than specified individuals. Moreover, legislation normally applies only prospectively, rather than to past actions as is true of case law. Like case law, however, a wealth of resources are available to assist you in your research. Each resource usually focuses on either federal law or an individual state's or municipality's laws.

1. FEDERAL

All public laws enacted by the United States Congress are published in the federal codes, as is the United States Constitution. The official federal code is United States Code (U.S.C.). It is the official code because it is printed and sold by the U.S. Government Printing Office. The U.S.C. classifies federal law into fifty topics, called "titles," that are further divided into chapters and subchapters. Each law ("statute") also is assigned a section number. To cite a statute, you give the title number, the code, and the section number. For example, 42 U.S.C. § 9607 refers to the statute printed as § 9607 in the United States Code volume that contains title 42. Because U.S.C. is the official code, you should cite to it in documents, rather than to an unofficial code, whenever possible.

Usually, the best way to find a particular statute in U.S.C. is to use its topic index. The index is reprinted only approximately every six years, so you also should check the annual supplement to the index. You also may be able to locate a statute by using U.S.C.'s popular name table, which lists statutes alphabetically by their commonly known name. When you find your statute in U.S.C., you will see that U.S.C. publishes only the text of the statute.

In addition to U.S.C., two unofficial federal codes are published by private companies. United States Code Annotated (U.S.C.A.) is published by West Publishing Company, and United States Code Service (U.S.C.S.) is published by Lawyers Cooperative Publishing. These unofficial codes are organized in the same manner as U.S.C., and their citation forms are very similar. The Bluebook details the exact forms. As with U.S.C., the easiest ways to locate a particular statute in U.S.C.A. or in U.S.C.S. are the code's topic index and the popular name table.

Unlike U.S.C., however, U.S.C.A. and U.S.C.S. publish more than just the text of statutes. They also publish information such as citations to legislative histories and to cases and other writings that analyze the statutes. U.S.C.A. also includes citations to West key numbers and publications. U.S.C.S., on the other hand, includes citations to A.L.R. annotations and to other Lawyers Cooperative publications.

U.S.C.A. and U.S.C.S. also are updated more frequently than U.S.C. Pocket parts are issued annually for U.S.C.A. and for U.S.C.S., and additional updates are provided in separate soft-cover form during the course of the year. Supplements to U.S.C., on the other hand, may not be distributed for more than a year after Congress has enacted a law.

Because Congress enacts hundreds of laws each year, immediately incorporating them into the bound code would be an almost impossible task. Therefore, just as with cases, temporary methods of cataloguing new statutes have been developed. When a law or an amendment to a law is first enacted, the U.S. Government Printing Office publishes it as a "slip law." Like a slip opinion, a slip law is a separately published copy of a new law. Slip laws are published monthly in the United States Code Congressional and Administrative News (U.S.C.C.A.N.). At this point, the new statutes are arranged by public law (P.L.) number, which is the number assigned to each new law. At the end of each congressional session, the slip laws are published by date of passage in United States Statutes at Large. Unfortunately, Statutes at Large usually is unavailable until more than a year after the session has ended. However, it is valuable because it contains every law passed by Congress, including "private" laws directed at a particular individual or individuals. The codes, on the other hand, generally include only the "public laws," which apply to the public at large. Both

U.S.C.C.A.N. and Statutes at Large have comprehensive indexes. Periodically, the session laws are
classified by topic and are added to the federal
codes.

2. STATE

State statutes and constitutions are published in
a manner similar to federal law. Each state has a
code that includes that state's statutes and constitution. The specific features of the state codes
vary, but they generally are organized by subject
matter, have topic indexes, and are updated to
include new legislation. Some codes are annotated
with information such as descriptions of cases interpreting each statute and legislative histories. Some
states have official codes, others have official and
unofficial codes, and the rest have only unofficial
codes. Some states also have published session law
reports, which contain the laws adopted during one
legislative session. In some states that do not,
private companies publish unofficial versions. Finally, your state may have a "legislative hotline"
that provides information about current legislation
or about the amendment or repeal of statutes. Before researching in a state's code, you should study
its format to ensure that you use it properly.

3. MUNICIPAL

Local units of government, such as cities, also
enact laws, which usually are called "ordinances."
Municipalities usually have a charter, which is the

municipal equivalent of a constitution. The charter
defines the municipality's powers. A municipality's
charter and ordinances may be published in a municipal code. Municipal codes vary greatly in their
organization, indexing, and types of information
that are included. Very few municipal codes include case annotations for the ordinances. If your
code does not, you can use the state digest to locate
cases that have interpreted an ordinance.

D. LEGISLATIVE HISTORY

Often, the terms of a statute are ambiguous in
their application to a particular case. To attempt
to determine how the legislature intended the statute to apply, you can research the statute's legislative history. The term "legislative history" includes a variety of materials concerning the statute.
It includes the statute's procedural history, such as
the committees that considered it, and materials
concerning the law's substance, such as committee
reports and transcripts of legislative debates.

The primary sources for federal legislative history
are United States Code Congressional and Administrative News (U.S.C.C.A.N.), which was first published in 1941, and the Congressional Record. In
U.S.C.C.A.N., you will find the texts of the most
important congressional committee reports regarding a statute. The easiest way to locate these
materials in U.S.C.C.A.N. is to look at the historical
notes and references following the text of the statute in U.S.C.A. They include citations to

U.S.C.C.A.N.'s legislative history section. The Congressional Record, on the other hand, focuses on House and Senate proceedings. For example, the Congressional Record publishes congressional debates and votes.

By researching a statute's legislative history, you may discover the legislature's reason for enacting a law, its intended scope, and the ways in which it has been amended. Unfortunately, the availability of legislative history for any given federal law varies greatly. At the state or municipal level, usually little or no written or recorded legislative history is available.

E. ADMINISTRATIVE LAW

As described in Chapter 3, Congress and state legislatures often empower administrative agencies to promulgate regulations, adjudicate disputes, or otherwise implement laws enacted by the legislature. The federal government publishes virtually all federal regulations in the Code of Federal Regulations (C.F.R.). The C.F.R. is organized using the same titles as in the United States Code, and the citation system is similar. For example, 12 C.F.R. § 509.1 refers to § 509.1 of Title 12 of the C.F.R. You can locate a regulation by using C.F.R. indexes, annotations in U.S.C.S. or U.S.C.A., or commercial indexes, such as the Code of Federal Regulations Index or the CIS Index to the Code of Federal Regulations.

Unlike the U.S.C., each C.F.R. title is revised and republished at least annually. The most recently promulgated regulations and amendments, as well as proposed regulations and amendments, are published in the Federal Register. The Federal Register is published on most business days. Therefore, when researching a federal regulation, you first should check the C.F.R. and then the Federal Register.

Researching agency adjudicative decisions is more difficult. Unlike judicial decisions, a comprehensive reporter for federal agency decisions does not exist. Some agencies publish their own reporters, and specialized reporting services for particular areas of law may include the text of an agency's decisions. To find judicial decisions concerning a regulation or the scope of an agency's authority, you can use the same methods that you use for any other type of case.

Most states publish their agencies' regulations in a comprehensive code and have a relatively current reporting service like the Federal Register. These codes and services may not be as well organized and indexed as the C.F.R. and Federal Register. The state statutory code may be helpful if it includes cross-references to relevant state agency regulations. If the state does not have a comprehensive regulatory code, you can request a set of regulations from the relevant state agency. State agency adjudicative decisions also may not be readily available, although some state agencies publish their decisions.

F. LEGAL PERIODICALS

Virtually every law school and many other law-related organizations, such as bar associations, publish one or more legal periodicals. A periodical may include articles from many areas of law, or it may focus on one subject. The articles range from abstract, scholarly analyses to concrete, practice-oriented discussions. Unlike cases and statutes, the articles in legal periodicals do not have the force of law, but they often have a significant impact on the law's development.

Periodical articles provide a useful starting point for a research project, as well as a means for staying current in the law. The articles provide references to the governing cases, statutes, regulations, and other research sources. They often provide a historical background and comprehensive analysis of a topic and make predictions and recommendations concerning the law's evolution. They generally are written by experts in the area, though law school reviews and journals often also include articles written by students.

To find periodical articles about a particular topic, you can use a periodical index. The two most comprehensive and commonly used indexes are the Index to Legal Periodicals (I.L.P.) and the Current Law Index (C.L.I.). The I.L.P. has been published since 1908, while C.L.I. has been published only since 1980. C.L.I. is somewhat more comprehensive than I.L.P.; C.L.I. includes over 700 periodicals, while I.L.P. includes over 500 periodicals and does not index articles that are less than five pages.

I.L.P. and C.L.I. both index articles by subject, author, case name, and statute. Both also use the standard citation form for articles—the author's name, the article's title, the volume number of the periodical in which the article is published, the name of the periodical, the page in the volume at which the article begins, and the year of publication. Thus, the citation Barry C. Feld, *Violent Youth and Public Policy: A Case Study of Juvenile Justice Law Reform*, 79 Minn. L. Rev. 965 (1995) tells you that this article, which was written by Barry C. Feld, begins at page 965 of volume 79 of the Minnesota Law Review. A complete list of abbreviations for periodicals is contained in The Bluebook.

G. TREATISES

A treatise is an in-depth examination of a particular area of law. It can range in size from a single volume to more than twenty volumes. The subject of a treatise may be broad, such as contract or property law, or more narrow, such as personal jurisdiction. Some treatises describe the law, while others interpret it and make recommendations for its future development. Your law library will contain a number of treatises on topics ranging from admiralty law to zoning.

When you research or study an issue, a treatise can be useful in a number of ways. It can provide an overview of the subject you are researching—the so-called "big picture"—and it normally will include citations to cases, statutes, and other research sources. A treatise also synthesizes the law in a given area and often describes the historic background and trends. This feature can be particularly helpful when researching an evolving area of law or a particularly complex subject.

Your library probably uses the Library of Congress or Dewey Decimal call number system to catalogue treatises. To find a treatise, check your library's index system for the treatise's call number. Your law librarian also can give you a range of call numbers for treatises dealing with a particular subject matter area. The most popular treatises may be on reserve in the library. There are treatises for the subject of many law school classes, especially for your first-year classes. You can ask your professor to recommend the best ones. It is important to remember that a treatise author may have a particular point of view on the subject. Therefore, you should read the underlying cases and statutes to determine whether you agree with the author's conclusions. You also should check for pocket parts and other update materials to ensure that you have the most current information.

H. LEGAL ENCYCLOPEDIAS

Corpus Juris Secundum (C.J.S.) and American Jurisprudence, Second Edition (Am. Jur. 2d) are the encyclopedias of the legal world. They provide an overview of virtually all federal and state law by dividing the law into separate topics, arranging them alphabetically, and further dividing them into subtopics. The encyclopedias provide a good starting point for research because they give an overview of each topic and cite relevant cases and other legal authorities. The encyclopedias are only a starting point, however, because their discussions are necessarily broad and generalized to incorporate all jurisdictions' laws and because they usually do not analyze the law but merely describe it. Therefore, when researching an issue in an encyclopedia, you must read the cited authorities to determine their applicability and effect. You also should check the encyclopedia's pocket part for any updates on the law.

While C.J.S. and Am. Jur. 2d cover federal and state law, a few legal encyclopedias deal only with the law of a particular state or subject. These more specialized encyclopedias sometimes are called "digests," though they are very different than the case digests described earlier in this chapter.

A citation to an encyclopedia entry should include the volume number in which it is published, the encyclopedia's name, the topic name, the section number for the relevant subtopic, and the year in which that volume of the encyclopedia was published. Thus, the cite to § 8 of C.J.S.'s discussion of the topic "Searches and Seizures," which is contained in volume 79, is 79 C.J.S. Searches and Seizures § 8 (1995).

I. AMERICAN LAW REPORTS

Although more limited in scope than legal encyclopedias, American Law Reports (A.L.R.) is another useful research source. A.L.R. reprints selected
appellate court opinions that present an issue about
which courts disagree or that is in a state of transi-
tion.   More important, A.L.R. also provides a discussion of the issue (an "annotation"), including a
brief description of all published opinions in which a
court addressed it.   Therefore, if you are researching an issue that has been the subject of an A.L.R.
annotation, it can provide a useful starting point.
As with legal encyclopedias, however, you should
read the cited cases to determine their applicability
and effect, rather than rely on the brief description
contained in the annotation.

To find an annotation on a particular subject, you
can use A.L.R. indexes that are arranged alphabetically by subject or by the name of cases that are an
annotation subject.   Federal laws and a few other
national legal resources also are indexed, and annotations are included in Shepard's Citations.   Annotations are supplemented with later cases on the
same subject, and an annotation may be replaced
when the law changes.   Therefore, you always
should check pocket parts and supplemental A.L.R.
volumes.

J. RESTATEMENTS OF THE LAW

Restatements of the Law are influential exposi-
tions of the law on a variety of subjects, including

contracts, property, and torts. Based on a review and analysis of the common law and legislation as it has developed in the different states, each Restatement sets forth a comprehensive statement of the law on a particular subject. Although the Restatements are not binding on courts or legislatures, they are cited frequently because they are written by eminent scholars who specialize in the areas about which they are writing and because the Restatements are reviewed and published by The American Law Institute, whose members are respected judges, practitioners, and professors.

Each Restatement section includes commentaries, illustrations, and citations to relevant cases, A.L.R. annotations, and West key numbers. A Restatement is particularly useful if you are researching an issue for which no controlling authority exists in the jurisdiction. You should be aware, however, that the jurisdiction may not follow the Restatement rule, especially if it is a new approach to the law, rather than merely a statement of existing law.

K. LAW DICTIONARIES AND THESAURI

As you read your class assignments, you will come across both unfamiliar words and familiar words used in an unfamiliar way. Many commonly used words have a different meaning when used as a legal term of art. It is essential to your understanding of a case and to your development as a lawyer that you learn the legal meaning of these words. Therefore, one of your first purchases as a law student should be a legal dictionary.

Many different dictionaries are available. The two most common are Black's Law Dictionary and Ballentine's Law Dictionary. Your law library has dictionaries available for your use while at school. Additionally, Black's Law Dictionary is available online.

Like other thesauri, a law thesaurus lists synonyms for legal terms of art and also may include antonyms and definitions. A thesaurus is especially useful in generating search terms for finding topics in a digest and online. This use will be particularly important as you begin the process of expanding your vocabulary of legal terms.

L. CITATORS

As discussed previously, each judicial opinion builds on the cases decided before it, and courts always are cognizant of the precedents in an area when rendering a decision. How do attorneys know if a decision on which they wish to rely has been overturned or modified? Traditionally, they would "shepardize" it. Shepard's Citations publishes lists of cases and other legal sources that have cited each published opinion. Shepard's is available in book form, and many of its titles are available online. By using Shepard's, you can discover (1) whether your case was appealed to a higher court or remanded to a lower court for additional proceedings, (2) more recent cases that have raised the same issues, and (3) cases in other jurisdictions that address the same issues. Using a citator is essential to good research. Imagine the horror of going to argue before the Supreme Court and discovering that the case on which your argument depends was over-ruled last month!

Shepard's is easy to use because it is organized in the same way as the case reporters. There are separate federal, regional, and state citators. To shepardize *People v. Walcher*, 42 Ill.2d 159, 246 N.E.2d 256 (1969), for example, you can use Shepard's Illinois Citations and Shepard's Northeastern Reporter Citations. Although state and regional citators are similar, some differences exist in the sources they include. Your research needs will dictate whether you use one or both citators.

Assuming that you use Northeastern Reporter Citations, you should page through the citator to find the listing for page 256 of volume 246 of N.E.2d. The listing includes a series of citations. These citations are to opinions that cite *Walcher*. Some citations are preceded by a lower case letter, such as "f" or "q." The lower case letter explains the court's treatment of the case you are shepardizing. For example, "f" means the case was followed, "q" means the case or its reasoning has been questioned, and "o" means the case has been overruled. A list of the meaning for each letter is in the front of each Shepard's volume. Each citation also includes a small number. This number is the head-note number for the issue in *Walcher* that is the subject of the cited case. These small numbers enable you to identify and to read only those opinions that address the particular issue you are researching, rather than every issue discussed in the *Walcher* opinion.

In addition to case citators, Shepard's citators are published for certain specialized areas of the law, such as labor law, evidence, and products liability. Shepard's citators also are published for constitutions, statutes, regulations, and a variety of other legal sources. Just as for case citators, these other sources are listed in numerical order by page or section number and include citations to subsequent amendments, cases, and other legal sources.

Shepard's citators are updated frequently so you might need to use one or more hardbound volumes and one or more paperback supplements. You will know which volumes and how many to use by finding the most recent paperback version. Its front cover will list all the volumes you need to check for a complete update. Despite its frequent updating, Shepard's is never completely current. To get the most current information and to save the time of looking through multiple volumes of citators, you can use an online citator service, as described in the next section on electronic research.

M. ELECTRONIC RESEARCH

Electronic research has become an important alternative method of legal research. Using a computer connected to a central database, you can find and retrieve cases, statutes, administrative regulations, law review articles, and many other materials. The two major online legal services are WESTLAW and LEXIS. Both services have extensive databases and provide comprehensive training materials for students. Personal training also may be available from a WESTLAW or LEXIS representative at your law school.

Law schools generally pay a flat rate for WESTLAW and LEXIS access, which includes individual passwords for students so that they can use the system free of charge. You may use the terminals at the law school or, if you have a modem on your personal computer, access the databases from your home. However, before embarking on computerized research, it is important to master the art of legal researching with books. Although as a law student you have free access to the databases, the office where you practice law may not use an electronic database or may limit its availability because of cost. Additionally, much of the information on the electronic databases is organized in a similar manner to the books.

A significant difference between electronic research and traditional research, however, is the method for locating source materials. With electronic research, rather than searching through digest entries, the "terms and connectors" approach is used in which the computer searches for one or more terms that you specify. To illustrate, consider the hypothetical corporal punishment issue discussed on page 78. After accessing the Iowa case law database in WESTLAW or in LEXIS, you would enter the following terms and connectors query: "corporal punishment" w/10 school. This query tells the computer to search for all Iowa cases in which the term "corporal punishment" appears within ten words of the word "school." The computer will find and display two cases that satisfy the query. The first case is an unrelated search and seizure case that mentions a federal corporal punishment case in a footnote. The second case is the same 1961 case found in the digest. On WESTLAW, you can enhance your search by supplementing the search terms with a key number.

To simplify the search process even further, WESTLAW has introduced "natural language" searching. With this type of search, terms and connectors are unnecessary. Instead, you can enter a query in sentence form. For our hypothetical issue, for example, you might enter: "May a child be subjected to corporal punishment in the public schools?" This natural language query will produce twenty cases. However, the system automatically lists the cases in order of relevance and importance to the issue. Thus, the first case presented in the natural language list is the same 1961 Iowa case. In contrast, the cases retrieved with the terms and connectors method simply are displayed in reverse chronological order.

WESTLAW and LEXIS also have online citator services. Both have Shepard's online. Both also supplement Shepard's with more recent case citations. Whereas Shepard's online is only as current as the printed citator, the WESTLAW citator includes a case within 24–36 hours after West Publishing receives it. Similarly, the LEXIS citator includes a case within two to three weeks.

Advances in electronic legal research, such as natural language searches, are being matched by advances in electronic research of non-legal sources. Both DIALOG and the Dow Jones News/Retrieval databases, which are available on WESTLAW terminals, and NEXIS, which is available on LEXIS terminals, provide electronic access to information on a great variety of subjects, and these databases are being expanded continually. They include newspapers, journals, market research, medical information, and a large collection of other types of sources. Understanding the context in which the law operates will enhance your legal studies and research significantly. DIALOG, Dow Jones News/Retrieval, and NEXIS put much of the necessary information at your fingertips.

N. YOUR LAW LIBRARIAN

Get to know your school's law librarians. Because they are knowledgeable about the law, as well as about library science, they are invaluable when you have a difficult legal research problem. A law librarian can help you develop a research strategy that will make the most effective use of the library's resources and of your time. The law is the most extensively catalogued body of knowledge. Law librarians' specialized training and experience make them the most effective guides.

CHAPTER 8

PREPARING FOR CLASS

Your law school classes will be different than any other class you have taken. Rather than reading textbooks and listening to lectures, you primarily will study judges' decisions in actual cases and will engage in Socratic dialogues about them with your professors and colleagues. This chapter will help unravel some of the mysteries of class preparation and will tell you the best way to prepare for class. In the next chapter, you will learn about the Socratic dialogue and the ways to make the most of your class time.

A. CASE METHOD

During the first year of law school and in many upper-level courses, your professors will use the case method. The assigned readings in your classes will consist largely of cases from the casebook for the course. Rather than reading a textbook description of the law, you will read the opinions that judges have written in actual lawsuits. Although technically the word "case" refers to the lawsuit itself, "case" also is used to refer to the judge's written opinion.

The case method is a reflection of the importance of judicial decisions in the common-law system. A great deal of the law comes from judicial decisions, and decisions in new cases are based on already decided cases. Therefore, learning to read and to analyze cases is essential. But cases teach more than just legal principles. By learning law in the context of actual lawsuits, you learn how disputes arise, the judicial procedures for resolving them, and available remedies. The case method also makes law come alive. Rather than reading pages of abstract statements of law, the principles are presented more vividly by real problems involving real people.

A case is included in the casebook either because it has been important in the law's development or because it is particularly useful in presenting a particular legal issue. The casebook author will include only the portion of the opinion that is relevant to the issue being studied. Sometimes, the opinion will be from a trial court. More often, however, the opinion will be from an appellate court because appellate courts primarily decide issues of law, which are the main focus of your classes. Trial courts, on the other hand, decide issues of fact and of law. Moreover, when deciding issues of law, trial courts are bound by the precedent of appellate court decisions, so trial court opinions less often include an in-depth examination of a legal issue. Finally, state trial court opinions usually are not published and, therefore, are less readily available to casebook authors.

An important lesson you will learn from reading cases is that more than one answer to a disagreement may exist, as demonstrated by concurring and dissenting opinions. In a concurring opinion, a judge agrees with the majority's decision but disagrees with its reasoning; in a dissenting opinion, a judge disagrees with the decision, too. The judges do not disagree because they cannot understand the law. They simply have different perspectives on how the law should apply. Therefore, do not be surprised or concerned if you disagree with the cases you read. To the contrary, independent and creative analyses of cases and of the governing law are important skills.

Beware! Your professors normally will post reading assignments for the first class session. Find out where assignments are posted, and be sure to buy your casebooks in time to get prepared. Although some professors will lecture on the first day of class, most professors will expect you to be prepared to describe the cases included in the reading assignment and to discuss the legal issues they raise. You will learn much more from class if you have done the reading beforehand.

B. READING CASES

Give yourself more time to read the assigned cases than you think you will need. Judicial opinions are not written with law students in mind. They are written for judges and for lawyers. Opinions are filled with terminology and concepts that will be new to you and may require several readings to understand them. A law dictionary will be an invaluable companion as you puzzle your way through the cases. You also will have to work to determine how each case fits with the other assigned readings. The reason your professor assigned the case may not be readily apparent.

The necessary class preparation time varies from person to person. At the beginning of the first year, everyone will be struggling to make sense of the cases and to keep up with the assigned readings. As you learn to read cases, you will become more efficient and will prepare for class more quickly. Like every other skill, some people will learn more quickly than others. Do not be discouraged if it seems to be coming more slowly for you. If you keep working at learning, you will learn. If you do not keep working, you may not become a lawyer and certainly will not become a good lawyer. If you fall behind in your assigned reading, catch up on the materials you missed only after preparing for each day's classes. Otherwise, you may stay behind for the rest of the term.

When you read a case, the first line will be a caption that identifies the parties to the lawsuit, such as *Shelley v. Kraemer*. In a trial court opinion, the plaintiff's name normally is first, and the defendant's is second. In an appellate court opinion, some jurisdictions put the appellant's name first and the appellee's second; others use the trial court caption. If the case has more than one plaintiff or defendant, the case name still will list only one party for each side. The "v." between the names is an abbreviation for "versus." Just beneath the case name will be a citation to the court that issued the opinion, the year in which the case was decided, and where it was published.

Usually, the next line will identify the judge or justice who wrote the opinion. For example, it might say: "Mr. Justice Stewart delivered the opinion of the Court." More frequently, just the author's name is given, such as "Zorotovich, J." This does not mean that the author's name is Janet Zorotovich. The "J." is an abbreviation for "Justice" if the opinion was issued by a court of final appeal or for "Judge" if issued by a trial court or intermediate appellate court. Similarly, "Madsen, C.J." refers to Chief Justice or Chief Judge Madsen.

Normally, the opinion then describes the parties to the case, the plaintiff's cause of action, and the relevant facts. Appellate court opinions also describe the lower court(s) decision, the procedural method by which the appellant brought the case to the appellate court, and the grounds for appeal. The court then begins its substantive discussion of the case by stating each legal and factual issue. For each issue, the court describes the governing law, how the law applies to the facts of the case, and its decision ("holding") concerning that issue. After discussing each issue, the court states its final disposition of the case. A trial court opinion describes the remedy, if any, the court is granting; an appellate court decision states whether the lower court decision is affirmed or reversed or whether the case is being sent back ("remanded") to the lower court for further proceedings.

The best way to read a case is a matter of personal style. Many people read the entire case quickly to get a sense of it and then re-read it more carefully as many times as necessary to fully understand it. You may understand the case after one reading, but that will be unusual during the first few weeks of law school. The opinion often will include unfamiliar words and terms, which you should look up in a law dictionary. Learning the language of the law is like learning any other language. When you do not know a word, look it up! You also should underline or otherwise highlight important passages, such as the court's statement of the applicable law.

Understanding the court's opinion is just the first step. The next step is analyzing its reasoning. Did the court apply the appropriate legal principles to decide the case? Did it properly apply the principles? Is this opinion consistent with relevant precedents? What are the legal, social, and political ramifications of the court's decision? Will it cause inappropriate results in future cases? Where does this case fit with the other cases you have read? Thinking about these questions will enhance your understanding of the case and of the legal process and will prepare you for the class discussion.

After analyzing the case, read the notes following it in the casebook. The notes often include questions about the case and brief descriptions of other cases that address the same or similar issues. The note cases may reach a different conclusion or may present a twist on the facts of the main case. Because there are so many note cases, you should not take time to find and to read the full opinions for them unless it would help your understanding of the subject or unless your professor tells you to do so. However, you should think about the note cases and attempt to synthesize them with the main case. If they reach a different result, are they inconsistent or are they distinguishable in some legally relevant way? Thinking about the note cases will illuminate new dimensions of the legal principles you are studying and will provide excellent practice at synthesizing cases.

C. BRIEFING CASES

You are now ready to begin a particularly important part of your class preparation. You now should "brief" the main case. A brief is a written summary of the case. To prepare one, you must distill the case's most important parts and restate them in your own words. The effort will provide a variety of important benefits.

First, to describe a case accurately, you must read it carefully and thoroughly. Describing the case in your own words forces you to determine exactly what the court said, which concepts and facts were essential to its decision, and the proper legal terminology and procedures. You do not understand a case simply because you can copy parts of it from your casebook. On the other hand, if you can describe the concept in your own words, you can feel reasonably confident that you do understand it.

Second, after reading so many cases in each course, your case briefs will help you remember the details of each case for class discussions and exam preparation. Case briefs are a particularly helpful study aid because they cover all the cases you studied in class, whereas most other study aids are not so carefully tailored to your coursework. To be most effective, case briefs must be brief. Otherwise, you will have difficulty discovering the salient points in your brief during class discussions, and you will have far too many pages to read for convenient exam review, because you may brief hundreds of cases each term.

Third, briefing cases exercises skills you will use throughout your legal career. As a lawyer, you will have to read and analyze cases with a careful eye to detail. You also will have to summarize cases when writing legal memoranda, briefs, and other documents and when making oral arguments to courts. Because case briefing is such a valuable skill, the time and effort you spend perfecting it in law school will be repaid many times over.

Because case briefing can be time consuming and difficult, especially when you are beginning, you may be tempted to use commercially prepared case briefs. By all means, resist the temptation. The primary benefit of a case brief comes from preparing it. The process of writing a brief forces you to exercise your analytic skills and to dig into all the procedural and substantive aspects of a case. Simply reading a canned brief will not provide this valuable exercise. Moreover, you cannot be sure that the canned brief is accurate or focuses on the same aspects of the case as your professor. Besides, canned briefs are not available for most of the cases you will have to read when you are a lawyer!

As you become more experienced at briefing, you will get faster. When you have become adept at briefing, you can consider dispensing with a separate written brief and briefing in the casebook instead. You can make the necessary notations in the margins of the casebook and can highlight key passages. You should keep this possibility in mind when you are deciding whether to buy new or used casebooks, because you will want room for your notations. You also can save time by developing a list of abbreviations. Some common law school abbreviations are "P" or "π" for "plaintiff," "D" or "Δ" for "defendant," and "K" for "contract."

D. CASE BRIEF FORMAT

There are many different ways to brief a case. You should use the format that is most useful for your class and exam preparations. Regardless of form, every brief should include the following information.

1. CAPTION

A brief should begin with the case name, the court that decided it, the year it was decided, and the page on which it appears in the casebook. The court is included to indicate the precedential value of the opinion. The precedential value depends on the court level—trial, intermediate appellate, or court of last resort—and on whether it is a state or federal court. Including the court also will be helpful when you are synthesizing the cases in that section of materials. The year of decision also is included to help assess the opinion's precedential value. Older cases may have been modified or reversed by more recent ones.

2. FACTS

Next, state the facts of the case. This section is necessary because legal principles are defined by the situations in which they arise. For example, assume you are briefing a case in which the defendant was convicted of murder. If your brief only states that killing is a crime without stating the facts of the case, you could mistakenly apply that principle to a case in which the defendant killed in self-defense. Only by stating the circumstances concerning the killing will you have an accurate picture of the law.

Include in your brief only those facts that are legally relevant. A fact is legally relevant if it had an impact on the case's outcome. For example, in a personal injury action arising from a car accident, the color of the parties' cars seldom would be relevant to the case's outcome. The defendant's liability will not turn on whether the injured party's car was green, rather than blue. Therefore, do not include that fact in your brief even if the court mentions it in the opinion. Similarly, if the plaintiff and defendant presented different versions of the facts, you should describe those differences only if they are relevant to the court's consideration of the case. Otherwise, just state the facts upon which the court relied. Because you will not know which facts are legally relevant until you have read and deciphered the entire case, do not try to brief a case while reading it for the first time.

3. PROCEDURAL HISTORY

With the statement of facts, you have taken the case to the point at which the plaintiff filed suit. The next section of the brief, the procedural history, begins at that point and ends with the case's appearance in the court that wrote the opinion you are reading. For a trial court opinion, identify the type of legal action the plaintiff brought. For an appellate court opinion, also describe how the trial court and, if applicable, the lower appellate court decided the case and why. In addition to setting the stage for the opinion you are briefing, describing the case's procedural history helps you learn judicial procedures.

4. ISSUES

You are now ready to describe the opinion you are briefing. In this section of the brief, state the factual and legal questions that the court had to decide. For example, assume the plaintiff claims that the defendant made a gift of a watch to her but now denies that he made the gift. For a gift to be legally enforceable, the person who claims it (the alleged "donee") must prove that (1) the person who allegedly made the gift ("the donor") intended to make a gift, (2) the alleged donor delivered the gift to the donee in accordance with the legal requirements for a delivery, and (3) the alleged donee accepted the gift. In this case, do not state the issue as: "Does the plaintiff win?" or "Was there a gift?" Instead, include in the issue statement each question that the court had to decide to answer the ultimate question of whether the defendant made a legally enforceable gift. If the court addressed all three requirements for a valid gift, you should include three issues in your case brief:

1. Did defendant intend to make a gift to plaintiff?;

2. Did defendant deliver the watch to plaintiff?; and

3. Did plaintiff accept the gift?

These are the questions the court had to answer to decide who is legally entitled to the watch.

Sometimes students think that they should consolidate all the issues in a case into one large issue.

That is the wrong approach. To analyze a case properly, you must break it down to its component parts. Otherwise, you will have a tangled skein of facts, law, and analysis. Dissecting the case allows you to deal with one question at a time, rather than trying to deal with all the questions at once.

5. HOLDINGS

In this section, separately answer each question in the issues section. For quick reference, first state the answer in a word or two, such as "yes" or "no." Then, in a sentence or two, state the legal principle on which the court relied to reach that answer (the "holding"). To do so, you must distinguish the holding from "dictum" (pl. "dicta"). The holding is the legal principle that was essential to the court's resolution of the issue. Dictum, on the other hand, is any nonessential principle that the court may have included in the opinion.

Dictum is not included in a case brief because it does not have precedential value. Although dictum can provide an insight into the court's thoughts about a related issue, the court is free to ignore it in future cases. Dictum is nonbinding because it was not directly related to the issue that the court had to decide and, therefore, may not have been considered by the court as carefully as a holding. Additionally, neither the plaintiff nor the defendant may have addressed the dictum's relevance and accuracy.

You must state the holdings as accurately as possible, because this section of the case briefs will be particularly important for exam preparation. Check whether your description of a holding is too broad by thinking of any exceptions or qualifications. For example, if you stated the holding as "killing is a crime," that holding would include a person who killed in self-defense. Therefore, narrow this statement of the holding. Similarly, check whether your description is too narrow by questioning the relevance of each part. For example, if the victim in the case was a man, the statement "killing a man without legal justification is a crime" is technically correct. However, no legally relevant reason exists for distinguishing between male and female victims, so broaden this statement. A hornbook or other study aid can help you determine the exact scope of the holding.

6. RATIONALE

You now should describe the court's rationale for each holding. This section of the case brief may be the most important, because you must understand the court's reasoning to analyze it and to apply it to other fact situations, such as those on the exam. Starting with the first issue, describe each link in the court's chain of reasoning. Begin by stating the rule of law that the court applied to decide the issue. Next, describe the facts of the case that were relevant to the court's analysis of that issue. Then, describe the court's holding when it applied the rule of law to the facts of the case. Repeat the same three-step process for each issue in the issue section.

After stating the court's rationale, give your analysis of it. Does it follow logically from point to point? Does the court assume facts that were not proved in the case? Has the court stated precedent too narrowly or too broadly? Does the court rely on improper analogies? You must be a critical and creative opinion reader. Note your criticisms and questions so that they are readily available during class and during other discussions with your colleagues and professors.

At this point, you also should synthesize the case you have briefed with other cases you have read for the course. As a lawyer, simply describing the holdings in individual cases is not enough. You must be able to give an overview of an area of law. If two or more cases seem inconsistent, perhaps you have stated their holdings too broadly. Check the cases for limiting language that you previously may have missed. Check to see whether the cases are from the same jurisdiction. If not, the earlier case was not binding precedent for the later case because jurisdictions generally are free to develop their own common law. Also check the years the cases were decided. If a substantial time gap exists, the later case may reflect changed societal, political, or legal conditions. Synthesizing the cases will give you an overview of the subject matter and will develop your analytic skills.

7. DISPOSITION

Describe the final disposition of the case. Did the court decide in favor of the plaintiff or the defendant? What remedy, if any, did the court grant? If it is an appellate court opinion, did the court affirm the lower court's decision, reverse it in whole or in part, or remand the case for additional proceedings?

8. CONCURRING AND DISSENTING OPINIONS

Concurring and dissenting opinions are included in a casebook when they present an interesting alternative analysis of the case. Therefore, you should describe the analysis in your case brief. It will help you see the case in a different light. Besides, professors love concurring and dissenting opinions almost as much as footnotes as a source for in-class discussion material!

E. SAMPLE CASE BRIEF

For practice, try briefing the following case. A sample brief follows the opinion against which you can check your brief. Remember, though, that briefing is an art and not a science. Use the format that works best for your purposes.

McAVOY v. MEDINA

Supreme Judicial Court of Massachusetts, 1866.

11 Allen (Mass.) 548, 87 Am.Dec. 733.

Tort to recover a sum of money found by the plaintiff in the shop of the defendant.

At the trial in the superior court, before Morton, J., it appeared that the defendant was a barber, and the plaintiff, being a customer in the defendant's shop, saw and took up a pocket-book which was lying upon a table there, and said, "See what I have found." The defendant came to the table and asked where he found it. The plaintiff laid it back in the same place and said, "I found it right there." The defendant then took it and counted the money, and the plaintiff told him to keep it, and if the owner should come to give it to him; and otherwise to advertise it; which the defendant promised to do. Subsequently the plaintiff made three demands for the money, and the defendant never claimed to hold the same till the last demand. It was agreed that the pocket-book was placed upon the table by a transient customer of the defendant and accidentally left there, and was first seen and taken up by the plaintiff, and that the owner had not been found.

The judge ruled that the plaintiff could not maintain his action, and a verdict was accordingly returned for the defendant; and the plaintiff alleged exceptions.

. . .

DEWEY, J. It seems to be the settled law that the finder of lost property has a valid claim to the same against all the world except the true owner, and generally that the place in which it is found creates no exception to this rule. 2 Parsons on Con. 97. *Bridges v. Hawkesworth*, 7 Eng. Law & Eq. R. 424.

But this property is not, under the circumstances, to be treated as lost property in that sense in which a finder has a valid claim to hold the same until called for by the true owner. This property was voluntarily placed upon a table in the defendant's shop by a customer of his who accidentally left the same there and has never called for it. The plaintiff also came there as a customer, and first saw the same and took it up from the table. The plaintiff did not by this acquire the right to take the property from the shop, but it was rather the duty of the defendant, when the fact became thus known to him, to use reasonable care for the safe keeping of the same until the owner should call for it. In the case of *Bridges v. Hawkesworth* the property, although found in a shop, was found on the floor of the same, and had not been placed there voluntarily by the owner, and the court held that the finder was entitled to the possession of the same, except as to the owner. But the present case more resembles that of *Lawrence v. The State*, 1 Humph. (Tenn.) 228, and is indeed very similar in its facts. The court there ... [distinguished] between the case of property thus placed by the owner and neglected to be removed, and property lost. It was there held that "to place a pocket-book upon a table and to forget to take it away is not to lose it, in the sense in which the authorities referred to speak of lost property."

We accept this as the better rule, and especially as one better adapted to secure the rights of the true owner.

In view of the facts of this case, the plaintiff acquired no original right to the property, and the defendant's subsequent acts in receiving and holding the property in the manner he did does not create any.

Exceptions overruled.

Sample Brief

McAvoy v. Medina

Supreme Judicial Court of Massachusetts, 1866

Page 63 of casebook

Facts

A customer of D's barber shop placed a pocket-book on a table in the shop and accidentally left it there. P found the pocket-book and gave it to D. P instructed D to give the pocket-book to its owner if he returned. The owner was not discovered. P demanded that D give him the money from the pocket-book, but D refused.

[Note: Several facts that were included in the court's opinion have been omitted from the case brief because they did not affect the court's holding.

For example, the court held for D although he twice denied that he had the pocket-book.]

Procedural History

P brought a tort action against D to recover the money. The trial court held for D. P appealed. [Note: The opinion does not state what type of tort action P brought, the basis for the trial court decision, or the grounds for P's appeal. If this information had been included in the opinion, it would have been included in the case brief.]

Issues

1. Was the pocket-book "lost" property?
2. If a customer voluntarily places an object in a shop and forgets it, is another customer who finds it entitled to possession?

Holdings

1. No. An object is not "lost" when its owner intentionally placed it somewhere and then forgot it.
2. No. When an object has been mislaid in a shop, the shop owner's right to possess the object is superior to the finder's.

[Note: Because the court held that the property in this case was not lost, its discussion of the law concerning lost property is dictum.]

Rationales

1. An object is "lost" only if its owner has unknowingly parted with it. In this case, a

pocket-book was found on a table in a barber shop. The court determined that the pocket-book's owner intentionally had placed it there. Therefore, the object was not "lost."

a. The court assumes that the owner of the pocket-book intentionally placed it on the table, which may be a reasonable assumption on the facts of this case. The court describes another case, however, in which an object was found on the floor of a shop. Because the object was found on the floor, the court assumed that the owner unintentionally parted with it and, therefore, that the object was "lost." As a result, the finder, rather than the shop owner, was entitled to possession. What if the object had been placed on a table or counter and then inadvertently knocked to the floor? What if a ring is found on the floor near a sink in a bathroom? The court's reasoning in this case causes completely different results based on assumptions about potentially ambiguous circumstances.

2. A shop owner who knows that an object has been mislaid in the shop has a duty to safeguard it until the owner of the object reclaims it. Giving possession to the shop owner increases the likelihood that the owner of the mislaid object will recover it.

Disposition

For D; affirmed lower court decision.

Concurring or Dissenting Opinions

[Note: No concurring or dissenting opinion was filed in this case. If one or both had been filed, you would describe them in the same way that you described the rationale of the main opinion.]

CHAPTER 9

CLASSROOM EXPERIENCE

The hours you spend in law school classes will be among the most intense learning experiences of your life. You will feel the full gamut of emotions—from exhilaration to frustration. You will be actively engaged in a learning process that requires you to deal with society's most profound issues, as well as with its most mundane. Unlike many college courses that you may have taken in the past, you will not be given a predigested diet of textbooks and lectures. You must make your own way through the thicket of the law. In this way, you will be best prepared for the practice of law.

A. THE SOCRATIC METHOD

To take you on this journey of discovery, the professors for most, if not all, of your first-year classes will employ the Socratic method. This method is named for the Greek philosopher Socrates, who educated his students by asking them questions, rather than by lecturing. During a typical class, your professor will begin by asking a class member to describe a case that was included in the day's reading assignment. Although professors vary as to the exact information that should be included in this presentation, typically it should include a statement of the legally relevant facts, procedural history, issues, holdings, and the court's rationale for deciding each issue.

Your case brief is invaluable for this part of class. If you are called on to present the case, you have all the information you need in your brief, and you already will have determined which facts are legally relevant and which legal principles are holdings, rather than dicta. Even if you are not called on to present the case, you can follow the presentation more effectively with your case brief and can take notes about the case on it.

If your professor asks you to present a case, do not read your case brief to the class no matter how brilliantly written it is. Reading a presentation is boring for the listeners and does not demonstrate that you actually have absorbed the case. Additionally, reading a case brief out loud will not help refine your public speaking skills. Therefore, review your case briefs immediately before class so that you can describe each case from memory.

Describing the case is merely the introductory step in the Socratic method. In fact, your professor may dispense with the case presentations after the first few weeks when the class members have become proficient at deciphering cases. The essence of the Socratic method is what comes next. Your professor will ask questions that are designed to explore the legal principles and policies that are raised by the case. Your professor may alter one or more facts of the case and ask you whether and how the result would change. To answer this question, you must know which facts in the case were crucial to the court's decision and how those facts affected the decision. You must recognize the goals sought to be served by the law to determine the best way to meet those goals under the changed facts. You must determine whether the same rule of law should apply or whether a different rule should apply. Finally, you must have determined whether the court's analysis in the case is correct.

After you respond to the hypothetical case (the "hypo"), your professor will ask another question that is designed to test the validity of your answer. For example, your professor might present another factual situation in which an undesirable result would be reached if your reasoning were applied. By doing this, your professor is asking whether you should refine your answer to the first question. You must determine how to state it more precisely or otherwise revise it to better serve the law's goals.

Alternatively, your professor might ask whether the case is consistent with other cases you have read or how the case fits within the subject you have been studying. These types of questions require you to synthesize the cases. Rather than viewing each case as an independent entity, you must learn to weave the cases together to get a comprehensive picture of that body of law. Your professor could tell you how the cases fit together, but you must learn that skill for yourself. Your professors will not be available to help you when you are a lawyer. Besides, how would you know whether you agree with their interpretations of the law?

At the next level of inquiry, your professor may ask you to explain how you reached your answer. Here, your analysis all gets laid bare. You may have been lucky and hit on an appropriate answer to the previous questions without really knowing why, but now you must explain your chain of reasoning. This exercise serves two purposes. It forces you to think through a problem step-by-step, and it enables your professor and colleagues to evaluate the soundness of each step.

If this process sounds intimidating, it can be, at least at first. Professors do not use the Socratic method because they hope to embarrass or to intimidate you, but because it serves important educational functions. As a beginner, you probably have not had any experience with legal analysis. Legal analysis is exactly what the Socratic method is designed to teach you. When you practice law, clients will not present you with factual situations that exactly replicate a case you studied in law school. Instead, you will be required to deal with many varying sets of circumstances.

Moreover, the law does not stay the same. It is constantly evolving as courts, legislatures, agencies, and other lawmakers perform their assigned functions. Therefore, your legal knowledge quickly would become outdated if you simply memorized legal rules in law school. The Socratic method is designed to teach you how to determine the current state of the law and how to apply it to any situation.

The Socratic method also creates a strong incentive to prepare thoroughly for class. To engage in the Socratic dialogue, you must understand the reading assignment. You must understand the stated rules, exceptions, policies, and procedures and should have thought through questions that the professor or your colleagues might ask. Even if the professor does not call on you, careful class preparation is essential so that you can understand and can evaluate the in-class discussion, contribute your observations, and ask questions. This process makes class much more interesting than a lecture-style class, in which you passively listen, take notes, and memorize what was said. You also will learn a great deal more.

The Socratic method requires you to formulate, explain, and defend a position on a variety of legal issues. This process not only hones your analytic and speaking skills, but also prepares you for the adversarial method, which is a key feature of the American legal system. Under the adversarial method, the parties to a dispute present the strongest possible arguments to support their positions. The prospect of having your position challenged in class provides an incentive to think it through before class, to refine it, and to prepare defenses to potential challenges. Each step is a valuable learning exercise.

In a similar vein, the Socratic dialogue teaches critical thinking. Few questions have just one clear-cut answer. Virtually any position that you take in class can, and probably will be, challenged by your professor or by a colleague who does not share your point of view or spots weak points in your argument. The existence of weak points does not necessarily mean that your position is wrong; few positions represent absolute truths. You must be able to explain, however, why your position is best despite its weaknesses. Denying that weak points exist can undermine your credibility.

You must learn that your professor and colleagues are not challenging you personally but only some aspect of your argument. This is difficult for some people to accept, but it is absolutely essential. In practice, other lawyers and judges often will challenge you. If you take it personally, your ability to respond will be hampered. Conversely, you must learn to challenge others without making it a personal attack. The person on the other side of an issue is not a bad person simply because you do not agree. Throughout your career, you will be on the opposite side from many people more than once; do not alienate each one the first time!

The Socratic method sometimes frustrates students because they are not given "the answer." Students sometimes complain that the professor is "hiding the ball" or that the class is unfocused. Neither is true. The Socratic method is designed to teach an approach and not a set of rules. The questions are the focus and purpose of the class.

Of course, you also must understand the law for exams and for the practice of law. If you do not understand a subject after class, read about it in a hornbook or other study aid or talk with your professor or colleagues.

B. CLASS ATTENDANCE AND PARTICIPATION

Because the skills taught by the Socratic method cannot be learned from a casebook, class attendance is crucially important. In fact, research on law students indicates that a positive correlation exists between class attendance and grades. When you go to class, take your casebook, any assigned supplementary materials, such as a statute book, your case briefs, and your class notes. If you must miss a class, be sure to borrow one of your colleague's class notes. If your professor requires class attendance, get an excused absence before missing class, if possible.

Class discussions can provide an important indicator of how well you are grasping the assigned materials. Other students' case descriptions and the related discussions will help you determine whether your assessments of the cases were accurate. The class discussion may go in a direction that you had not anticipated. This does not necessarily indicate that your assessment was incorrect but only that the professor chose to focus on a different aspect of the case. If you had not been in class, you would have missed that perspective, which could hinder your understanding of future class discussions and your exam performance.

Although you will learn a great deal by listening to others and by thinking about their questions and answers, you will learn other important skills by actively participating in class discussions. Even if you do not become a trial lawyer, you will have to speak in public when you are in practice. For example, you will have to speak before neighborhood groups, corporate boards, and governmental bodies, such as legislative committees and zoning boards. Those should not be your first public speaking experiences. Instead, use the time in law school to learn to control the butterflies in your stomach and to speak effectively. Virtually everyone feels nervous when speaking in public, including your professors. Learning to speak effectively is just a matter of practice.

Even if you already feel comfortable speaking in public, you should participate in class for a variety of other reasons. The class will be much more interesting and issues will be presented from a variety of perspectives if all class members contribute their observations and experiences. By speaking in class, you give your professors a better basis for evaluating your understanding of the materials. In the typical law school class, your professor will have only the final exam on which to base your grade. If you regularly have spoken in class, however, your professor will have a broader basis for evaluating your performance. In fact, some professors may increase your grade based on the quality of your class participation. Additionally, you will need references and letters of recommendation from your professors for job and scholarship applications. You are far more likely to get a strong letter if the professor knows something about you other than your final exam grade.

Speaking in class early in the semester is particularly important. The longer you wait to speak for the first time, the harder it will be. During the first week of class, you may decide to sit back and check out your professor and colleagues. During the second week, you may not speak because you are waiting for a question that you would feel comfortable answering. By the third week, you may think that you have to wait for a question on which you are particularly strong because you want to make a good first impression. In the fourth week, if you have not yet spoken, you may feel pressure to make a very good impression the first time you speak. The burden you feel to perform well the first time you speak will become heavier with each week that passes. Break the ice early and get past that first time.

What if you answer incorrectly or say something that is strongly challenged? So what? Everyone makes mistakes, even your professors, and your challengers may be the ones who are wrong. Of course, everyone would prefer to make unimpeachable proclamations and to be honored for their wisdom, but that is not likely to happen in your first year of law school. In fact, if you are mistaken about something, it is better to find out about it and correct it now, rather than in practice or on your final exam.

On the other hand, do not talk unless you think that your comments will advance the class discussion. If your remarks would be tangential to the discussion or would raise a very minor point, wait to talk with your professor after class. Otherwise, you risk irritating your colleagues and professor, because class time is too valuable to waste and because everyone in class should have the opportunity to speak. Unless your professor has said otherwise, you should not speak until you have raised your hand and been recognized. This is the means by which the professor can direct the flow of the class discussion.

Unfortunately, some people are socialized to be particularly reticent about speaking in class. They may believe that they have nothing to contribute to the class discussion or that they already have taken too much of the class' time when, in fact, they have spoken less than their colleagues. Research has shown that these feelings are particularly strong for members of groups who traditionally have been underrepresented in law schools. The professor unintentionally may reinforce these feelings by treating class members differently from a misplaced concern about embarrassing someone who appears to be less assertive than other students.

Another common reason students avoid speaking in class is their belief that everyone else is smarter and more articulate. These students are sure that speaking in class will reveal their ignorance to their professors and colleagues. This common fear is understandable. After enjoying years of academic success, law students are thrown into a difficult new field and are beginners again. Professors who are experts in the law challenge their thinking and, to make matters worse, do so in the public forum of the classroom. But the fear is as wrong as it is common.

Do not let yourself fall into these traps. Lawyers are called "mouthpieces" for a reason. Clients hire you to represent their interests, including in public. In fact, the client may have hired you because the client is afraid to speak in public. Therefore, even if you do not want to speak in class and can slide by without doing it, resist the temptation. You are entitled to the same opportunities as every other student, and you have a responsibility to take advantage of those opportunities. It will get easier with practice. By the end of the term, you will have come a long way in overcoming your fear.

C. CLASS NOTES

A few students have such excellent memories that they do not need to take class notes. They can listen to the class discussions and think about them without the interruption of writing. For the great majority of students, however, class notes are essential. Normally, the final exam will cover fourteen or more weeks of classes, and you probably will take four or more courses each semester. As you prepare for exams, class notes can be very helpful for refreshing your memory.

Your notes will be most helpful if they are not just literal transcriptions of class discussions. Unless you are proficient at shorthand, you cannot write everything that is said. Even if you could, your time is better spent listening closely to the class discussion and thinking about it. Moreover, if you copy everything that is said in class, the enormous quantity of notes for each course will make exam preparation even more burdensome.

Rather than writing down as much as you can, focus on identifying the most important parts of the class discussion and include only those parts in your notes. You should include your professor's questions and hypos, as well as the main discussion points about them. Your professor obviously thinks that the questions and hypos raise important issues. If your professor thinks they are important, you normally should too.

Pay particular attention to information that is not in the casebook. For example, if your professor describes other jurisdictions' laws on an issue that is raised in the assigned reading, make a note of those laws. If that issue appears on the exam, analyze it under each type of law. If a lucid explanation is given in class of a concept with which you have been struggling, include that explanation. Also include the insights you have had as a result of the class discussion. In this way, your class notes will supplement your casebook and case briefs, rather than replicating them.

Well prepared case briefs can reduce the time you spend taking notes. If you already have written a description of the case, you need not repeat it in your class notes. Instead, you can think about the case presentation, absorb the additional insights it offers, and determine whether you agree with the presenter's analysis. Leave room on your case brief for notes so that all your information about the case will be in one place.

Do not become consumed by note-taking when you are in class. By intently focusing on your notes, you may stop listening critically to the class discussion with sometimes disastrous results. For example, when a speaker states the elements of a legal doctrine, a student who is overly absorbed in note-taking sometimes grafts the first part of one element onto the last part of the next element because note-taking impairs one's ability to listen. The student does not realize that the resulting notes are nonsensical because s/he is not thinking about the material. Such notes are worse than useless, and the student has lost the benefit of the class discussion.

People taking notes on a lap-top computer seem to be more prone to this problem. At times, a lap-top user may become so engrossed in the screen's glow or in editing and organizing the notes that s/he does not respond when called on by the professor. This lack of response does not seem to be attributable to the age-old gambit of studiously taking notes to avoid being questioned by the professor. Instead, the student seems to be concentrating more intently on the computer than on the class discussion. This is not progress.

Read your notes immediately after class to find any holes or unclear statements. You also should edit your notes and include your more fully formed thoughts about the materials based on the class discussion. This process will be much easier when the topic is fresh in your mind, rather than weeks or months later. Your colleagues and a good study aid can help clear up any errors or omissions.

CHAPTER 10

LEARNING AFTER CLASS

Despite the importance of attending classes, most of your learning will occur outside the classroom. An important way to learn is by spending time talking with your colleagues and professors. Rather than disciplining yourself to spend all your time studying alone in the library, take time to talk about the law in the halls or over a cup of coffee. By talking with people in a less structured setting than the classroom, you will get a variety of new perspectives on issues. Inevitably, you will kick around hypotheticals that will exercise your analytic skills and will reveal gaps in your knowledge. You also will improve your speaking skills and your abilities to formulate and to defend positions on issues.

Of course, you also will spend a great deal of time alone, reading your casebook and study aids and preparing case briefs and course outlines. Research on law students has shown that no method of studying is inherently superior to the others in terms of exam performance. However, research also has indicated that two types of activities can enhance performance: (1) regular review of course materials and (2) studying in an organized manner.

This chapter will explain how to do both, including how to prepare a course outline.

A. DAILY REVIEW

After each class, take a few minutes to review your notes and case briefs. Make sure that they are accurate and complete. Finish incomplete sentences, correct misstatements, and clarify ambiguous statements. Think about the class discussion and add your new insights. By routinely reviewing your class notes and case briefs, you will remember more of each class and will be better prepared to understand the next day's reading assignment and class discussion.

If you are still uncertain about a subject that was covered in class, take time to clarify it now. Clarifying a subject is easier and faster when it is fresh in your mind, and you will save time at the end of the semester, when time becomes extremely precious. If you have questions, you can talk with your professor immediately after class. You normally should not ask your professor to help fill in the gaps in your notes; instead, ask a classmate. You may want to stay after class even if you do not have questions. Other students' questions may present a problem that you had not recognized or may provoke an interesting discussion.

If you cannot stay after class, you can go to your professor's office. Check whether your professor has specific office hours or is willing to respond to questions by telephone or electronic mail. Before going to your professor's office to discuss a subject, familiarize yourself with the material in the casebook concerning it. You do not want to ask questions that are answered in the assigned readings, and you will learn more if you can discuss the subject knowledgeably.

Do not be put off if your professor cannot see you immediately. In addition to teaching, professors have a variety of responsibilities, including research, writing, and administrative duties for the law school and for other professional organizations. Professors also must travel to testify before legislative bodies, to present papers at conferences, and for a variety of other purposes. However, effectively educating students is a top priority for your professors. So take advantage of their expertise about the law, course selections, legal practice, and maintaining a balanced life while in school.

B. OUTLINING

Your daily review, like your case briefs and class discussions, generally will focus on the law in bitesized pieces. Therefore, the next step in learning is putting the pieces together. The best way is to prepare a written outline of the materials you have studied. This outline is not just a list of topics you have studied or a collection of your case briefs. Instead, it is your synthesis of the course materials.

The analytic process that is required to prepare an outline is at least as valuable as the completed product. Organizing the materials requires you to determine the exact contours and focus of each doctrine. By working with the concepts, rather than just reading them, you will have better comprehension and recall and will hone your analytic skills. Comprehensively stating the law that you have studied also will reveal weaknesses and gaps in your knowledge.

Although you may be tempted to rely on a commercial outline, do not succumb. It will not provide the benefits that come from preparing your own. Moreover, a commercial outline will not be tailored to your course. Even if it includes the cases in your casebook, it will have a different focus and approach than your professor's. If you try to avoid that problem by using an outline prepared by someone in your class or who has taken it previously, you cannot be certain that the outline is accurate and complete. Therefore, set aside time to prepare an outline for each course. The time and effort you invest will be rewarded.

Begin an outline as soon as you have finished a chapter of the casebook, and supplement the outline as you finish each additional chapter. A chapter ending is a good time to outline because the materials in a chapter normally all relate to the same subject and provide a natural organizational unit. By outlining at the end of each chapter, you also will stagger the task of outlining among your courses; normally, you will finish chapters on different days in different courses. You also will spread the work of outlining over the entire term, rather than trying to prepare complete outlines for each course in the days immediately before finals.

To begin outlining, review your notes and case briefs for the chapter to identify its main topics. The casebook's table of contents can help you in this process. For each topic, gather the following information:

1. Definitions of any terms of art;
2. Relevant rules of law, including a description of each element that must be satisfied for the rule to apply and any differences among the jurisdictions;
3. Exceptions to each rule;
4. Available remedies;
5. Underlying policy considerations;
6. Any important historical background; and
7. Any important reform proposals.

Because the number of class sessions for each course is limited, you may have studied only parts of each topic. For example, you may not have studied all the exceptions to a rule. You are responsible only for the information in the assigned readings and in the class sessions. You are not required to research and to outline additional materials.

Case names and fact patterns from cases usually need not be included in the outline. You should include a case name, however, if it is closely related with a legal doctrine. For example, you will learn in your civil procedure course that the *Erie* doctrine is named for *Erie v. Tompkins*, the case in which the United States Supreme Court first stated the doctrine. Similarly, you should include a fact pattern in your outline only if necessary to describe or to illustrate a rule.

After culling the necessary information from your notes and case briefs, you must synthesize and organize them. You must determine how the topics included in the chapter relate to each other and to the topics you previously have outlined. For example, if the chapter dealt with an intentional tort and you previously outlined another intentional tort, group them together in the outline and note their similarities and differences. If a problem on your torts exam involves intentional wrongdoing, the possible torts will be grouped together in your outline and their unique features will have been identified.

A hornbook can be particularly helpful in organizing and synthesizing the course materials. As described in Chapter 11, a hornbook is a treatise that describes and analyzes a body of law. It can help you put the pieces of the course together, fill in gaps, and clarify ambiguities. Other types of study aids can be useful, although they are not as thorough and are more prone to error. Ask your professor to recommend an outside source.

There is not one proper outline format. The best format depends on the course materials and on the organization that is most helpful to you. To keep the outline to a usable length, avoid including tangential materials no matter how interesting they are. Despite the need for conciseness, however, you should include an example of how a rule applies if the rule is particularly complex or abstract. An example can make the rule more understandable and memorable.

Outlining will be slow going at first. Just as with case briefing, however, you will become more proficient. As your outlining skills improve and as you cover more material in each course, review the earlier portions of the outline to correct and to supplement them. If you have access to a computer, it can be quite helpful as you edit and reorganize your outline.

C. SAMPLE OUTLINE

For practice, try outlining the following materials. They deal with finding lost or mislaid property, which takes us back to the issue used for the case briefing example in Chapter 8. Assume that, after reviewing your notes and case briefs for the casebook chapter on finding property, you identified the following case descriptions, analyses, and questions to include in your outline. Please note that the case descriptions have been abridged for the purpose of this illustration.

Armory v. Delamirie

— A finder of property does not become its owner but has the right to possess it.

— The owner of the property has the right to recover it.

— D, who was not the owner, took a jewel from its finder and would not return it to him. D was held liable to the finder for the value of the finest jewel of the same size unless D presented the jewel and showed that it was worth less.

Bridges v. Hawkesworth

— P found bank notes on the floor in D's shop and gave them to D in case the owner returned. The owner did not return, but D refused to give the notes to P.

— P sued to recover possession of the notes.

— P was entitled to possess the notes because, before being found, they were not in D's possession and had not been left in his shop for safekeeping.

South Staffordshire Water Co. v. Sharman

— P hired D to clean a pond on P's land. D found two gold rings in the mud at the bottom of the pond and refused to give them to P.

— P sued D to recover possession of the rings.

— A person who possesses a house or land with intent to control it and the objects on or in it is entitled to possession of any found object.

  — The land's possessor need not be aware of the object's existence to be entitled to possess it.

— The court distinguished *Bridges* on the ground that the shop in that case was open to the public.

  — Where is the line between public and private places?

    — Is an exclusive, members-only club public or private?

McAvoy v. Medina

— A customer in a barber shop found a pocketbook that a previous customer unintentionally left on a table.

— The court distinguished between "lost" and "mislaid" property.

  — "Mislaid" property is property that is voluntarily placed but accidentally left.

  — "Lost" property is involuntarily placed.

— The owner of the premises where an object is mislaid has the right to possess it.

— A shop owner has a duty to use reasonable care to safekeep mislaid property for its owner.

— The underlying public policy is to restore property to its owner.

  — The owner of mislaid property is more likely to recover it if it is held by the owner of the place where it was mislaid.

  — But the owner of the bank notes in *Bridges* also would be more likely to recover them if the shop owner had them.

— The lost v. mislaid property distinction causes completely opposite results based on ambiguous circumstances.

   — A finder of fact cannot always determine whether an object's owner voluntarily placed it.

   — Would the result in *McAvoy* have been different if someone had knocked the pocketbook to the floor before it was found?

   — In *Bridges*, the bank notes may have been voluntarily placed on a counter and then knocked to the floor.

   — What if a ring is found on the floor near a bathroom sink?

To outline these materials, begin by thinking about the key points that must be included. You know that the property's owner does not lose ownership even if the property is lost or mislaid. In determining the finder's rights, the courts have created distinctions based on the place where the property was found (public v. private) and whether the owner voluntarily parted with possession (lost v. mislaid). How do these distinctions fit together? If the property is mislaid on private land, who is entitled to possession? If it is lost on public land, who is entitled to possession? Work through all the combinations to discover the hierarchy of values and to fill in any gaps in your notes and case briefs. If the cases have not have addressed a particular combination of facts, use the reasoning and policy statements from the cases to analyze the situation.

Then pull all the results together and organize them in outline form.

Sample Outline

I. Found Property

A. Owner

The owner retains ownership of property even after someone else has found it. The owner can recover the property from anyone who has possession.

B. Finder

The finder's right to possess the found property depends on whether it was:

1. Lost or mislaid; and

2. Found in a public or private place.

1. Lost v. Mislaid Property

   a. Property is "lost" if its owner involuntarily parted with possession.

   b. Property is "mislaid" if its owner voluntarily parted with possession and accidentally left it, such as a pocket-book left on a table in a shop.

      i. This distinction will not always be clear. For example, a ring might be found on the floor near a bathroom sink.

   c. If property is mislaid, the owner of the premises where it was found has the right to possess it.

       i. Underlying theory is that the owner is more likely to recover the property if it is left with the owner of the premises.

      ii. This theory is better served by characterizing property as being "mislaid" in unclear cases.

    d. If property is lost, the right of possession depends on whether the property was found in a public or private place.

  2. *Public v. Private Place*

    a. A "public" place is one that is open to the public.

    b. A place is "private" if its possessor intends to exercise control over it and everything found on or in it, such as a private home.

       i. These definitions leave a large middle ground.

    c. If property is found in a public place, the finder is entitled to possess the property.

    d. If property is found in a private place, the owner of the premises is entitled to possess the property.

C. Remedies

A person who wrongfully has possession of an object is subject to the following remedies:

  1. Monetary damages in the amount of the object's value; or

2. An order to return the object to the person who is entitled to possession.

Repeat this process of gathering, synthesizing, and outlining the materials for each topic covered in the course, and prepare a table of contents for quick reference. By keeping up with your outlining, you will have the best possible tool for studying for exams. The outline will be tailored to the materials covered in the course, and the process of preparing and of reviewing the outline will have taken you a long way in your exam preparation. You can spend the days before the exam studying the outline, rather than attempting to read and to synthesize all your notes and case briefs.

After finishing the outline, prepare a very brief version of it. This shortened version should be a checklist that includes just the key words from your outline. For example, a checklist for the sample outline on found property could be written as follows:

Found Property

Owner

Finder

Lost v. mislaid property

Public v. private place

The checklist can be useful both when you are preparing for exams and during an exam. By listing all the topics in the course on two or three pages, you will have a picture of the forest, rather than of the trees that are contained in your outline. In this way, the checklist can help you get an overview of the course and see the ways in which the different topics are interrelated. If you can use the checklist during the exam, it can help you spot issues and answer problems thoroughly. Review the checklist before writing an answer to a question to see whether it triggers in your mind any additional issues that must be addressed. Given the time pressures of an exam and the anxiety you may feel, the checklist can provide an important supplement to your thinking.

D. STUDY GROUPS

A popular image of law school includes students working in study groups. In fact, many students do work in study groups, but many others do not, and study groups take a variety of forms. Some groups meet throughout the semester, while others only meet just before exams. Some people work with the same study group for every class, while others work with a different group for each class. You should study in whatever way works best for you.

If you decide to work with a study group, two to four people is the optimal size. If the group is larger, each person will have only limited time to raise questions, and the discussions can get bogged down. The group members should agree to be prepared for each session, so that each one can contribute to the discussion and not slow the others down. The members also should agree that discussion will be focused on the subject matter, rather than on movies and other diversions.

Do not divide case briefing or outlining among the group members. A very substantial part of the benefit of case briefs and outlines comes from preparing them. Besides, you might lose a group member or discover that a member has done a poor job, which could leave you in bad shape just before finals. Instead, the group members should prepare their own materials, which can be shared and discussed within the group.

In fact, group discussions are the primary benefit of belonging to a study group. The group members will provide a variety of perspectives and problem-solving techniques. As a group, they can spot issues that no one person would spot and can brainstorm to solve problems, to understand cases, and to synthesize the course materials. They also can help clarify confusing class notes and class discussions. For all these reasons, you should be sure to discuss issues with your classmates on a regular basis even if you decide not to join a study group.

CHAPTER 11

STUDY AIDS

A great variety of commercial study aids are available, and many students use them. Some study aids focus on the subject matter of a particular course, while others focus on exam preparation. The most commonly used study aids are hornbooks, subject summaries, subject outlines, case briefs, computer-based exercises, exam reviews, and flash-cards. Each one is described in this chapter.

Study aids are popular with law students for a variety of reasons. The primary reason is that study aids describe the law in a straightforward manner. A student who feels at sea about the substance of the law after reading cases and discussing them in class may view the study aid as a life ring. Study aids often provide illustrative examples of various points of law and may include practice questions and answers with explanations. Additionally, after studying the law in class-sized pieces, study aids can help provide an overview so that you can see how all the pieces fit together. Finally, study aids may provide a different perspective on a subject, which can help you understand its many dimensions.

Although study aids can be helpful, they also present certain dangers and should be used only as supplements to—and not as substitutes for—assigned readings and class discussions. Exclusive reliance on study aids will not prepare you for classes, exams, or the practice of law. In part, this is because study aids present an overly simplified view of the law. To provide a straightforward, concise description of the law, study aids necessarily omit a great deal of detail. When you read a case for class, on the other hand, you must focus on the particular facts of the case, the court's precise statement of the holding, and the nuances of the court's reasoning. Only in this way will you truly understand the case and be able to engage in meaningful class discussion. Your professors use assigned cases as mere points of beginning for their questions and hypotheticals. Simply knowing the holding in a case from a study aid will not prepare you for this type of discussion.

In addition to the potential problems presented by the substance of study aids, the process by which you learn from them can be detrimental. Study aids generally present a fully digested statement of the law, thereby eliminating the necessity for independently analyzing and organizing it. In contrast, law school courses are designed to teach analytic skills. Rather than merely memorizing rules that may change even before you graduate, the case method requires you to evaluate cases, organize them into a comprehensible body of law, and apply them to new situations. Some students fall into the trap of believing that they understand the law because they have read an entire study aid or that memorizing the rules in a study aid is sufficient exam preparation. The exam can be a rude awakening for them. To understand the law, you must do more than read an outline of it.

A final danger is that a study aid's perspective and focus often will differ from your professor's. A law school course can cover only a small portion of the law in the area, and the cases described in the study aid often will be different than the cases in your casebook. Moreover, every body of law is subject to different interpretations. Because your professor, rather than the study aid author, will be grading your exam, you must prepare for and attend class to make sure you know exactly what subjects may be covered on the exam and the approach that your professor has taken. Otherwise, you may find that you are marching to a different drummer than the rest of the class. To find a study aid that is most compatible with a class, ask your professor to recommend one. You should need no more than one.

Despite the potential dangers described above, study aids can be useful supplements for your class and exam preparations. Study aids can reveal important aspects of a topic and can assist your exam preparation by refreshing your memory and by summarizing the topics you have studied. The best type of study aid to use for each course depends on the purposes for which you will be using it and on your individual learning style. Because you want to make the most of your study time and of your

budget, consider the unique features of each of the
following types of aids.

A. HORNBOOKS

Hornbooks are the most thorough and scholarly
type of study aid. They provide a detailed description of the law in a given subject matter area and
include citations to all the leading cases, statutes,
and other sources of law. Although hornbooks do
not have the binding force of law, courts and lawyers often cite them as authority because they usually are written by an established scholar in the
field and often are kept current by a pocket part or
supplemental volume.

A hornbook is particularly helpful when you are
beginning a research project or are confused about a
particular topic. The hornbook will provide a thorough and synthesized discussion and analysis of the
topic, including its historical development, current
status, underlying policies, and potential future development. The hornbook also will cite other
sources, such as law review articles and books, for
additional discussions of the same topic. The hornbook's coverage is sufficiently detailed to provide a
precise view of the law, rather than the more generalized view provided by other types of study aids.

Because hornbooks provide in-depth discussions,
they normally are longer and more detailed than
other types of study aids. If you are looking for an
overview of an entire body of law, rather than a
discussion of a particular topic within that area, a

less detailed type of study aid, such as a subject outline, may be more useful. Other types of study aids also may be more useful in the few days immediately before your exams, though a hornbook can be very helpful in outlining the course in preparation for the exam.

Cost is another consideration. Hornbooks normally are more expensive than other types of study aids, especially because hornbooks are hard-bound. Cost usually does not have to be an issue, however, because your law library's collection will include the best hornbooks. In fact, hornbooks often are kept on reserve in the library because such a great demand exists for their use. Moreover, a hornbook can be viewed as an investment for the future; unlike other types of study aids, you will use hornbooks in the practice of law, as well as in law school.

B. SUBJECT SUMMARIES

Subject summaries, such as West Publishing Company's Nutshells, are a shorter and less expensive alternative to hornbooks. Like hornbooks, subject summaries are written by experts in the area, provide an overview of an area of law in narrative form, and are available for a wide variety of subjects. Some summaries include sample questions and answers, which provide an opportunity to test your understanding of the subject. Because conciseness is a feature of subject summaries, they are necessarily less detailed than a hornbook and do not provide an extensive citation of authorities.

However, subject summaries do discuss the key cases in the area and provide some historical background.

Subject summaries are particularly useful in providing an overview of a subject before studying it in class. By reading the summary before beginning a new topic, you will have a better sense of what to look for in the cases and in the class discussions. For example, if you are about to begin considering the *Erie* doctrine in your civil procedure class, you would be well served by reading that chapter in a civil procedure summary. Without going into a great deal of technical detail, the summary's discussion should be sufficiently descriptive to provide a grounding in the topic.

Subject summaries also can be helpful in preparing for exams. Because an exam can test three or more months of course materials, remembering and organizing them can be challenging. A subject summary can help refresh your memory about the key cases and put the different parts of the course into a coherent whole. The concise narrative style permits relatively fast reading, which is important in the last few days before finals. The drawback, however, is that the discussion may be rather general and may not address all the concepts covered in the course.

C. SUBJECT OUTLINES

Subject outlines, such as Black Letters, Emanuel Law Outlines, Gilbert Law Summaries, and Legalines, come in a variety of formats. The central feature of each is a narrative outline of the basic principles and issues covered in a law school course. The outline explains the rules and the theories behind them and gives examples. Many subject outlines also include practice exam questions and answers and abbreviated summaries and outlines that condense the narrative outline into its most basic and critical components. Some outlines also include cross-references to the leading casebooks in the area so that you can see where the cases in your casebook fit in the subject outline.

Subject outlines are popular with law students for three main reasons. First, outlines organize their subject matter in a straightforward manner. In this way, they provide an overview that helps students see how the different pieces of the subject fit together. Second, the outline is relatively brief. Therefore, students can read an outline section quickly, which is helpful for class and exam preparations. Third, because outlines present the material in more than one way, including summaries and practice questions, the material may be more readily understood and remembered.

You must be careful, however, not to let these benefits become detriments. Because this type of study aid provides an outline of the subject matter, you may be tempted to rely solely on it, rather than preparing your own outline. As described in Chapter 10, outlining is an important step in learning the subject matter, especially during your first year of law school. Additionally, because the outline is relatively brief, it often states the law in a simplified form. Your professor will expect you to have a more detailed knowledge of the law from your course work.

D. CASE BRIEFS

Commercial case briefs are an entirely different type of study aid. Rather than providing a comprehensive description of a particular area of law, Blond's Law Guides, Casenote Legal Briefs, and other commercial case briefs are primarily collections of briefs of cases included in the major casebooks. The case briefs are designed to help students understand and interpret the cases. They also can help students learn to brief cases by providing examples.

Students normally use commercial case briefs to supplement their reading of cases in the casebook. After reading a case and interpreting it, students may check their interpretations of the case against the case brief. In this way, students first independently analyze the case, thereby strengthening their issue spotting and analytic skills. They then further strengthen those skills by comparing their conclusions with those of the study aid author and by assessing the merits of the author's conclusions.

Commercial case briefs may provide a tempting alternative to reading and analyzing the cases in your casebook, especially when you are pressed for time. By reading a commercial brief, however, you will not learn the essential skills that come from independently analyzing and briefing cases, as described in Chapter 8. Moreover, cases can be interpreted in different ways. Relying on a commercial brief eliminates the opportunity to find a better or more creative interpretation. In class, you also will be unable to cite specific language in the case to support the position you have taken based on the case brief because you will be unfamiliar with the opinion.

E. COMPUTER-BASED EXERCISES

Of the various types of study aids, computer-based exercises provide the most interactive and individualized form of learning. The major provider of computer-based exercises is the Center for Computer-Assisted Legal Instruction (CALI), which is a consortium of over 125 law schools. CALI has created a large number of exercises on a variety of subjects, and the exercises are available for all major types of computers. The exercises are available in many law school computer labs, oftentimes free of charge to students.

The exercises come in a variety of formats, including simulated trials. The most common format is a series of questions and answers on a particular legal subject. In this format, the computer asks you a question. If you answer correctly, the computer asks another question. If you answer incorrectly, the computer asks you to give another answer. After the correct answer has been identified, the computer explains why the answer is correct.

After every ten questions, the computer displays your score for those ten questions and for the entire exercise. At the end of the exercise, the computer asks whether you want to review the questions you answered incorrectly and compares your final score to those of other students who have completed the exercise.

Like other types of study aids, computer-based exercises should be viewed as supplements to, and not as substitutes for, assigned readings and class attendance. The exercises normally do not cover all the topics studied in a class. In this way, they are less useful than other types of study aids. The exercises are excellent tools, however, for testing knowledge and for reinforcing weak areas. Plus, many students enjoy using the exercises as a change of pace from reading casebooks and more traditional types of study aids.

F. EXAM REVIEWS

The primary focus of exam reviews, such as FI-NALS, Ryan Law Capsules, and Siegel's Answers to Essay and Multi–Choice Questions, is preparing students for exams. Although some exam reviews include brief outlines or summaries of the law, they primarily consist of sample essay questions, multiple-choice questions, and answers. The exam reviews explain the answers and the underlying reasoning process.

The better exam reviews, however, do more than simply provide practice questions and answers.

They also attempt to teach exam-taking skills. As discussed in Chapter 12, knowing the subject matter of a course may be insufficient to guarantee a good grade. You also must be proficient at the skills required for law school exams. Although these skills come naturally for some students, many other students could improve their performance by studying and practicing exam-taking skills. For these students in particular, an exam review could be helpful.

Unlike other study aids, exam reviews are not designed to teach the substance of a course. Substantive discussions tend to be brief and basic, and some subjects may not be discussed at all. Many questions may address subjects not covered in your class, and few or none may address subjects that were covered in great detail. Therefore, if you do not know or understand the course materials, an exam review is not the resource to use.

On the other hand, if you know the materials, an exam review can be useful as you prepare for exams. The multiple-choice questions in an exam review can help you understand the basic components, as well as the details, for a great deal of material. The essay questions will give you practice spotting issues and organizing and writing answers within a set time limit. By working through both types of questions, you can fine tune your skills and learn from your mistakes before taking the final exam.

G. FLASHCARDS

Flashcard sets, such as Law in a Flash and Study Partner Flashcards, are available for many courses in the law school curriculum. Each set of flashcards is indexed and follows an organizational outline. Normally, a set of flashcards includes several hundred black letter and hypothetical questions. The front of the card asks the question, and the back gives a relatively brief answer. Flashcards also sometimes include mnemonic devices to aid retention.

Some students who have difficulty remembering what they have read find flashcards to be a useful tool. By being forced to think through an answer before reading the answer, the cards require more focused attention than do other, more passive types of study aids. Repeatedly drilling with flashcards also can help students retain what they have read on the cards.

Flashcards also provide an opportunity for studying in groups, which adds variety to your study routine and helps you learn from your peers. After reading a question, the group members discuss the best answer to the question. In this way, you will be actively involved in learning and will be forced to stay alert and attentive. In fact, the group often will formulate a better answer than the one on the card.

Some students find flashcards to be most helpful before beginning a new subject in class. The materials on the flashcards can inform your reading of the class assignments and your participation in class discussions. Other students find the cards to be most helpful when reviewing for exams. Whichever way you use them, you should be careful not to let them create a false sense of confidence. The statements of law on the cards often can be simplistic. Because the law is complex, slight factual differences in a problem can lead to very different results.

CHAPTER 12

EXAMS

Perhaps no subject strikes as much terror into the heart of a law student as exams. In most law school courses, the final examination will be the only written test of your knowledge and skills. Some professors may base your grade in part on your classroom performance and on written or oral exercises, but in most classes your grade will depend largely on your final examination. After working so hard to master the subject matter of a course, you owe it to yourself to acquire the skills necessary to write a successful exam. Contrary to many students' belief, exam taking skills can be learned, just as you have learned to brief a case and to prepare a course outline.

Although the questions on a law school exam may take a variety of forms, the most common is the essay question. An essay question gives a fact pattern and requires you to apply the law you have learned to the fact pattern to reach a legal conclusion. The methods that you must use are the same as those you will use as a practicing lawyer. When a client tells you about a problem, s/he will describe the facts of the situation to you. Your job as a legal counselor is to analyze your client's situation in light of the governing law. To do so, you must understand the relevant body of law, determine the legally relevant facts, elicit any additional necessary information, and determine the outcome of applying the law to the facts. Therefore, a law school exam tests not only your mastery of the subject matter of the course, but also how well you have learned to think like a lawyer.

A. PREPARING FOR THE EXAM

Exam preparation consists of two parts: learning both the substance of the course and the form the exam is likely to take.

1. THE SUBSTANCE OF THE COURSE

Each person's method for learning differs. In preparing for exams, you should stay with the method that has worked best for you during the school term. Regardless of the study method you use, briefing each case that has been assigned in your classes, as described in Chapter 8, and preparing an outline of each course, as described in Chapter 10, are particularly useful, especially during your first year. Once you have briefed the cases and outlined the materials, your primary study tools are complete. Your job at this point is to become thoroughly familiar with their contents.

Do not be lulled into a false sense of security by your ability to read through the case briefs and outlines and to recite them verbatim. Mastery of the material means that you can explain each concept in plain language. Imagine that you are trying to explain the concept to a friend who is not in law school. Can you explain it in a way that your friend will understand? Can you give your friend an example of a situation in which it will apply? Can you tell your friend the purpose of the rule? Only by engaging in this type of exercise will you know whether you truly understand the material. The same advice applies if you are relying on commercially prepared case briefs and outlines. You may experience a false sense of security because you can read through them without seeing any words that you do not understand.

Thinking about the course as a whole also is important to your exam preparation. During the rush of the school term, you may fall into a pattern of learning the law in discrete pieces as you study them in each class. In fact, with the onslaught of new vocabulary and concepts, you often will feel that you have accomplished a lot just to master each day's assignments. But the law is a seamless web. To understand and apply it, you must understand how all the strands weave together. Law professors often refer to this as understanding the "big picture." To see the big picture, think about these questions:

- What are the policy considerations in this area of law?

- Which rules take precedence over others?

- What roles do the different branches and levels of government play in shaping and in applying the law in this area?

- What are the most effective tools for redressing injuries to the rights recognized in this area of law?

By considering these and similar questions, you will synthesize the course materials. This process of synthesis is the most challenging and the most satisfying part of studying law. It enables you to understand the real workings of the law and to develop an informed philosophy about it.

Hornbooks and law review articles can be particularly helpful to you in this endeavor, because they systematically examine an area of law and pull together its many strands. Based on the authors' expertise in the area, they will discuss the current state of the law, the directions in which it is moving, and the ways in which it can be improved. Take advantage of that expertise, as well as of the insights of your professors and fellow students.

2. THE FORM OF THE EXAM

In addition to learning the substance of a course, you should prepare for the form of the exam. An important first step is to talk with your professor. Ask what materials, if any, you can use during the exam. The answer to this question will affect how you prepare for the exam. For example, if the exam will be completely closed book, you may want to allocate time for memorizing some of the course materials. If you can bring a copy of the relevant statutes into the exam and can annotate them before the exam, you should allocate time for that purpose. Therefore, ask as early in the term as possible what materials, if any, you will be allowed to use as a reference source during the exam.

You also should ask your professor to describe her grading philosophy.

- Will your grade be based in part on how well your answer is organized and written?

- Should you cite case names and statute numbers or are descriptions of the relevant legal rules sufficient?

- Should you discuss each element of an applicable rule if only one element is questionable in its application, or should you merely state that all but one element is satisfied and discuss only that element?

- Should you discuss the law only as it currently exists or also as you think it should be changed based on the underlying policies?

The answers to these and similar questions will help you to understand the criteria by which your answers will be evaluated.

In addition to talking with your professors, you should find out whether copies of past exams are available. Many law schools keep files of exams, usually in the law library. You should look for exams given by your professors for the courses in which you will be tested. In this way, you can learn the type of test your professor has given in the past, such as essay, short answer, or multiple choice, and the types of questions your professor may be likely to ask.

- Does your professor routinely test particular topics?

- Does your professor often test the ability to construe statutes, to apply policy to decide issues not yet clearly governed by the law, or to apply the established common law to a fact situation?

- Does your professor normally ask the examinee to act as an advocate or as a neutral evaluator of the facts and law?

As will be discussed later in this chapter, your approach in answering each of these types of questions will be similar, but a review of past exams will give you a better sense of what to expect from the exam you will be taking.

Past exams also are an excellent tool for reviewing the course materials and for practicing your test taking skills. By preparing answers to a previous year's exam, you will discover how well you understand the subject matter, particularly if you work on the exam with other students. Working with other students also helps you spot all the issues raised by a question and demonstrates different methods for approaching an exam question. You should write out answers to past year's questions within the time allocated for them to get a sense of the speed with which you will have to work during the exam and to practice budgeting your time. If your professor's past exams are unavailable or if you want additional practice and insights into the types of questions that might be asked, you can look at exams given by other professors who have taught the course at your law school and find out whether exams from other law schools are available.

3. LAW SCHOOL POLICIES

As a first-year student, you also should investigate whether any school policies concerning exams exist. For example, your school may have an honor code that includes provisions about taking exams. If so, you should get a copy of these rules and carefully study them to avoid violating them and facing possible sanctions. Your ethical responsibilities in the legal profession begin when you are a law student, and ignorance of the rules is not a defense.

Policies also may exist to deal with special circumstances. For example, if English is a second language for you or if a physical or other condition makes reading or writing the exam more difficult for you, you may be given additional time for taking the exam. If you unexpectedly cannot take the exam because of a family emergency or because you are ill, you should immediately notify the law school administrator responsible for administering the test. Do not wait until after the exam. Find out what, if any, documentation you will need to excuse your absence from the exam.

4. ANXIETY AND PROCRASTINATION

Many people, if not all, experience anxiety about law school examinations. Anxiety can be useful as a motivation for studying. If anxiety is interfering with your ability to study, however, you should take time to learn to control it. Many books and audio tapes are available on the subjects of dealing with anxiety and procrastination. Additionally, many schools offer help in dealing with these problems, often through the campus health service or counseling center. If you are experiencing one or both of these problems in law school, the chances are that they will continue to be problems for you when you practice law. Therefore, just as you are learning how to study law and to take law school exams, learn how to master anxiety and procrastination. These patterns of behavior can be changed.

B. TAKING THE EXAM
1. THE NIGHT BEFORE THE EXAM

Many people recommend that you go to a movie or otherwise relax the night before an exam, rather than staying up all night cramming. All other things being equal, you probably will perform better on an exam if you are well-rested. If cramming has been your most successful study method in the past, however, you should feel free to stay with it. Research concerning first-year law students' study methods indicates that grades are not affected by whether a student crams for a test or spreads his study time more evenly over the course of the semester. You should take into account, however, that law school exam periods normally are longer in length and test greater amounts of material than you previously have experienced. Therefore, keep these differences in mind when planning your preparation strategy so that you can maintain your performance level through the end of the exam period.

2. DURING THE EXAM

Feeling nervous during the exam is absolutely normal. Work to channel your adrenaline into taking the exam. The adrenaline will help you focus your full attention on the questions and on the course materials. If you are too panicked to focus your thoughts, take a few deep breaths and remind yourself that you have worked hard in the course, all you can do at this point is give the exam your best effort, and you only have to get through the next few hours and then you can go home and forget about the exam. Take a minute to think through the following rules about reading the questions and about organizing and writing your answers. If you can follow these rules, you will avoid many of the common test-taking errors and will write answers that best demonstrate your knowledge and abilities.

a. Reading the Exam

The first step is to read the exam instructions carefully.

- Are you required to answer all the questions?
- Are there limits on the length or form of your answers?
- How much time do you have for each question?
- Should you discuss a particular jurisdiction's laws?
- Will points be deducted for incorrect answers?
- Can you write an explanation of your answer on a multiple-choice exam?

If an instruction is unclear, ask for a clarification, rather than hope that you have interpreted it correctly.

After you understand the exam instructions, you are ready to read the questions. Some people prefer to read all the exam questions before they begin to write any answers to get a sense of the exam's overall structure and to allocate time among the questions if the times have not been specified. Reading all the questions immediately also can allow your thinking to begin on the answers to all the questions. Additionally, if you are not required to answer the questions in the order in which they are given, you can find the question that is easiest for you to answer. In this way, you can take a running start into the exam and warm up for the more difficult questions.

People often immediately read the entire exam for another reason, however, that actually may hurt their performance. Because an exam is testing a limited universe of knowledge—the materials covered in the course being tested—some people think that they can determine which questions are designed to test each of the course topics. In a property law exam, for example, they might think that the first question is the concurrent ownership question, the second question is the landlord-tenant question, and the third question is the license question.

To a degree, this approach is accurate. Because of the time constraints of an exam and the large body of knowledge to be tested, professors usually will not test the same topic in depth in more than one question. This assumption is a dangerous one, however. First, if you incorrectly believe that a question raises a particular issue, you may then incorrectly believe that the issue is not raised in any other questions. Second, the professor may test different aspects of the same topic in different questions. Third, and most serious, this approach may cause you to be less comprehensive and creative in your answer to each question. By neatly categorizing the questions by subject matter, you will constrain your thinking about the problem.

You also may prefer not to read the entire test immediately to avoid increasing your feelings of confusion and panic. If you are having difficulty focusing on the exam or keeping the facts and parties straight, reading several more sets of facts probably will increase your confusion. Additionally, while you are writing the first answer, your thoughts about the later problems may disappear. In this case, the time spent reading the entire exam will have been wasted. As with the other aspects of taking exams, you should determine the method that works best for you and stay with it unless special circumstances dictate otherwise.

Once you have selected a question to answer, you should read it three times before beginning to write. The first time, focus on the facts and on the exact question you have been asked. The exam question usually will not ask you simply to discuss the applicability of a particular legal rule to the facts. Instead, the question usually will be framed more generally. For example, the question may ask: "Does your client have any causes of action against the manufacturer of the product that injured her?" Before reading the question a second time, start to identify the issues that the facts may raise. Based on the course materials you have studied, you will recognize that certain relationships between people and certain types of conduct create legal rights and liabilities. You must determine which of those rights and liabilities are involved in the exam question. If the question does direct you to consider the applicability of a particular rule of law, think about the elements that are necessary to satisfy that rule and about potential defenses.

As you now read the question a second time, your mind will be focused on the issues that the problem potentially raises. Look for the facts that have a bearing on those issues. In addition to the issues you spotted during the first reading, new issues may appear to you now that you have the complete fact pattern in mind. With respect to these additional issues, follow the same process of considering the necessary elements and any potential defenses. Think also about any related causes of action. For example, if a landlord who fails to provide a lock on a lobby door may be liable for negligence, consider whether that failure also constitutes a breach of the lease.

You are now ready for the third reading. With this reading, ask yourself why each fact is in the question. If the problem states that someone is seventeen years old, ask yourself why the person's age is mentioned. Is the issue of legal capacity relevant to the problem? If the problem states that a person is married, is an issue of marital rights in property involved? Of course, the professor may have added these details merely to dress up the problem or even to mislead the unwary. But never assume. Instead, search for the reason for each fact.

As one further check of the completeness of your issue spotting, run through an outline of the subjects you have studied in the course. If the test is open book, you can use the index of the casebook or a written list that you have prepared. If the test is closed book, memorize the list of topics. Not every topic will be included in the exam, but thinking through them will help ensure that you have not overlooked a relevant issue.

b. Taking Notes

As you go through each of these reviews, taking notes is critically important. The notes need not be elaborate. You should write just enough to remind yourself of issues that you have spotted and of the facts that are relevant to those issues. Depending on the rules your school may have about note taking, you can write the notes in the margin of the test or on a separate sheet of paper. By doing this, you will have a checklist for organizing and writing your answer.

The importance of taking notes cannot be overstated. Under the stress and hurry of taking an exam, you may spot an issue and then forget it or forget to write about it. Often a student who believes that his grade on an exam does not reflect his knowledge of the subject matter is shocked when he reviews his bluebooks after the exam and finds that he failed to write about an issue that he was sure he had discussed. This situation is especially frustrating because it is so easy to avoid. Note taking requires very little time and can have a significant effect on your exam performance.

c. Common Errors

Unfortunately, failing to take notes is only one type of error that commonly occurs in the process of reading the exam questions. You also should be careful to avoid the following pitfalls.

i. Misreading the Question

Whether due to stress or fatigue, students often misread one or more critical parts of the question. For example, students sometimes jumble the parties in the problem, discussing the plaintiff as though

she were the defendant and vice versa, or overlook
the word "not" in a statute that must be construed.
By changing the question in these or other ways,
you inevitably will lose points even if your professor
can salvage part of the answer. Force yourself to
read the question carefully before you begin analyzing it and writing your answer.

ii. Ignoring Facts

Virtually every exam question requires more
analysis than the straightforward application of
black letter law to a clear-cut set of facts. Questions generally include both facts that support application of a particular rule of law and facts that
are inconsistent with application of that rule. Your
professor puts inconsistent facts in the question for
three reasons. First, your professor may be testing
your knowledge of the elements of a particular legal
rule by seeing whether you can spot the facts that
create a question as to the rule's applicability. Second, your professor may be testing your ability to
determine whether inconsistent facts create defenses and whether you can rebut those defenses.
Third, your professor may be testing your ability to
identify and to apply the policy considerations that
a court would weigh to resolve the question created
by the conflicting facts. You will need all three of
these abilities when you practice law because the
resolution of actual issues often requires balancing
conflicting facts and policies. Therefore, if a fact in
an exam problem is contrary to your position, identify that fact in your answer and give your analysis

of its legal effect no matter how great an urge you feel to pretend that it does not exist.

iii. Assuming Facts

Two types of errors can occur when you assume facts that are not in the exam question. The first error can occur when the question does not include all the facts that you need to reach a conclusion. Your professor may have omitted the fact to test your diagnostic skills. As a lawyer, you must be able to determine the information you need to respond to a client's problem. Therefore, in your exam answer, you should identify the information that is missing and describe its relevance to your analysis.

By omitting a necessary fact, your professor also may be testing your ability to analyze the problem under more than one fact scenario. For example, if the answer to a contract law question depends on whether the agreement was written or verbal but the question does not include this information, you first should answer the question based on the existence of a written agreement and then based on the existence of a verbal agreement. Do not assume away half the answer by stating that you assume the agreement was in writing. Although you may get credit for having noticed that the question did not specify whether the agreement was in writing, you will miss the points allocated for your analysis of the outcome based on the absence of a written agreement.

The second type of error occurs by assuming a fact that changes the question. For example, if the question involves a killing, do not state in your answer that you assume the killing was committed in self-defense unless the question provides some basis for that conclusion. This type of assumption obviously substantially changes the complexion of the problem. As a result, your answer will bear little relationship to your professor's grading outline. Remarkably, students often make such unjustified assumptions that eliminate issues or simplify their resolution. Therefore, before writing your answer to a question, compare your assumptions to the stated facts of the problem to ensure that each assumption is warranted.

iv. *Answering Questions That Have Not Been Asked*

The final pitfall that can occur when reading an exam question is failing to focus on the exact question that has been asked. This problem arises when you either discuss issues beyond the scope of the question or fail to answer in the manner specified. The first problem can arise in two ways. Obviously, you should discuss only those issues that relate to the subject matter of the course. If you are taking a torts exam, for example, you should not spend time writing about an issue of procedure unless you also have studied that issue in your torts course.

The second situation in which it can arise is when the question asks you to discuss the rights of a particular party or a particular issue. For example, assume that the question describes a car accident involving three people, Adams, Baker, and Chen, and then asks: "What causes of action does Adams have against Baker?" Even if you have identified causes of action that Adams has against Chen or that are available to Baker or Chen, suppress the urge to show that knowledge. It is irrelevant to the question that has been asked.

Similarly, assume that the question asks: "Does Adams have an action for negligence against Baker?" Even if you believe that Adams has other causes of action against Baker, discuss only the negligence action. Although answering questions that have not been asked normally will not lower your grade directly, it will do so indirectly by wasting time that could have been spent on relevant issues.

You also can lose time and points by failing to answer in the manner specified in the question. Focus on whether the question asks for a neutral evaluation of the problem or for an advocate's presentation. If the question asks that you determine whether a person has acted negligently, you should evaluate the problem as a judge would. You should discuss objectively the facts and legal principles indicating that the party acted negligently and those indicating that he did not. You then should state your overall conclusion concerning the issue of negligence.

On the other hand, if the problem directs you to act as an attorney for one of the parties or to make the best possible argument for a particular position, you should discuss the problem as an advocate. You should present the facts and law in the light most favorable to your position. Even as an advocate, however, you cannot ignore facts and legal doctrines that undercut your position. Part of being an advocate is recognizing the arguments against your position and explaining why those arguments do not require a result contrary to your client's best interests. Therefore, writing as an advocate is similar to writing as a judge; you must address all the relevant facts and legal doctrines. The difference is in the focus of your answer.

By carefully reading each exam question and by avoiding the pitfalls described above, you will have passed a big hurdle in taking the exam. You will be prepared to answer the question that your professor has asked and on which she has based her grading scale. Your knowledge of the subject matter and your analytic abilities will not help you receive the grade that you should unless you take time to focus your full attention on each question as it has been written.

d. Thinking Through and Organizing Your Answer

Carefully reading the exam question is just the first preparatory step to writing your answer. The other crucially important steps are thinking through your answer and organizing its presentation. You should use at least one-quarter of your time for each question on this process. Some peo-

ple advise that you use as much as one-half of your
time. Although you probably will feel a strong urge
to start writing your answer immediately after
reading the problem, especially when everyone
around you seems to be furiously writing, curb that
urge. Overall, you will save time because you will
avoid writing about irrelevant issues, writing an
answer that you later decide is incorrect, and losing
yourself in the convoluted presentation of an argument.

The easiest and best format for you to use is the
one that you have used in class and in your legal
writing program:

- Identify each issue raised by the problem;

- Identify the legal rule that governs that issue;

- Analyze the facts in light of the legal rule; and

- Reach a conclusion.

Just as you did when reading the problem, take
notes as you think through and organize your answer. By doing so, you will remember to include
each part of your answer and you will be sure to
follow the organization you have developed. The
outline need not be extremely detailed. Rather, it
should include just enough information to serve as a
check list.

i. Identifying Issues

When reading the problem, you will have identified issues that potentially are raised by it. As you
now think through the problem and your answer,

ask yourself which of these issues must be resolved to answer the question. In other words, identify the legally relevant issues. Although the facts in the problem may raise many issues, you should address only those that have a bearing on the specific question you have been asked. This process of identifying the legally relevant issues is the same one you have used in your classes and on your legal writing assignments. You are distinguishing the relevant facts and law from the irrelevant. Writing a brilliant discussion of an irrelevant issue will not increase your grade.

Assessing an issue's relevance is inextricably linked with analyzing the question. For example, assume that the exam includes the following question:

> Adams sold a parcel of land, Blackacre, to Baker and Chen, who are unmarried. The deed stated: "Adams hereby conveys Blackacre to Baker and Chen as joint owners." Chen subsequently transferred his interest to Dale. What is the current state of title to Blackacre?

Recognizing that the deed language may have created either a joint tenancy or a tenancy in common, you might be tempted to address that issue. If you first analyze the problem, however, you will discover that the issue is irrelevant to answering the question. Whether a joint tenancy or tenancy in common was created, Chen had the legal power to transfer his interest to Dale, and Baker and Dale own Blackacre as tenants in common.

When writing your answer to this question, you should state that the deed language is ambiguous with respect to whether a joint tenancy or a tenancy in common was created. A detailed analysis of that issue is unnecessary, however, because it does not affect the current state of title. You simply should state that Chen could transfer his interest regardless of whether he was a joint tenant or a tenant in common and then analyze the state of title after the transfer. By thinking through the problem in this way before beginning to write an answer, you will avoid writing about an irrelevant issue.

No magic formula exists for knowing which issues to discuss. You are better served, however, by erring on the side of overinclusiveness. For example, if you think that a legal principle does not apply clearly to the situation described in the exam problem but that the policies underlying the principle would be served by applying it, you should discuss that issue. Similarly, if you are applying a rule that includes three elements, two of which are clearly satisfied but one of which arguably is not, you should include a discussion of the rule and its elements and explain the ambiguity in the application of the third element. When discussing issues that are not clearly relevant, you should spend less time than you do for the more clearly relevant issues. By including at least a brief discussion, however, you will demonstrate that you considered the issue and will have addressed it in case your professor disagrees with your conclusion that the rule may not apply.

ii. Identifying the Legal Rule

After identifying the relevant issues, you should identify the legal rule that applies to each issue. This step includes identifying:

- The distinct elements of each rule;

- Any relevant exceptions to the rule;

- Relevant case names and statutes if your professor wants those citations; and

- The policies and trends in the rule's application.

The sources for these rules are your casebook, any other assigned materials, and your class notes. Unless your professor directs otherwise, you should identify the majority and minority rules if a split exists among the jurisdictions.

iii. Analyzing the Problem

Analysis is the most important part of an exam answer. No client will be satisfied if you merely identify the legal issues raised by the client's situation and describe the relevant rules of law. Instead, a client correctly expects you to explain how the law applies to his situation. This process of analysis is the process of "thinking like a lawyer" that you have been developing in your classes. Your analysis is particularly important for an open book exam, because your professor knows that you will have the legal rules before you. Therefore, you will receive few, if any, points for merely reciting the rule. Instead, the professor will be focusing on how well you can apply the rules to the facts of the problem.

Few essay questions require only the straightforward application of an established rule to an unambiguous fact pattern. By thinking through your analysis of the problem before beginning to write, you can avoid some common exam errors. You will avoid pursuing lines of analysis that lead to a dead end. The presentation of your analysis also will be more cogent; rather than careening from point to point, you can present a consistent and comprehensible line of analysis. Moreover, as discussed above, reasoning the problem through to its conclusion is a necessary predicate to determining which issues are relevant.

The most common and serious error that occurs when analyzing a problem is assuming that only one right answer exists and giving the analysis for that answer only. The obvious danger to this approach is that you have reached an incorrect conclusion. Equally important, your professor probably wrote the question so that it could be answered in more than one way. Professors often test whether you can spot ambiguities in the facts and in the law. They also want to test your creativity in applying the law in new ways and to new situations.

In fact, the adversarial nature of our legal system indicates that more than one view of the applicable facts and law is very common. Therefore, be creative in your approach. If you have been asked to construe a statute, do not limit your analysis to the

interpretation that is most obvious to you. Instead,
think about other ways the language could be construed. As a zealous advocate for your client, you
must search for the interpretation that best serves
her legal interests. Imagining that you are the
attorney for a party opposing your interpretation
may be helpful to you in this process. Ask yourself
how you would interpret the facts and law differently from the original conclusion that you reached.
For each possible interpretation, determine which
facts and legal rules are relevant to that interpretation. In this way, your answer will be as complete
as possible.

iv. *Reaching a Conclusion*

After analyzing an issue, you should determine
the most likely outcome of applying the law to the
facts. Again, place yourself in the position of an
attorney advising a client. The client will want
your professional opinion as to the likely outcome of
her case. She will not be satisfied with just your
analysis of the strong and weak points of the case.
If the probable outcome of a court's determination
of an issue is unclear, you can state that it is
difficult to predict and explain why. However, you
still should reach an overall conclusion for each
issue that you address.

After reaching a conclusion for the first issue, you
should repeat the process described above. For
each issue that you have spotted, you should identify the relevant legal rules, analyze the application
of the law to the facts, and reach a conclusion as to

the outcome of the issue. After completing this process for each issue, you should reach an overall conclusion to the question. By approaching the problem in this way, you will greatly facilitate your ability to reason through the problem, and you will be thorough and comprehensible in your written answer.

e. Writing the Exam Answer

With your outline complete, you are ready to write your answer. Beginning with the first issue, you should state the issue, identify the relevant legal rule, apply the law to the facts, and state your conclusion. Then address the next issue in the same way and continue to follow the same format until you have addressed each issue. After discussing all the issues, you should state your final conclusion concerning the problem. Unlike a legal memorandum, you should not restate the facts at the beginning of the problem or include an introductory statement of issues and conclusions.

In many, if not most, exams, you will feel significant time pressure. Therefore, you should not expect to write a brilliant and polished analysis of each issue. It is more important that you discuss each issue in the format described above and that you not exceed the time you have for each question. If the allotted time for a question is running out faster than your ideas, outline the rest of your answer in as much detail as you can. Your professor then can see that you spotted the issue and that you could give at least a brief statement of the governing law and of your analysis. Normally, you will receive more points on an exam by addressing all the issues than you will by writing an extremely detailed analysis of a limited number of issues.

i. *Common Errors*

In writing exam answers, the two most common errors are overinclusiveness and underinclusiveness. The problem of overinclusiveness is also known as "treatise-itis." The main symptom of treatise-itis is writing a treatise on the law generally surrounding each issue, rather than discussing just the question that has been asked. For example, if the question involves a tenant's right to terminate a lease, the sufferer of treatise-itis will write about the legal requirements for a valid lease, the types of tenancies that may be created by a lease, and the landlord's and tenant's obligations during the lease term, rather than writing only about the situations in which a tenant can terminate a lease.

After working hard all term to learn a subject, a strong desire to show off all that knowledge in the bluebooks is understandable. It is a mistake for two reasons, however. First, you will waste time writing about irrelevant material. Second, students who are suffering from treatise-itis often get so wrapped up in writing a treatise of legal doctrine that they often fail to reach the steps of analyzing the problem and stating a conclusion. This omission is particularly serious because, as described above, analysis is the most important part of an exam answer. Therefore, limit your description of legal rules to those you have identified in your outline as being directly relevant to the issue. Otherwise, the relevant material that you discuss may be lost in a sea of irrelevant material.

The problem of underinclusiveness also is quite common. This problem occurs when the bluebooks contain only a conclusory statement of the answer to a question. Because your bluebooks are the only means by which your professor can evaluate your exam performance, you should give thorough statements of the relevant issues and legal rules and of your analyses and conclusions.

For example, assume that a question on your property law exam asks you to classify a future interest and that you conclude it is a contingent remainder. Do not simply state that the interest is a contingent remainder. Instead, describe the relevant rules of law for classifying the interest and describe the analytic steps that you took to determine, first, that the interest is a remainder and, second, that the remainder is contingent. Otherwise, your professor may think that you simply made a lucky guess and will not award you the points allocated for your statement of the law and for your analysis. Similarly, do not substitute a statement that a conclusion is "clear" or "obvious" for a description of your analysis in reaching that conclusion. Unless you explain why the conclusion is apparent, your professor will not know whether you can perform the necessary analysis.

f. Form of the Answer

Although the substance of your answer is of primary importance, the form also can play an important role. If your professor cannot decipher the flow of your logic, your discussion will be pointless. To help ensure that the form of your answer is comprehensible, observe the following recommendations:

- Begin your discussion of each issue with a heading that briefly identifies it. By doing so, you will provide a clear guidepost for your professor and flag your discussion of the major points.

- If you use abbreviations, include a description of them at the beginning of your answer. Otherwise, your professor may be unable to follow your answer.

- Define a term of art when the result in a problem turns on the precise meaning of the term. For example, if the question involves an issue of fraud, define that term to demonstrate your understanding of the concept and to help focus your discussion of the issue. Similarly, if a relevant legal rule involves more than one element, state the elements and address each one in your discussion.

- Do not expect your professor to refer to your answer to another question. Even if you think that the same issue has been raised in a previous question, do not write: "See my discussion of this issue in Question 1." Instead, you should state a legal rule in each problem in which it is relevant and should present your analysis of the rule's application to the particular facts of the problem.

- If you have difficulty writing legibly, type your answers. Although a professor usually will not consciously reduce your grade for illegible bluebooks, you run the risk that parts of your answer will be difficult or impossible to read. If you plan to use a personal computer, check your school's policies to determine whether you can do so.

- Do not misspell words, especially terms of art. If you cannot spell a term, a question arises as to whether you really understand the concept it represents. If you have difficulty with spelling, treat English as you would a foreign language that you are trying to learn. When you are uncertain about the spelling of a word, look it up in the dictionary. It is no answer to say that, when you are a practicing lawyer, you will have a secretary who will worry about the spelling for you. Your secretary will not always be available, and, besides, your secretary may not spell very well either! Two commonly misspelled words are judgment (only one "e") and "defendant" (only two "e"s).

C. AFTER THE EXAM

Immediately after taking the exam, you should forget about it. Otherwise, you may distract yourself from studying for the next exam by worrying about the one you have just taken. As you think about an exam you have taken, you unintentionally may start changing the facts and worrying because you did not address issues presented by the altered fact pattern. Little, if anything, can be gained by worrying about a past exam. Instead, direct your energy and attention to the next one.

If you are disappointed with the grade you receive, you should ask to see your answer and the model answer or grading outline for the exam, if one exists. If you still are uncertain about the mistakes you made, make an appointment with your professor to discuss your exam. Although this may be embarrassing or difficult for you, it is the best way to improve your performance. Only by seeing the errors that you made will you know how to improve. Exam skills can be learned, and you will learn them more quickly if you know your weaknesses.

CHAPTER 13

OTHER ACTIVITIES DURING
THE FIRST YEAR

Undoubtedly, most of your time and attention
during the first year will be occupied by your
classes. There are many extracurricular activities
in law school, however, and you should participate
in these activities, even during your intense first
year of law school. You also need to save some time
for yourself and for your family and friends.

A. LAW STUDENT ORGANIZATIONS

There will be a student governance body, often
known as the Law School Council, at your law
school. This Council usually has representatives
from each of the three law school classes, including
the first-year class. If you are interested in participating in law school governance work, you should
become involved with the Council activities. You
can get involved either by running for election as a
class representative or by serving on one of the
committees of the Council. These committees deal
with a variety of law school subjects, such as the
curriculum, faculty hiring, or the placement program. All of these subjects are critically important
to your law school experience. Participation in

193

these activities will give you a better understanding of the resources available from your law school and a more informed perspective on your law study. In addition, you typically will become better acquainted with faculty members and administrators at your law school, who also may serve on these committees.

In addition to law school governance activities, your law school will have many other student organizations available for your active participation. The following is a list of some of the organizations that you may be able to join at your law school:

American Bar Association Law Student Division

Asian American Law Student Association

Black Law Student Association

Catholic Law Student Association

Christian Law Student Association

Entertainment Law Society

Environmental Law Society

Federalist Society

Gay and Lesbian Law Student Association

High School Law Teaching Program

International Law Student Association

Islamic Law Student Association

Jewish Law Student Association

Justice Foundation

La Raza Legal Alliance

Law Student Newspaper

Legal Fraternities

National Lawyers Guild

Native American Law Student Association

Sports Law Association

Women Law Student Association

If your law school does not have a student organization in an area of your interest, you should speak with the Dean of Students about how to create such an organization at your school. Participation in student organizations helps to develop organizational and leadership skills. It also will make your law school experience more enjoyable as you interact with other law students who share a common interest with you.

B. ATHLETIC ACTIVITIES

In addition to the many student organizations, athletic activities are available at most law schools. These activities may be operated as part of the intramural program of the larger university or college of which the law school may be a part. These intramural sports activities provide an opportunity for coeducational participation in sports programs, which are an additional way of building friendships with your law school classmates.

C. LECTURES AND SPECIAL EVENTS

Your law school will present several lectures and other special events, such as debates, panel discus-

sions, and films. Plan your schedule to attend
these events and to take advantage of these opportunities. The speakers will be leading advocates
and commentators about current legal and political
issues. Attending these events will contribute im-
portantly to your intellectual growth as you are
exposed to new ideas and have an opportunity to
analyze critically the presentations with your classmates. Rarely during your entire legal career will
you have a comparable opportunity to attend so
many interesting presentations about the law and
government.

D. FIELD TRIPS

There are many places and activities in the community that will be instructive for you to visit. You
should take time to visit the courthouse in your
community—both federal and state if they are located there. While at the courthouse, sit in and observe a trial and talk to the court administrator
about judicial administration issues in that court.
Oftentimes, your law school will make it easy for
you to observe a trial or appellate hearing by arranging for an actual court session to be held in
your law school.

Other interesting and enjoyable trips in the community include visiting a legislator or the legislative
clerk, visiting an attorney practicing in an area of
your interest, and observing a foreclosure sale. Be
creative. Think about ways to add variety to your
schedule by observing the law in action. You will

find that the lawyers and judges you seek to visit usually will be very happy to talk with you.

E. LAW SCHOOL EMPLOYMENT

If you will be attending law school full-time, you should try to avoid employment during your first year. Your hours will be more than consumed by your class preparation and attendance, as well as by other law school activities.

If it is essential for you to be employed to meet your expenses, however, you should limit your employment hours as much as possible. The American Bar Association accreditation standards require that accredited law schools have a policy limiting outside employment to twenty hours per week. Of course, if you are attending night law school part-time, you may work full-time during the day. Your night law school educational program has been designed with your employment needs in mind.

If you must work, try to find employment that does not conflict with your study schedule. Look for work close to the law school to limit your commuting time. In fact, some excellent work opportunities are in the law school itself, such as working as an assistant in the law library or as a research assistant for a professor. A research assistant job with a faculty member is an excellent educational experience and will enable you to develop a close relationship with a faculty member who can serve as a reference for you when you seek permanent employment after graduation. Because research assistant positions are highly sought after, however, it may be difficult to obtain such a job in your first year of law school.

If possible, find a law-related job so that you can learn on the job by seeing the law in practice. The best way to begin your search is with a visit to your law school Career Services Office. Law firms and other employers post notices of part-time jobs there, and the Office may be able to assist you in obtaining part-time employment while you are a law student. It also can be of great help to you in obtaining summer employment after your first and second years of law school.

Law firms traditionally hire law students to work as law clerks at the firm during the summer break period. Firms frequently use the services of the Career Services Office to identify the summer clerks they will employ. These law firm summer clerkships are in great demand by law students, because they are an excellent educational experience and because law firms frequently hire their permanent associate attorneys from the firm's summer clerkship program. Usually, the second-year students have first priority on the summer clerkship jobs, but the Career Services Office at most law schools will assist the first-year students during the second semester of the first year.

F. TAKE TIME FOR YOURSELF

While you pursue your studies intensively during the first year, it is important to reserve some time for relaxation. Schedule time to go to a movie, do a run, or engage in some other activity that you enjoy to keep yourself well rounded and physically and mentally healthy.

It also is essential to take care of relationships that are important to you. Law school can be a time of great stress as you feel the pressures of the educational experience. You will be changing in the way you think about problems, and you probably will not have as much free time as previously. Those changes will affect others with whom you have a relationship. You should work on keeping those relationships strong. It may take some special effort, but it is well worth it. If you invest the time and effort, relationships that are important to you can grow even stronger during the years of your study of law.

G. PRO BONO ACTIVITIES

We hope that early in your law school experience you will develop a commitment to pro bono (literally, "for the good") legal services. A lawyer's obligation to perform pro bono service is one of the principal characteristics that distinguishes law as a profession. This obligation may be discharged by providing legal services without fee to those who cannot afford to pay for those services or by working to broaden access to justice for groups that historically have been excluded.

Your law school experience should help you develop this commitment. There will be many opportunities to volunteer your time for pro bono service in law school. A good place to look for these opportunities is the Student Justice Foundation in your law school.

Whenever your commitment to pro bono service begins, it should remain with you throughout your entire career in the law. It is an important part of your responsibilities as a lawyer.

H. VALUES

Do not lose sight of the values that brought you to law school in the first place. The nature of the study of law will cause you to analyze cases and the legal process in very technical ways. Always remember, however, that behind the cases and concepts you discuss are real people with real problems. Through your law training, you will be in a position to assist people seeking justice. This is an enormous opportunity and responsibility. Don't forget it.

CHAPTER 14

BEYOND THE FIRST YEAR

While this book is intended to guide you through the study of law and the writing of examinations during the first year of law school, it will be helpful to look briefly beyond the first year.

A. LAW JOURNALS

It is very likely that your law school publishes one or more student-edited journals. The journal may be a traditional law review that covers all legal subjects or a specialized journal that publishes articles on a specific legal topic. These law journals are the major scholarly journals for the legal profession. Law is unique in this respect among all disciplines in having its major scholarly journals edited by student editors.

A law journal writing experience is a very valuable educational experience. During your first year on the journal, you will research and write on one or more subjects. Journal editors, who are third-year students, will evaluate and edit your work. The best student-written articles will be published in the journal, along with articles by professors, judges, and practicing lawyers.

During your second year on the journal, you will evaluate and edit the research and writing of the new journal staff members. Editing another's work also will improve your own organizational and writing skills. This unique educational experience will sharpen the very skills that a law school education seeks to develop.

Because of the important training that writing for a journal provides, you should apply to participate as a member of the staff of one of the law journals at your school. At most law schools, you cannot do so until you have completed your first year. Normally, near the end of your first year, information will be posted as to how you can apply to become a member. The selection criteria vary from journal to journal. At some schools, some students are invited to join a journal staff based on their high grades. But virtually every journal gives all students an opportunity to petition to become a member of the student editorial board by submitting a writing sample.

Law journal work is a highlight of the law school experience. You will be required to make a substantial time commitment to the journal, but the rewards are great. A law journal writing experience is highly regarded by law firms in hiring law school graduates. Employers recognize the value of the intensive research and writing experiences you will have as an editor of the journal. The experience is particularly important if you plan to seek a judicial clerkship or become a law professor.

B. CLINICAL EDUCATION

Clinical education programs are excellent educational experiences that permit you to apply your legal knowledge in the context of live client representation. Clinics give you a good perspective on the career for which you are preparing and help you see the relevance of your course work. The importance of clinical training is strongly supported by a very significant report recently published by the American Bar Association, *Law Schools and the Profession: Narrowing the Gap* (known as the Mac-Crate Report after New York lawyer Robert Mac-Crate, the chair of the committee that wrote it). The report urged law schools to provide more lawyering skills training opportunities in their curriculum. Because many law school clinics serve low income clients, they also help you develop your commitment to pro bono legal services.

Clinical education will be especially important if you are planning to be a solo practitioner or if you intend to enter a practice in which you will have immediate responsibility for cases after graduation. You will receive individualized instruction and supervision from a clinical faculty member. Like law journal work, clinical courses require a substantial time commitment, but the benefits greatly outweigh the extra time demands.

There are many different kinds of clinical programs. Some are general practice clinics in which students handle all types of cases, and some are specific subject matter clinics that focus on a single area of practice, such as:

Bankruptcy Law Clinic

Child Advocacy Clinic

Domestic Abuse Clinic

Elder Law Clinic

Employment Discrimination Clinic

Environmental Law Clinic

Family Law Clinic

Federal Prosecution Clinic

Human Rights Clinic

Immigration Law Clinic

Landlord–Tenant Law Clinic

Misdemeanor Defense Clinic

Misdemeanor Prosecution Clinic

Prisoners Rights Clinic

Social Security and Workers Compensation Claims Clinic

Tax Law Clinic

In a live client clinic, you will represent an actual client in connection with a variety of transactions, in a trial, or in a proceeding before an administrative agency. There are also clinical courses that do not involve live clients, which are sometimes called simulated clinic programs. In such a course, a student represents a hypothetical client in a hypothetical fact situation. Examples of such courses include a trial advocacy course or an estate planning seminar. An important goal of clinical programs, whether live or simulated, is to help a law student develop lawyering practice skills—such as advocating, counseling, negotiating, and writing.

At most law schools, you cannot participate in the law school clinical program during your first year. You should take time during your first year, however, to identify the various clinical programs at your law school and find out what you need to do to participate in your later years in law school.

C. MOOT COURT

Another valuable learning experience in law school is participation in the moot court program. Moot court is a program in which students act as appellate advocates in a hypothetical case that is based on a real case or a prepared set of facts. The students learn valuable appellate written and oral argument skills and participate in appellate argument competitions.

Participation in moot court is especially valuable if you plan to be a litigator after graduation. Employers value moot court experience because of the oral advocacy training and because your research and writing skills will be strengthened by writing the appellate briefs.

While your law school may have some instruction in appellate advocacy in the first year, most moot court programs will be in your upperclass years.

You will normally participate as a team of two students, arguing either for the appellants or for the appellees in a hypothetical case. In addition to intramural competition, your law school very likely will participate in a national or international competition in one or more of its moot court programs. Find out which programs offer national competition, and you may have an opportunity to match your appellate advocacy skills against the top competition from law schools throughout the United States.

As with clinical programs, you should take time during your first year to identify the various moot court programs at your law school and find out what you need to do to participate in them during your upperclass years in law school. Like law journals and clinical education courses, moot court programs require a substantial time commitment. For this reason, students usually are not able to participate in all three of these programs during their law school years.

D. COURSE SELECTION

The Professional Responsibility course is a required upperclass course at most law schools. Other than that course, there will be few, if any, required courses in your second and third years of law school. Your choice of courses largely will depend upon your interests and career choices.

There are several upperclass courses that a large number of law students normally take, however, that are foundational for other advanced courses and that provide a well-rounded legal education. They include commercial paper, corporations, criminal procedure, evidence, family law, jurisprudence, real estate transactions, sales, secured transactions, tax, and wills and trusts. Other courses that are important to a well-rounded legal education include bankruptcy, conflicts, and employment law. Because of the increasing globalization of the practice of law, it is also important for you to take one or more courses that will expose you to international law or comparative law. Your law school may have several courses that you can take in sequence as a specialty track.

Rather than being guided by subject matter alone in selecting your courses, you also should take into consideration the professors who are teaching the courses. If you have had an especially successful learning experience with a professor in your first year, you should take a course from that professor in your upperclass years. In addition, your law school may have faculty members who are renowned for their expertise or views in a particular field, and it would benefit your legal education to have an opportunity to be exposed to those views by taking a course from that professor.

You also should seek to have one or more small class or seminar learning experiences in your upperclass years. A seminar experience typically enables you to focus in an intensive way on a narrow subject matter. In this setting, you will have the benefit of intense examination of an issue in a small enrollment class in which you can participate actively. In addition, you will be directed to conduct research into that issue and prepare a paper reporting the results of your research. This experience will further develop your research and writing skills.

If your law school grants academic credit for courses taken in other departments, consider taking some non-law school courses in your upperclass years. After having the benefit of training in critical thinking in your law school education, you will be astounded at how enriching the courses in other disciplines will be with your new perspective. These courses also can expand the context in which you evaluate issues in your law school classes. Some helpful non-law school courses include accounting, economics, finance, history, political science, and public policy.

Students often think it is important to take courses covering subjects that are tested on the bar examination. While that is a natural temptation, we believe that factor should be a minor consideration in course selection. You can prepare adequately for the bar examination in your bar review preparation, even for subjects you did not study in a law school course. It is more important that you take a wide variety of courses. Seek to become well educated in the law, so that you can counsel your clients most effectively. Furthermore, in taking a wide variety of courses, you unexpectedly may discover a subject that you really enjoy and that will become a practice speciality for you.

E. INTERNATIONAL PROGRAMS

You should participate in a program of international study offered by your law school or by another law school if at all possible. Studying abroad will give you a better understanding of how common legal issues are addressed by different legal systems in different cultures. You also will learn a great deal about the country in which you study, including its political and legal systems and its culture. The insights you gain will be valuable to you as the practice of law becomes increasingly globalized, and they will help you look at the American legal system from a broader perspective. International study programs often take place during the summer, but some schools also offer semester study abroad programs.

F. JOINT DEGREE PROGRAMS

Joint degree programs provide opportunities for interdisciplinary study and for a course of study specifically suited to your particular career goal. In a joint degree program, you can obtain a law degree and a degree in another discipline in less time than would be required to pursue the degrees separately. Some examples of these degree programs include:

Law and Business Administration (JD/MBA)

Law and Economics (JD/MA or PhD)

Law and International Relations (JD/MA or PhD)

Law and Public Policy (JD/MPP)

Law and Medicine (JD/MD)

Law and Public Health (JD/MPH)

Law and Journalism (JD/MA)

A joint degree can be an outstanding credential for a career that bridges the two subjects.

G. SUMMER CLERKSHIPS

Law firms traditionally hire students to clerk at the firm during the summer break between your law school years. These law firm summer clerkships are in great demand by law students, because they are excellent educational experiences and frequently law firms hire their permanent associate attorneys from their summer clerkship program. In a summer clerkship, you will do legal research and write memos, and you will have an opportunity to attend real estate closings, trials, depositions, client meetings, and other practice-related events.

You should seek such a clerkship during at least one, if not both, of your law school summers. It is a good opportunity to explore questions you might have about your career decisions, such as type of firm, geographic location, and type of practice specialty. In addition to law firm summer clerkships, summer employment opportunities may be available with judges, administrative agencies, or corporate law departments.

Typically, larger law firms will conduct interviews for their summer clerkships at your law school during the fall semester. From these interviews, they invite some students to their offices for more extensive interviews. Smaller law firms normally interview during the spring semester when their hiring needs have been defined more clearly. But do not wait for employers to come to you at the law school. As with all types of job searches, you should take the initiative. Send a letter expressing your interest in employment and a resume to the employers for whom you would like to work. Talk with family members and friends about employment possibilities, and take advantage of the resources of your law school's Career Services Office. You should get acquainted with the services and resources of that Office at the beginning of your second year of law school, if you have not already done so. During your second and third years of law school, you will be busy juggling job interviews with all of the many other time demands of your course work and extracurricular activities.

H. NEW ADVENTURES

There are many new adventures awaiting you in your future years in law school. You have made a wonderful career choice, and we wish you well in your study of law.

SAMPLE EXAM QUESTIONS AND ANSWERS

This section of the book includes two exam questions and model answers for each of the six most common first-year courses: Civil Procedure, Constitutional Law, Contracts, Criminal Law, Property, and Torts. These questions are from actual law school examinations, and the model answers have been prepared by law professors. The questions are of varying lengths and types, and each includes a note that explains the best way to approach the problem.

You will benefit most from these sample questions by writing your own answer before reading the model answer. After reading the question, follow the steps described in Chapter 12 for analyzing the question and for writing an answer. Each question states the amount of time the professor allocated for the question when it was given during an actual exam. Therefore, in addition to practicing your analytic and writing skills, these questions provide an opportunity to practice time management. Force yourself to stay within the stated time limits. By practicing on these questions, you can develop your method for answering exam questions, rather than trying to develop one during an actual exam. Practice will improve your exam performance.

Because the law changes—sometimes quite rapidly—do not rely on the statements of law included in the model answers for their substance. Instead, use the model answers to learn the method for taking exams. Because the material covered in any first-year course will vary significantly by professor, you may not have studied the doctrines or cases included in these answers. Therefore, do not worry if some of the material is unfamiliar to you. Also keep in mind that these answers were prepared by law professors, rather than by students writing under the time pressures and stress of an actual exam. These model answers do not represent the norm for student examination answers. Instead, the model answers are designed to give you the best possible examples of organization and analysis.

Good luck!

CIVIL PROCEDURE I

(One hour)

On September 21, 1994, attorneys from the law firm of Goode, Better & Best filed a products liability action on behalf of Belle Plaine. The suit was filed against nine pharmaceutical manufacturers and unknown defendants in the state district court for the County of Minneapple, which is located in the State of Northstar. Northstar has a Code of Civil Procedure that is identical to the Federal Rules of Civil Procedure, but Northstar courts are not bound by federal interpretations of the rules. On the same day, the same attorneys from Goode, Better & Best filed seven other actions on behalf of other plaintiffs against the same nine manufacturers. These defendants manufacture, publicize, sell, and distribute felzene-based antibiotic drugs. These drugs allegedly caused permanent staining and discoloration of each plaintiff's teeth. Goode, Better & Best specializes in products liability cases, particularly in felzene litigation.

Plaine's complaint contained adequate jurisdictional allegations and a prayer for damages and injunctive relief. In her complaint, Plaine alleged that, during her infancy and teeth-forming years, she ingested drugs that had a felzene base and that the drugs were manufactured, publicized, distributed, and sold by the named defendants and by possible unknown defendants who may have been in the same business. She alleged that each defendant was strictly liable to her for all adverse consequences and injuries resulting from the use of the drugs. She further alleged that, although she did not know the brand name or manufacturer of all the drugs that had caused discoloration of her teeth, "one or more of the Defendants herein did manufacture, publicize, distribute, and sell said drugs so used and ingested by Plaintiff."

Plaine alleged that the defendants were jointly and severally liable. Because she did not know which defendants manufactured, publicized, sold, and distributed the drugs that she ingested, she claimed that each defendant had the burden to exculpate itself by proving that its drug did not cause her injuries. No Northstar decision addresses the issue of whether, in a multiple-defendant products liability case, a defendant must prove that it did not cause a plaintiff's injury to escape liability; this is a question of first impression in Northstar. Finally, Plaine alleged that she first discovered that her injuries and damages were caused by felzene-based drugs on September 22, 1993, when a local newspaper published an article concerning another lawsuit filed against felzene manufacturers.

The defendants, including Acme Drugs, each filed a separate answer in which they denied most of the essential allegations. They denied the allegations that they had "manufactured, publicized, distributed, and sold the drugs used and ingested by Plaintiff." They also denied that they had the burden of proving that their drug had not caused her injury. Moreover, they answered that, even if they had manufactured, publicized, distributed, and sold the drugs ingested by the plaintiff, the drugs were not the cause of her injuries.

During discovery, Acme and the other defendants served Plaine with interrogatories and a request for production of documents. In response to an interrogatory question, Plaine stated: "During Plaintiff's infancy and teeth-forming years, physicians prescribed various antibiotic drugs for her, including felzene. Felrex, Declozene, and Disteclin are the only brand names of felzene drugs that Plaintiff knows she ingested." All the medical records in Plaine's possession were attached to her answers to interrogatories. The records of Dr. Roberta Kidd, which Plaine had obtained shortly after reading the article about felzene, showed that Dr. Kidd had prescribed these drugs for Plaine between 1967 and 1972. Acme did not manufacture or have any other connection with the drugs prescribed by Dr. Kidd.

Plaine also stated in her answers to interrogatories that she had been treated in 1971 or 1972 by Dr. Wolf, a dentist who had extracted four of her teeth as part of orthodontic work. Plaine stated that she believed that Dr. Wolf had prescribed some antibiotics for her, but she could not recall which types. She stated that she did not know the location of Dr. Wolf's records and that Dr. Wolf is deceased and his practice dissolved. Plaine's answers to interrogatories included a signed authorization permitting the defendants to obtain her medical records from all her physicians.

On June 8, 1995, Acme moved for summary judgment on the ground that it had not been identified as a manufacturer, publicist, distributor, or seller of any felzene drugs taken by Plaine. Acme also moved for sanctions under Rule 11 of the Rules of Civil Procedure against the law firm and individual attorneys representing Plaine. The trial court granted both motions and awarded $20,000 in attorneys' fees against Goode, Better & Best and its individual attorneys as Rule 11 sanctions. Plaine and her attorneys have appealed.

You are the law clerk to Justice Diesterheft, a member of the Northstar Supreme Court. Advise Justice Diesterheft:

1. Whether the trial court erred in granting Acme's summary judgment motion; and

2. Whether the trial court erred in granting Acme's motion for Rule 11 sanctions.

Note: Because you do not know whether this jurisdiction will impose the burden of proof on Plaine or on Acme, you must analyze the problem both ways and must discuss the underlying policies and their bearing on the problem.

MODEL ANSWER

A. Summary Judgment

As the movant, Acme had the burden of proving that the standard for a summary judgment is satisfied. Acme had to prove that no dispute exists concerning the subject matter of the summary judgment motion even if Plaine would have the burden of persuasion at trial. The trial court must view the evidence in the light most favorable to Plaine and must resolve all doubts in her favor. If Acme failed to establish that no genuine issue of material fact exists, the court should have denied the summary judgment motion even though Plaine presented no additional evidence. *Adickes v. S.H. Kress & Co.*

The exact scope of Acme's burden depends in part on whether it will have the burden of persuasion at trial. Whether a defendant in a multiple-defendant products liability case has the burden of proving that it did not cause the plaintiff's injury has not yet been decided in Northstar. The Northstar Supreme Court will have to resolve it by considering factors such as which party has better access to information and which party is in a better position to prove the issue. Because the issue of the burden is unresolved, I will provide alternative analyses based first on Acme and then on Plaine bearing the burden of persuasion at trial.

1. If Acme has the Burden of Persuasion at Trial

If Acme has the burden of persuasion on the issue of its liability to Plaine, Acme will avoid liability only if it presents evidence proving that it was not responsible for her injuries. Plaine could prevail at trial even if she presents no evidence. The same reasoning should apply to the summary judgment motion.

Acme presented no evidence to support its summary judgment motion. Instead, it relied on Plaine's failure to allege a specific connection between Acme and a drug she already knew she had taken. Therefore, Acme did not meet its burden of proving that no genuine issue of material fact exists, and the trial court erred in granting the summary judgment motion.

2. If Plaine has the Burden of Persuasion at Trial

Even though Plaine has the burden of proving liability at trial, Acme had the burden of establishing the absence of a genuine issue of material fact for the summary judgment. The courts have not developed a uniform standard for determining whether a movant has satisfied that burden. *In Adickes v. S.H. Kress & Co.*, the United States Supreme Court held that, to win a summary judgment motion under the Federal Rules of Civil Procedure, the movant must present affirmative evidence that a genuine issue of material fact does not exist. If the movant fails to do so, a court must deny the motion for summary judgment even if the respondent does not introduce any evidence to the contrary. In this case, Acme did not produce any evidence to prove that it was not a manufacturer, publicist, distributor, or seller of any felzene drug taken by Plaine. Therefore, if the Northstar Supreme Court adopts the *Adickes* standard, the trial court erred in granting the summary judgment motion.

The more recent United States Supreme Court case, *Celotex Corp v. Catrett*, reflects a more expansive view of the situations in which a federal court should grant a motion for summary judgment. The Court was divided in that case, however, concerning the standard to be applied. The majority stated that the movant does not have to introduce additional evidence to support its motion for summary judgment if it can demonstrate that the respondent cannot prove an element of its claim against the movant. The respondent then would have the burden to refute that assertion.

In this case, Acme correctly asserted that Plaine had not established any connection between Acme and the felzene drugs she had taken. Moreover, Plaine did not offer any evidence in response to Acme's motion to show that a genuine issue of material fact exists concerning Acme's potential culpability. Therefore, without more, the *Celotex* majority's standard was not satisfied. Of course, Northstar courts are not bound by federal courts' interpretations of the Federal Rules of Civil Procedure.

Even if the Northstar Supreme Court finds the *Celotex* majority's reasoning to be persuasive, Rule 56(f) of the Northstar Rules provides a potential avenue of appeal for Plaine. Rule 56(f) provides that a motion for summary judgment can be defeated by showing that the respondent did not have access to the information necessary to show the existence of a genuine issue of material fact. In this case, Plaine has been unable to locate the records of a doctor who may have prescribed felzene-based drugs for her. On the other hand, nearly two years have elapsed between publication of the newspaper article about the earlier felzene lawsuit and Acme's motion for summary judgment. If it appears that Plaine may never be able to locate evidence establishing a link between Acme and a drug she took, the court may grant the motion for summary judgment. In any event, it does not appear that Plaine made a Rule 56(f) argument to the trial court.

Because the Northstar Supreme Court is not bound by the majority opinion in *Celotex*, the Court may wish to consider adopting Justice White's approach in the concurring opinion. In his concurring opinion, Justice White interpreted Rule 56 to require the movant to do more to satisfy its burden than merely assert that the plaintiff has no evidence to prove the case. If the Northstar Supreme Court adopts this approach, the summary judgment should be reversed; Acme introduced no evidence to support its motion.

Pursuant to some other states' rules of civil procedure, the respondent does not have to prove the existence of a genuine issue of material fact even if the respondent has the burden of pleading and proof. Under those states' rules, the movant has the burden of proving that no genuine issue exists. If the Northstar Supreme Court decides to adopt this approach, the summary judgment in favor of Acme should be reversed.

3. *Conclusion*

This case presents countervailing considerations. On one hand, if a summary judgment is not permitted in this case, even though Plaine has not produced any evidence of Acme's involvement after two years, a summary judgment seldom will be available in this type of products liability case. To help relieve congestion in the court dockets, the judicial trend has been to grant summary judgments more liberally, thereby forcing respondents to do more than simply rest on their pleadings. The summary judgment motion should be used to pierce the pleadings to determine whether a cause of action really exists. Moreover, determining all the felzene-based drugs that Plaine ingested may be impossible. She is unsure whether Dr. Wolf prescribed any, and locating his records may be impossible.

On the other hand, when medical causation is not discovered for many years, this type of case often is plagued by stale records and by other difficult problems of proof. Because the issue of the burden of proof in this case is unclear, it may be best to reverse the summary judgment and permit this case to go to trial or at least to require Acme to produce some evidence that it is not linked to any drug that may have caused Plaine's injuries.

B. Rule 11

Rule 11 requires that at least one attorney of record in a case must sign every pleading. By signing the pleading, the attorney is certifying that a reasonable inquiry has been made concerning those matters specified in Rule 11(b)(1)-(4). The trial court may have granted Acme's motion under three separate provisions of Rule 11(b): (1) subdivision (b)(1), which applies to pleadings presented for an improper purpose, (2) subdivision (b)(2), which applies to legal contentions, or (3) subdivision (b)(3), which applies to factual contentions. Each will be considered. The Supreme Court can overturn the trial court's decision only for an abuse of discretion.

As an initial matter, the current version of Rule 11 makes clear that law firms, as well as individual attorneys, can be held liable for Rule 11 sanctions.

1. *Subdivision (b)(1)*

Unless Acme proved that Plaine's suit against it was merely a strike suit to get a settlement, the trial court probably did not grant Rule 11 sanctions pursuant to subdivision (b)(1). That subdivision applies to pleadings that are presented "for any improper purpose, such as to harass or to cause unnecessary delay or needless increase in the cost of litigation." Although it can be argued that a violation of subdivision (b)(2) or (b)(3) also violates subdivision (b)(1), that argument is weak because of the rule of statutory construction that each provision of a statute should be interpreted so as not to be superfluous.

2. *Subdivision (b)(2)*

Subdivision (b)(2) provides that a court can impose Rule 11 sanctions if the claims and other legal contentions made in a suit are not "warranted by existing law or by a nonfrivolous argument for the extension, modification, or reversal of existing law or the establishment of new law." Sanctions arguably are appropriate under this subdivision because no precedent supports Plaine's contention that Acme should have to prove that it was not connected with a drug that Plaine ingested. On the other hand, if Acme prevailed in the Rule 11 motion based on that argument, the common law's evolution would be hampered significantly. Arguments that are unsupported by precedent frequently are made either because a new situation has arisen or because changed conditions have rendered the former rule inappropriate.

Moreover, Plaine's legal position is a nonfrivolous argument for an extension or modification of the law. Acme is in a better position than Plaine to prove that it should not be held liable. The medical records that would establish which drugs Plaine took are old and may be impossible to find, whereas Acme should have access to its records about its drug manufacturing, distribution, and other activities. Moreover, a company that profits from the sale of a drug should bear the burden of pleading and proving that it is not liable for injuries resulting from that type of drug. Therefore, the trial court should not have imposed Rule 11 sanctions pursuant to subdivision (b)(2) because a reasonable basis exists for the legal theory on which Plaine has sued Acme.

3. *Subdivision (b)(3)*

Subdivision (b)(3) provides for Rule 11 sanctions if allegations and factual contentions do not "have evidentiary support" or are not "likely to have evidentiary support after a reasonable opportunity for further investigation or discovery." Acme could have supported its Rule 11 motion by arguing that the only records Plaine had before filing suit were Dr. Kidd's and that Dr. Kidd's records did not implicate Acme. Although Dr. Wolf's records might supply the necessary link, one year elapsed between the time Plaine discovered her cause of action and filed it, and she did not locate Dr. Wolf's records during that time. Another year has elapsed since Plaine filed suit, and she still has not located the records.

Acme also may have argued that, because Plaine's law firm and lawyers specialize in products liability cases and in felzene cases in particular, they should be held to a higher standard in evaluating the merits of potential claims and in conducting investigations. Additionally, Acme may have argued that the firm's filing of eight suits on the same day against the same nine manufacturers indicates that the firm simply is trying to extort settlements. Presumably, not all nine manufacturers were involved in all eight sets of underlying facts, and it seems unlikely that the firm and its lawyers could have investigated each claim adequately if all the suits were filed on the same day.

Plaine's lawyers will respond that finding records for an injury that occurred over twenty years ago is difficult and that this difficulty is common in cases in which medical causation may not be discovered for many years. Plaine did all she could to assist discovery by authorizing the defendants to obtain all her medical records. Moreover, Acme very likely is linked to at least one drug Plaine took because Acme is a large pharmaceutical company. Acme did not deny that it was connected with the drugs Plaine may have taken; it simply asserted that Plaine had not yet discovered a link between Acme and the drugs she took. Particularly because of the uncertainty concerning which party bears the burden of proof in this type of case, the trial court should not have granted Rule 11 sanctions pursuant to subdivision (b)(3).

4. *Subdivision (c)(1)(A)*

In addition to the substantive provisions discussed above, the court should determine whether Acme complied with the procedural provisions of subdivision (c)(1)(A). That subdivision provides that a Rule 11 motion may not be filed with the court unless the respondent is given 21 days after service of the motion to withdraw its claim. The record does not indicate whether Acme provided this notice.

5. *Conclusion*

Although abuse of discretion is a high standard of review, it is met in this case. Therefore, the Supreme Court should overturn the Rule 11 sanctions.

CIVIL PROCEDURE II

(One hour)

Plaintiff Patty Peterson filed a wrongful death action in federal district court against Red Cross of America and Hilldale Hospital. Peterson's infant son, Calvin, died of AIDS after receiving blood transfusions at Hilldale Hospital. Red Cross had solicited and processed the donated blood that was used in the transfusions. Peterson alleged *inter alia* that Red Cross and the hospital had been negligent in transfusing her son with blood from an HIV-positive donor. Peterson served Red Cross with interrogatories and a request for production of documents concerning the identity and medical history of each donor whose blood may have been received by Calvin. Peterson also sought a description of and any documents relating to the specific procedures followed during the donation process.

Red Cross responded with a description of the blood donation process, including a detailed description of the screening process that it follows to test for HIV-positive donors. Red Cross further responded that, of the six donors whose blood had been used in Calvin's transfusions, only one donor might have been HIV-positive when the blood was donated. However, Red Cross refused to provide the name or any other information about the donor, citing the confidentiality of donor medical information.

Peterson moved for an order to compel Red Cross to respond to the interrogatory concerning the blood donors. Peterson also moved for an order for a physical examination of the potentially HIV-positive donor to be identified by Red Cross.

Red Cross opposed Peterson's motion to compel and moved for a protective order. Red Cross admitted that, under the jurisdiction's law, it does not have standing to raise the donor's right to privacy, so you should not consider that issue. Instead, Red Cross argued that, if the court grants Peterson's motions, the blood supply will become dangerously depleted because many potential donors will fear becoming involved in litigation. According to Peterson's and Red Cross' moving papers, courts and experts are divided on the effects of revealing donor identities and histories. Some courts and experts believe it will cause a depletion of the nation's blood supply; an equal number say it will not.

At oral argument on the motions, Peterson indicated her intention to serve a subpoena duces tecum to depose the potentially HIV-positive donor following receipt of his or her name and the results of the physical examination.

You are the law clerk to Judge Neumann, who must decide these discovery disputes based on federal law. Advise Judge Neumann concerning:

1. Peterson's motion to compel further responses to the interrogatories;

2. Peterson's motion for an order for a physical examination; and

3. Red Cross' motion for a protective order.

Be creative and consider all possible alternatives.

Note: In addition to applying the Federal Rules of Civil Procedure and federal case law, this question requires you to balance competing policies—the federal procedural interest in full discovery and the desire to prevent harassment and the invasion of individual privacy. The question also requires you to craft creative solutions to attempt to protect each party's interests. Finally, because you are advising a judge, you must be neutral in your evaluation of the case.

MODEL ANSWER

A. Peterson's Motion to Compel and Red Cross' Motion for a Protective Order

Rule 26(b)(1) provides that a party may obtain discovery regarding any matter that is relevant to the subject matter of the suit, including "the identity and location of persons having knowledge of any discoverable matter." In this case, Peterson wants information about blood donors to obtain additional information concerning Red Cross' process for screening out HIV-positive donors. Peterson wants to discover whether Red Cross, in fact, has a procedure and whether that procedure was followed for each donor who contributed blood used in her son's transfusions. Peterson also wants to determine whether more than one donor is HIV-positive, rather than rely on Red Cross' evaluation of the donors. If Red Cross does not have an adequate procedure or if the procedure was not followed, Peterson will have a good case that Red Cross acted negligently. Pursuant to Rule 37(a)(2)(B), Peterson was entitled to move for an order to compel disclosure when Red Cross failed to answer her interrogatory questions.

Red Cross has opposed Peterson's motion to compel and has moved for a protective order pursuant to Rule 26(c). The court may grant a protective order when justice requires it "to protect a party or person from annoyance, embarrassment, oppression, or undue burden...." Red Cross has the burden of proving good cause for the protective order. To satisfy this burden, it must show that disclosure will result in a clearly defined and very serious injury. General allegations are insufficient to satisfy the burden; Red Cross must make a particularized showing of the alleged injury. If Red Cross satisfies this burden, the court then should consider Peterson's interests, the interests of persons who are not parties to the action, and the general public interest. In a significant opinion, Judge Posner has argued that courts should give more weight to these social interests than to merely private interests.

Red Cross has supported its motion for a protective order with evidence that disclosures concerning donors will cause the national blood supply to become seriously depleted because potential donors will fear becoming involved in litigation. Red Cross also could argue that Peterson does not have a good faith reason for requesting the information; she merely wants to harass any potentially HIV-positive donors who contributed blood used in her son's transfusions.

On the other hand, Peterson has submitted evidence that disclosures concerning donors will not affect the blood supply. She also has argued that she has good faith reasons for wanting the information. In light of this conflicting evidence, Red Cross has not satisfied its burden of proof, and the court should not grant an order that completely shields Red Cross from responding to the interrogatory questions.

Because of the conflicting evidence concerning the potential impact on the national blood supply, however, the court may wish to consider an intermediate ground in ruling on Red Cross' motion for a protective order. Pursuant to Rule 26(c), the court can order that discovery "be had only on specified terms and conditions," "be had only by a method of discovery other than that selected by the party seeking discovery," or "be conducted with no one present except persons designated by the court." Additionally, Rule 26(d) provides that, upon motion and in the interest of justice, the court can control the timing and order of discovery. Pursuant to these provisions, the court could attempt to satisfy the interests of both Peterson and Red Cross. For example, the court could:

1. Order *in camera* review of the documents by the court;

2. Permit Peterson to submit only written inter-
    rogatory questions for the donor to answer,
    appoint a lawyer for the donor, and have the
    donor's answers, with verification deleted, de-
    livered to Peterson; or

3. Require Peterson to depose or otherwise con-
    duct discovery on the Red Cross personnel
    involved in screening donors during the rele-
    vant period and allow her to conduct discov-
    ery on the donor only if she could not obtain
    necessary information from the Red Cross
    personnel.

As a final, technical matter, the court must verify
that Peterson's motion to compel included a certification that she in good faith conferred or attempted
to confer with Red Cross to secure the information
without court action, as required by Rule
37(a)(2)(B). The court also must verify that Red
Cross' motion for a protective order was accompa-
nied by a certification that it in good faith conferred
or attempted to confer with Peterson in an attempt
to resolve the discovery dispute without court action, as required by Rule 26(c).

B. Peterson's Motion for Order
for Physical Examination

The court should deny this motion. Pursuant to
Rule 35(a), a court may order a physical examination only "of a party or of a person in the custody or
under the legal control of a party." The potentially
HIV-positive donor is not a party to the action. No
evidence has been presented that the donor is in

Red Cross' custody or under its legal control. Even if the donor is a Red Cross employee, donating blood probably is not within the scope of employment, and, therefore, the donor would not be within Red Cross' control for that purpose.

An additional reason for denying the motion is that Rule 35(a) requires the movant to show good cause for the examination. Good cause does not exist because, even if the exam shows that the donor is HIV-positive, it probably would not prove that the donor was HIV-positive when the blood was donated. Therefore, the motion should be denied both because the donor is not within the class of people who can be ordered to submit to a physical examination and because Peterson does not have good cause for the exam.

CONSTITUTIONAL LAW I

(Ninety minutes)

Center County, the largest county in the State of Arcadia, includes Metropolis, the largest city in the state. Metropolis has about 300,000 residents, and Center County as a whole has about 600,000 residents. Approximately 30% of Metropolis' adult residents are African American. Before the Voting Rights Act of 1965, very few African American citizens of Arcadia were registered to vote. As a consequence, very few African Americans served as jurors in criminal cases, because an Arcadia statute provides that only registered voters are eligible for jury service.

Under the Arcadia statutes, jury pools are generated by randomly drawing a certain number of registered voters. Voir dire by the attorneys to choose the jury is conducted in the order in which the jurors were randomly identified. Since adoption of the Voting Rights Act, the percentage of African Americans registered to vote has increased dramatically. However, a racial difference in the percentage of registered voters in Center County still exists: about 50% of the African American population is registered to vote, as compared to 75% of the Caucasian population. Other non-Caucasian groups in Center County are quite small in number and have voter registration patterns similar to that of the African American community.

Largely because of the relatively small size of the African American community, but also in part because of its lower voter registration percentage, many juries in criminal cases in Center County have been all-white. During the past few years, several criminal trials of African American defendants by all-white (and, in several instances, predominately male) juries have caused significant controversy. In response, the Metropolis City Council and the Center County Commissioners are attempting to find ways to increase African American representation on juries in criminal cases. If the City Council and the Commissioners can agree on a method for populating juries other than by exclusively using the voter registration lists, they will propose their reform to the Arcadia Legislature as an amendment to the state statutes. Three different proposals have been identified.

The first proposal would retain the system of randomly identifying potential jurors from the registered voter lists but would supplement the lists with the names of people who are listed on electricity bills and who are not registered to vote. Each person added to the pool by examination of the electricity bills would be required to prove American citizenship to qualify to be a juror. Proponents of this proposal argue that it would have two benefits: (1) it would increase the number of African Americans drawn for jury service, and (2) it would increase the number of women because of the some-

what higher percentage of female-headed households in the African American community, which
presumably would be reflected by the names on
utility bills.

Opponents of this proposal argue that it would do
too little to increase the number of African Americans on juries. They have made a second proposal:
utility bills would be used only for residents of
Metropolis' Fourth Ward, which is predominantly
African American, and not for the whole county.
Several City Council members support this idea not
only because it probably would increase the relative
number of African Americans on juries, but also
because it would save money; the court clerk would
not have to examine utility billing lists throughout
the rest of the county but could continue to rely on
the existing computerized voter registration lists to
identify potential jurors from those areas.

A third proposal would continue exclusive use of
voter registration lists to create a pool of potential
jurors for criminal cases. Instead of creating an
initial pool of thirty people, however, as is currently
done, the pool would be increased to seventy-five
people. Increasing the pool size should increase the
number of African Americans in the pool, although
not the relative percentage. The voir dire procedure also would be changed. Although voir dire
still would be conducted in the order in which the
potential juror's name was randomly generated, at
least every fourth person subjected to voir dire must
be African American until either the jury of twelve

has been selected or the number of African Americans in the pool has been exhausted.

Note that none of these proposals guarantees any African American a spot on the jury. Each potential juror, regardless of race, would be subjected to voir dire and would be excusable in two ways: (1) for cause (a decision made by the judge presiding at voir dire on the motion of counsel that the potential juror is unfit for jury service because of an inability to evaluate the evidence objectively) or (2) by peremptory challenge (under Arcadia law, the prosecutor and the defense counsel in a criminal case have two peremptory challenges). Note also that the potential jurors would not be told how or in what order their names were generated.

The Metropolis City Council and the Center County Commissioners have retained your services to assess the constitutionality of each proposal under the equal protection clause of the federal Constitution. Provide your advice.

Note: It is important to discuss each proposal separately. If you group all three proposals under the heading of affirmative action and try to analyze them as a group, you quickly will have analytic difficulties because two proposals are facially neutral, while the third proposal is not. Normally, your professor presents separate proposals to see whether you can spot the relevant analytic distinctions among them. Therefore, do not combine different parts of an exam question unless you are certain that they are analytically indistinguishable.

MODEL ANSWER

Obviously, there is no problem finding state action or a general legislative police power to authorize legislation along the lines of the three proposals. The following discussion analyzes the validity of each proposal under the equal protection clause.

A. Proposal 1

Proposal 1 is facially neutral. It applies to minorities and to non-minorities alike. It discriminates against no one in an invidious way. Indeed, although it may increase the percentage of African Americans and other minorities eligible to serve on juries, it almost certainly will mean that more non-minorities than minorities will be added to the pool. For example, if this proposal increases the percentage of minorities who are eligible for jury service by 20% and the percentage of non-minorities by 10%, the greater number of non-minorities in the population will mean that more non-minorities than minorities will have become eligible for jury service.

Before *Shaw v. Reno*, such a proposal was unquestionably constitutional. It is facially neutral, produces no impact harming racial minorities, and is not motivated by a desire to harm minorities. For these reasons, *Washington v. Davis* would be inapplicable. That case is very clearly about covert discrimination against racial minorities.

Thus, the issue posed by Proposal 1 is whether *Shaw v. Reno* changes this analysis. To be sure, one can make a mechanical argument that it does.

The statute is facially neutral. Therefore, the next question is whether it has a disparate impact along any racial lines whatsoever. This is a significant modification of *Washington v. Davis*, which presumed that only an impact harming minorities was of constitutional significance. This proposal may have a disparate impact against non-minorities, although this is not clear from the facts of the problem. Under the *Washington v. Davis* standard, the question then becomes whether this harm to non-minorities was intended. The statute clearly was intended to produce a disparate impact against non-minorities. Therefore, strict scrutiny applies.

I submit that this chain of argument is nonsensical. The problem with the question of whether the statute has any disparate impact along any racial line is that lots of statutes—probably nearly every statute—has some racial impact. For example, increasing the progressive income tax harms non-minorities disproportionally. Can that possibly mean that it raises serious equal protection problems? Of course not. This question of disparate impact ignores the zero-sum nature of legislation.

Moreover, the facts may not support the argument that Proposal 1 may have a disparate impact against non-minorities. But even if the proposal will produce a greater percentage increase in minority than in non-minority participation in juries, the absolute number of non-minorities who become eligible for jury service almost certainly will exceed the number of minorities who become eligible. It is hard to consider this to be a disparate impact at all, particularly since virtually any adult citizen can circumvent this plan entirely and become eligible for jury service simply by registering to vote.

If Proposal 1 raises any serious equal protection problems, all legislation designed to help minorities is constitutionally suspect, which is precisely the impact of asking whether the harm to non-minorities was intended. Consider Title VII of the Civil Rights Act of 1964, the Voting Rights Act of 1965, or any statute prohibiting discrimination. They were motivated by a desire to help minorities, and they disproportionally help them. They are not unconstitutional for this reason.

What, then, is the proper analysis of *Shaw v. Reno*? After the Supreme Court's decision in *Miller v. Johnson*, the best analysis is that it will invalidate a facially neutral scheme because of its extreme disparate effect against non-minorities, if that effect was the sole legislative intention, cannot be explained nonracially, and causes dignitary harm to its "victims." Thus, *Shaw* does not invalidate Proposal 1. Proposal 1 probably helps more non-minorities than minorities. Proposal 1 is easily explainable on grounds other than race: it is designed to open jury service to all adult citizens and to diversify the jury to better reflect the overall community. That is a valid, nonracial reason—one that a city council easily could adopt in an all-white city, for example. Finally, it is hard to see any dignitary harm to non-minorities resulting from Proposal 1, which also distinguishes it from *Shaw*.

Proposal 1 clearly is constitutional. The Court would apply rational basis review of the minimal *Railway Express* variety. The goal of expanding jury service is not unconstitutional; indeed, it is legitimate and important. The means chosen to effectuate the goal are not terrific; using drivers' licenses, for example, would be much more efficacious. But the means are rationally connected to achieving the goal.

B. Proposal 2

Proposal 2 presents more difficulty. Although this proposal is facially neutral, it has the gerrymandering qualities that the Court arguably condemned in *Shaw* and in *Miller*. The proposal does not benefit anyone living outside the Fourth Ward. To be sure, non-minorities, as well as minorities, in that Ward will benefit from it, but it will help more minorities than non-minorities. It also is clear that race is the only reason this proposal was developed. The scheme is quite underinclusive, because it fails to bring in people, whether minority or otherwise, from outside the Fourth Ward.

The general defense of underinclusive regulation, the "one step at a time" argument, will work for rational basis review but not for any higher level of scrutiny. Nor will a defense of administrative convenience or cost savings work if higher scrutiny is applied. The proposal does not respect "communities of interest" that cut across racial lines, *cf.* Justice O'Connor's opinion in *Shaw*; instead, the proposal assumes that race is a good proxy for interest and behavior. In addition, this approach would get some publicity, which could cause irritation, anger, and perhaps other forms of dignitary harm to non-minorities in general and to minorities who live outside the Fourth Ward. In *Shaw*, it seemed critical that the use of race produced anger or other dignitary injuries. For these reasons, I advise against implementing Proposal 2. It may well be subject to strict scrutiny, and, while diversifying the jury is probably a compelling state interest, the means chosen here are quite underinclusive and thus are not "the least restrictive."

C. Proposal 3

Proposal 3 has two parts: (1) increasing the number of jurors in the initial pool, which is facially neutral and is easily supported by a rational basis, and (2) requiring that each fourth potential juror subjected to voir dire be African American, which probably is unconstitutional. The question is not as easy as it seems, however. The narrowest way to invalidate this proposal is based on the proposal's use of a racial classification, which triggers strict scrutiny under *Croson*. Although diversifying the jury is probably a compelling government interest, the means chosen are underinclusive because the proposal applies only to African Americans and not to all racial minorities who reside in the county.

If the proposal were modified to say "racial minority," rather than "African American," it gets closer to the constitutional line. Because a facial racial classification is used, the majority of the current Supreme Court would apply strict scrutiny. But the proposal's classification is a very soft kind of quota. It does not compel proportional representation on any jury; potential jurors can be eliminated through challenges for cause and peremptory challenges, though supposedly not for racial reasons under *Edmonson*. Moreover, the clear goal is to diversify the jury.

Diversity—a forward-looking justification for affirmative action—is probably a much better purpose for this measure than any remedial, backward-looking notion, because it will be very hard to show that the current composition of juries is linked to at least a prima facie constitutional or statutory violation, as *Croson* commands. Indeed, Proposal 3, if expanded to include all racial minorities, could look a lot like the Harvard Plan upheld by Justice Powell in *Bakke*: it could be seen as more of a plus factor than as a quota. Moreover, it is hard to think of a "gentler" approach that more clearly would be a plus factor and less clearly a quota. In other words, if one wanted to craft the jury inclusion policy along the lines of Justice Powell's opinion in *Bakke*, this may be the best possible plan.

In his *Metro Broadcasting* concurring opinion, Justice Stevens said that diversity in education and on the police force strikes him as being a compelling government interest. Although the Supreme Court overruled *Metro Broadcasting* in *Adarand Constructors, Inc. v. Pena, Adarand* still leaves open the possibility that diversity can be a compelling government interest. If so, I think that Justice Stevens would consider diversity in juries to be as compelling as in education and on the police force. The question for Justice Stevens would be whether the means are sufficient. How he would come out on that issue is unclear. Perhaps he would prefer that a facially neutral approach be attempted first. Justice Blackmun surely would have upheld this measure as well, assuming that the means chosen are substantially related to the achievement of diversity. Although Justices Scalia, Thomas, Rehnquist, and Kennedy surely would condemn this approach, Justices O'Connor, Souter, and Ginsburg might join Justice Stevens and vote to uphold diversity approaches in limited circumstances. Although this approach may look too much like a quota for Justice O'Connor, she may not vote against affirmative action on these facts. Compare her decisions in the abortion cases.

Finally, the problem briefly mentions a gender impact. Gender should not cause any of the proposals to be unconstitutional. First, none of these proposals necessarily would help women. Proposals 1 and 2 might benefit women who are heads of households; however, in households containing a man and a woman, the man's name probably is more likely to be on the electric bill. In any event, gender considerations seem pretty far removed from any dominant legislative intent here.

CONSTITUTIONAL LAW II

(One hour)

The City of Aquamarine is a lovely, small community in southern California on the Pacific coast. It has wonderful beaches, and its economy is largely based on tourism. Recently, several merchants who have shops fronting on the sidewalks running toward the beach and who cater to tourists have complained to the city council about competition from sidewalk vendors. These vendors have been setting up tables on the sidewalks adjacent to the merchants' shops and have been selling tourist-oriented merchandise. The merchants have complained that they are at a competitive disadvantage because, unlike the vendors, they must pay rent for their shops and must comply with costly municipal regulations. The merchants also complain that the vendors' tables obstruct pedestrian traffic and degrade the beauty of the area.

All but one of the sidewalk vendors are for-profit entrepreneurs. The exception is a group called One World Together (OWT), which is a nonprofit environmentalist organization. OWT sells message-oriented merchandise for tourists. For example, it sells t-shirts that are embroidered with sayings such as "May all the world have the beauty of Aquamarine beaches." Unpaid volunteers staff

OWT's tables, and all sales proceeds are used to disseminate the group's viewpoints concerning environmental protection.

The merchants have suggested to the Aquamarine City Council that it prohibit all sidewalk vending. In response, the police chief has suggested that, instead of prohibiting all vending, a permit system be implemented under which only a vendor with a city permit could operate legally. The police chief suggested that the simplest way to implement the system would be to give the chief authority to draft the permit application and to grant or to deny an application after personally speaking with the applicant.

The City Council has asked you to assess the constitutionality of the suggestions of the merchants and of the police chief. The Council also wants your advice concerning any preferable alternatives. Provide that advice.

Note: This problem involves two different types of sidewalk vendors—for-profit and nonprofit. Although this type of distinction in a problem may be irrelevant, it usually is not. Normally, your professor is testing your ability to analyze both types of situations and the analytic distinctions between them. The clearest way to organize your answer usually will be to discuss the legal implications for one group and then for the other.

MODEL ANSWER

The for-profit vendors have virtually no first amendment right to set up tables on the sidewalks.

Distinguishing these vendors from any other merchant is virtually impossible, except that the vendors have set up shop on government property—the sidewalk. Perhaps displaying a sign that indicates what is being sold and for how much is a kind of minimal commercial speech. But that is the sole extent to which the first amendment might apply to the for-profit vendors, because selling goods is not speech. Therefore, with respect to the for-profit vendors, a court probably would characterize a vending ban as a prohibition on pure conduct and not on speech.

Even if the commercial-speech cases have some relevance, the test for regulating commercial speech turns on whether an important government interest is involved. Presumably, protecting government property from "free rent" merchants, enhancing pedestrian flow, and preserving the area's beauty are sufficient. Moreover, a prohibition on for-profit sidewalk vending is like a zoning requirement; the vendors can sell their merchandise but only in a shop. As such, the prohibition would be subject to only rational-basis due process and equal protection scrutiny.

A harder question arises with respect to OWT, because it is a nonprofit vendor that uses its sales proceeds to disseminate its political and social message. A good case could be made that OWT should be treated like the other vendors. If OWT were giving away t-shirts or leaflets that advocated environmentalism, the first amendment obviously would apply in this public forum. But selling the goods is different, especially when the vendor is encroaching on public property. Is OWT any different from a bookstore that puts tables on the sidewalk in front of the store and sells books that way? Indeed, if OWT as a vendor is treated different than the other vendors, an equal protection problem would exist, although presumably it would be subject only to rational-basis review.

On similar facts, two lower courts have assumed that the first amendment applies to the nonprofit sale of goods that contain a message by a group that advocates the message. However, even if the first amendment does apply, a court might uphold a prohibition of sales on a public sidewalk under an *O'Brien/Rock Against Racism* approach; it is a prohibition on conduct, and it promotes various government interests, such as fairness to other vendors, pedestrian access, and preservation of the beach's beauty. A court is particularly likely to uphold the prohibition because the mere selling of goods is not really symbolic speech. Thus, even if the prohibition is considered to be a ban within a public forum, which is presumptively unconstitutional with respect to "speech," selling goods is not speech either in the direct or in the symbolic sense. Moreover, obvious alternative avenues of expression exist, such as distributing leaflets, giving away t-shirts, and selling the goods in a shop.

The counterargument turns on a variety of factors. First, as suggested by the court in *Gilleo*, venues may exist in which a particular kind of expression is especially effective. Selling these goods at this location is related to the message that OWT intends to convey. This distinguishes it from the bookstore example, in which the communicative items (the books) have no single message and in which the bookstore is not attempting to send any single message. Second, the profits are used to promote the exchange of ideas on the environment. If OWT's sidewalk vending is banned, it will have to open a shop in a building, which may be economically infeasible, or cease operations. Either alternative will reduce the amount of speech that OWT can contribute to the marketplace of ideas. Indeed, OWT's activities may be somewhat analogous to religious groups' distribution of materials and solicitation of contributions in airports. Banning all such activities is unlikely to be constitutional, *Lee*, especially on public sidewalks where the interest in unimpeded pedestrian movement is less important than in a crowded airport where people are hurrying to catch their planes. Moreover, unlike the airport in *Lee*, sidewalks are a traditional public forum.

Assuming that OWT's sales are somewhat protected by the first amendment, we must deal with the supposed rule that a ban on expression in a public forum is presumptively unconstitutional. The proposed ban on vending is quite removed from the situation in *Frisby*, in which a ban on targeted picketing was upheld largely for "captive audience" reasons. If a court viewed OWT's sales as being somewhat like a religious group's solicitations at an airport, noted that sidewalks are traditional public forums, and considered the weaker regulatory justifications for regulating on public sidewalks, it probably would hold that the ban is unconstitutional, unless the city makes a very strong showing that no alternative means exists for promoting pedestrian movement and for protecting the beach's beauty. Protecting store merchants from sidewalk competition is a very weak interest in this context, because OWT is unlikely to take away much of their sales and because economic protectionism is probably not a substantial government interest when weighed against a free speech interest.

The proposed permit system is clearly unconstitutional. Under *Shuttlesworth* and other precedents, permit systems are treated as prior restraints that are presumptively unconstitutional. To be constitutional, a permit system must identify with particularity the criteria that are used to judge applications, and the decision-maker must have very narrow discretion. Otherwise, overbreadth and vagueness problems will invalidate the permit system. Here, granting the police chief essentially complete discretion is similar to the approach invalidated by the court in *Shuttlesworth*.

A better approach to the problem might be to ban for-profit vending and to issue permits to nonprofit groups with cognizable free speech interests, such as OWT. The permit system would have to meet the requirements of *Shuttlesworth*. Alternatively, for-profit and nonprofit sidewalk vending might be allowed under a permit system that limits the number of tables, designates particular spaces for tables, and imposes other time, place, or manner restrictions that allow pedestrians to move about easily and that preserve the area's beauty. Indeed, the tables' appearance could be regulated so that they are attractive and enhance the area's appearance rather than detracting from it. The permit also could be conditioned on payment of a fee for the city's administrative expenses to establish and to maintain the system. The fee requirement also might lessen the sidewalk vendors' competitive advantage over the shop merchants.

CONTRACTS I

(One hour)

You are an attorney in Westville, which is a small suburban town. A young couple, Evelyn and Steve, just moved to town. They are living in Eastgate, which is an apartment complex owned by Evelyn's mother, Maria. Evelyn is a psychologist and is employed as a consultant by the Westville school system. Steve is a physician. He is going into general practice with Dr. Prince, a local doctor nearing retirement age. You are representing Steve in the negotiations to buy Dr. Prince's practice and take it over. Today, you have dropped in at Evelyn and Steve's apartment in Eastgate to discuss some questions about his proposed contract with Dr. Prince. As you are about to leave, Steve, at Evelyn's urging, asks you to read the following letter from her mother, which is dated four months ago.

Dear Evie,

Your father and I were overjoyed to hear that Steve and you are seriously considering moving back to Westville. We have hoped for some time that you would, now that you finally have completed your educations and Steve his residency. We hesitated to say anything because we didn't want you to think that we were pressuring you.

As your father and I get older, particularly with your father's chronic health problems, it would be nice to be able to go to Steve for medical advice and treatment. Anyway, we'd both be delighted to welcome you back.

I had a long talk with your father last night about what we might do for Steve and you over the next few years. As you know, when your sister Chris moved back to Westville with Roger, we gave them the house on Orchard Street as a welcoming gift. My business was doing very well then, and it gave us pleasure to see them living in such a nice place, especially because they would have had trouble affording it on their own. Things aren't quite so flush for me now, but we would still like to do something special for Steve and you to show our love for you both. We haven't forgotten how quick you were, Evie, to take a semester off from college so that you could stay home and nurse your father when he broke his hip. Of course, Chris couldn't be as much help as she would have liked with her twins being so little then. I don't know what we would have done without you.

Your father and I have decided that if you move back to Westville, you can count on a rent-free apartment in Eastgate for as long as you want it. Maybe you'll need to buy a home later, but since there are just two of you for now, you might appreciate a nice apartment. You know I've kept Eastgate in A-1 condition. Also, for the next five years, I will give you a check for $5,000 on

January 1 of each year. I know it isn't easy to get started in a career, as you both are doing. If you decide to have children, that will be a financial strain, too. This money is something you can count on, so don't be ashamed to talk about it, and don't be afraid to make your plans taking it into account. This is something we've thought a lot about, and we know that at our age we'll get more pleasure out of watching Steve and you use this money than we would get from it ourselves.

Love,
Mom

"Naturally, I wrote Mom and told her that we were pleased and very grateful and that we would move back to Westville," Evelyn says. "Steve piled up a lot of debt going through med school, and neither of us believes in looking a gift horse in the mouth. On the other hand, human nature being what it is, I know that living in the same town with my parents is taking a risk. People can change, and sometimes relationships that seem great at a distance sour when you see each other frequently. If we can count on this money, we can commit a greater portion of our incomes to buying out Dr. Prince. We can buy him out in three years, rather than in six as originally planned. So Steve and I couldn't help wondering about the legal status of Mom's letter. Suppose Mom gets mad at Steve or me for some reason. Can she just change her mind and keep the money? Could she evict us from the apartment? I'm not saying that we would ever dream of taking Mom to court. But for our own information and as a lawyer's opinion we could quote if it ever actually came to that, does Mom's letter give us any legal rights?"

What will you tell Evelyn and Steve and why?

Note: To answer this question, you must identify the types of promissory obligations that are enforceable and the elements of each type of promissory obligation. Your answer then can be organized by discussing each element separately. Because the question asks you to advise Evelyn and Steve concerning their legal rights, you should provide an objective evaluation of the merits of their claim. Therefore, discuss the strengths and weaknesses of their position and provide an overall conclusion concerning the merits.

MODEL ANSWER

Because the transaction does not involve the sale of goods, the Uniform Commercial Code does not apply. Therefore, the question must be analyzed under the common law of contracts and other promissory obligations.

A. Traditional Contract

For the letter to be legally enforceable as a contract, three elements must be satisfied: (1) the letter must constitute a valid offer; (2) the offer must have been accepted; and (3) there must be consideration.

1. *Offer*

From the facts in the question, the letter appears to be the only basis for arguing that Evelyn's mother made an offer. To constitute a legally sufficient offer, the letter must evidence a desire to enter into a bargain and must have reasonably caused Evelyn to believe that her agreement would conclude the bargain. Restatement (Second) of Contracts § 24.

The letter contains language of commitment or promise: "you can count on." The letter is also fairly specific as to what is being proposed. Maria states that you will get a rent-free apartment. Exactly what type of apartment is less clear, but you are told that you can have it "as long as you want it." You also are told that all this will be yours "if you move to Westville."

Concerning the five $5,000 checks, the letter also is very clear in its commitment: "I will give you a check for $5,000 on January 1 of each year." The letter is less clear, however, whether this promise is being made in anticipation of a traditional contract or bargain. Unlike the sentence about the apartment, the sentence concerning the money does not include the condition "if you move back to Westville." Moreover, an offer of a rent-free apartment contemplates that the offeree will be living in the apartment. A check, on the other hand, can be sent anywhere. Even if you had not moved to Westville, Maria may have wished to give you the money because of the previous gift to Chris or because Evelyn helped her father. Therefore, it is

unclear whether the offer to form a traditional
contract included the money. With respect to the
apartment, however, the offer was unambiguous
and could be accepted without further negotiation
or clarification. Therefore, the letter constitutes a
valid offer for the apartment and possibly for the
money.

2. Acceptance

The letter did not indicate how the offer was to
be accepted. Therefore, you could have accepted it
by promising to perform or by performing. Restatement (Second) of Contracts § 32. You did
both. Evelyn wrote to her mother and said that
you two would move to Westville, and you in fact
moved there. Because the power of acceptance was
not terminated before acceptance, you validly accepted the offer.

3. Consideration

Without consideration, a promise is characterized
as a donative promise and normally is unenforcea-
ble. At least two parts of the letter indicate that
Evelyn's mother merely made a donative promise.
The letter refers to a "welcoming gift" that Evelyn's parents made to Chris when she moved to
Westville. This reference indicates that the apartment and annual payments also were intended to be
a gift. Additionally, the letter states that the promise was motivated by Evelyn's parents' desire to
"show our love."

On the other hand, at least the promise of the
rent-free apartment was conditioned on your mov-

ing to Westville. Moreover, the letter indicates that the move would benefit Evelyn's parents; the letter states that they were "overjoyed" at the prospect of your moving to Westville and that they would like to go to Steve for medical treatment. However, this argument would be weakened significantly if you already had decided to move to Westville, as indicated by the statement in the letter that you had been "seriously" considering moving. If that is the case, the move to Westville was not in return for the promise and does not constitute consideration.

The argument that Steve's future medical treatment is adequate consideration is weak. The letter does not condition the offer on Steve's agreement to treat Evelyn's parents; the letter merely states that "it would be nice" to be able to become Steve's patients. Additionally, the letter does not indicate that Evelyn's parents are expecting Steve to treat them for anything less than his usual fee. Finally, the facts of the problem do not indicate that Steve agreed to provide medical treatment for them, though perhaps his agreement could be implied from his acceptance of the apartment or by virtue of the family relationship.

If neither the move to Westville nor Steve's agreement to provide medical treatment constitutes consideration, we could argue that Evelyn's assistance to her father when he broke his hip is sufficient consideration. The letter indicates that Maria's promise was made at least in part because of Evelyn's prior help. Generally, however, past consideration will not make a donative promise enforceable.

B. Promissory Estoppel

Promissory estoppel (promises causing reliance) provides an alternative, or an additional, basis to enforce the promises in the letter. That is, even if the consideration requirement is not satisfied so as to allow the finding of a traditional contract, a court might enforce Maria's promises based on the common law doctrine of promissory estoppel. Under that doctrine, a promise that the promisor reasonably should have expected to induce reliance and that does induce reliance is enforceable if necessary to prevent injustice. Restatement (Second) of Contracts § 90.

1. The Apartment

We can argue that Maria made a promise of a rent-free apartment, that she wanted you to rely on that promise ("you can count on"), and that you moved to Westville. However, you may have decided to move to Westville before receiving the letter, which would undercut the extent of your reliance on that promise. Even if you relied on the promise, your remedy may be limited. You both have been able to begin your careers in Westville, which indicates that you will not suffer an injustice if the promise is not enforced. Therefore, a court probably would not require Maria to continue to provide you with an apartment. However, you may get to keep the apartment until you find a new one and may be able to recover the costs of finding a new apartment.

2. *The Money*

Maria also promised you $5,000 each year for the next five years. She wanted you to act on that promise: "[t]his money is something you can count on, so don't be ashamed to talk about it, and don't be afraid to make your plans taking it into account." If you can show reliance on that promise, a court may enforce it to some extent. Entering into a three-year, rather than a six-year, contract with Dr. Prince would help because you could argue that you did so in reliance on Maria's promise, although you have not done so yet. Also, what other plans have you made on the assumption that this money would be yours? Is there any other evidence of reliance? A court may enforce the promise of money based on promissory estoppel but only to the extent of your actual reliance.

C. Promise For Benefit Conferred

Restatement (Second) of Contracts § 86 states that a promise made in recognition of a benefit previously conferred may make the promise enforceable even though the benefit constitutes past consideration. Maria's promises in the letter were prefaced by a recognition of the care Evelyn provided when her father was ill. Maria said: "I don't know what we would have done without you."

Such promises are enforceable only "to the extent necessary to prevent injustice" and will not be enforced on this basis if the past consideration was "conferred ... as a gift." No evidence exists that Evelyn expected to receive any compensation for nursing her father. Rather, she apparently acted from love for her parents and intended to make a gift of her services. Therefore, this past consideration is probably insufficient to make Maria's promises enforceable.

D. Conclusion

Although a court probably would find that Evelyn's mother made an offer, at least with respect to the apartment, and that you accepted the offer, the court would be unlikely to hold that you gave consideration. Moreover, the court probably would not enforce either promise based on promissory estoppel, although some enforcement of the apartment promise is possible. Finally, the past consideration you supplied is unlikely to provide a means to enforce either promise. Therefore, I advise you to enjoy the gifts you have been given and hope that they will continue but not to rely on continued rent-free use of the apartment or on the $5,000 checks as enforceable promissory obligations.

CONTRACTS II

(Ninety minutes)

William White is the owner of a twenty-six acre plot of land. Until recently, the land had been the site of a pig iron manufacturing plant. In addition to various industrial and office buildings, the site had a 60–ton blast furnace, large lifts, hoists and other equipment for transporting and storing ore, railroad tracks, cranes, diesel locomotives, and various other implements and devices used in the business. In November 1995, reduced demand for pig iron and increased foreign competition caused White to decide to close the plant and to sell the land.

White determined that the land would sell for much more if he razed the structures on the site. In December 1995, he signed an agreement with Greta Green, a demolition and excavation expert. Under the contract, White agreed to pay Green $15,000 and also agreed that Green could keep all the items removed, which had a scrap or resale value of approximately $5,000. In return, Green promised to remove the equipment, demolish the structures, and grade the property as specified.

Paragraphs 6 and 7 of the parties' written agreement provide:

6. After the Closing Date, Contractor [Green] shall remove all the equipment and demolish all the improvements on the Property included in the transfer to Contractor. All structures and equipment, including foundations, piers, and headwalls, shall be removed to a depth of approximately one foot below grade lines, as set forth above, in order to provide a reasonably attractive vacant plot for resale.

7. Any payment otherwise due hereunder is subject to Contractor commencing work no later than April 1, 1996 and completing performance by August 31, 1996. Owner [White] will pay Contractor $15,000 for the removal.

Because of unusually heavy rains that began on March 31, Green did not begin the demolition work until April 20, 1996. She first knocked down several structures and began hauling away material. In mid-June, she began to work on excavating subsurface structures. She quickly discovered that subsurface structures from earlier industrial configurations still existed. She estimated that to remove these structures completely to one foot below the surface would cost $50,000 more than the $12,000 she had estimated as the cost of removal.

After discovering these difficulties, she told White that she would complete all the demolition work but would be unable to complete the excavation as specified in the contract. She also stated that, even if she could do both the excavation and demolition work, she could not complete the job until mid-

September. White said that he expected full compliance with the contract specifications. Green continued the demolition work but stopped removing the subsurface structures.

On July 1, White notified Green that he planned to withhold payment under the contract because she was not performing her contractual responsibility to remove the subsurface structures. He also mentioned her failure to begin work on April 1 as required by the contract. Green and White continued to negotiate through the month of July, and Green continued her demolition work. The negotiations came to an impasse when White demanded that Green either perform the excavation work or not get paid under the contract. Green refused, removed her equipment from the job site, and informed White that she considered him to be in breach and that the contract was terminated.

White subsequently hired another contractor to level the property. After Green's three-month effort, little was left to demolish. White conveyed the remaining structures, which had an estimated scrap value of $1,000, to the new contractor and agreed to pay an additional $1,000 to remove the structures. After inspecting the subsurface foundations revealed by Green's earlier excavation work, the new contractor quoted an additional price of $80,000 to remove them to a depth of one foot below grade. White did not contract for their removal.

The new contractor has finished leveling the land. White believes that the fair market value of the leveled land is now $165,000 and that the land's value with the subsurface structures removed to a depth of one foot below grade would have been $190,000.

What are the rights and liabilities of the parties? Discuss claims, counterclaims, defenses, likelihoods of success, and policy considerations.

Note: This problem illustrates the importance of thinking through your answer before beginning to write. First, it is essential that you recognize that Green may have breached two separate contractual provisions—the time provision and the excavation provision. The analyses of the two potential breaches differ substantially. Therefore, failing to separate them will confuse your thinking and writing and will cause your answer to be less thorough.

Second, by thinking through your answer before writing it, you can avoid addressing irrelevant issues. For example, although this problem presents an issue of anticipatory repudiation, that issue and its implications need not be discussed completely to answer the question that has been asked.

Third, under the Uniform Commercial Code, there is a potential sale of goods because Green was granted the right to keep the removed items. Under whatever test a court would apply, such as predominance of purpose or substantial nature of the contract, the U.C.C. probably does not apply. If you studied the U.C.C. in your Contracts course, however, you should discuss this issue in your answer. The following answer applies the common law of contracts.

MODEL ANSWER

White and Green entered into a valid contract. White's promise to pay $15,000 and to convey various items of property constituted consideration for Green's excavation and demolition promises. Both parties accepted the contract, as evidenced by their signing the agreement.

A. Performance Dates: Condition or Promise

The legal effect of the contract provision concerning the commencement and completion dates turns on whether the provisions are conditions or promises. The characterization is based on the parties' intent, the language used, and the court's consideration of the effect of one characterization compared to the other. In case of ambiguity, courts will construe a contract provision to be a promise and not a condition to avoid forfeiture of the right to recover under the contract.

In this case, the contract expressly provides that payment "is subject to" Green satisfying the specified dates. Courts normally construe this language as creating a condition. If the starting date is a condition, White could have terminated the contract initially because the condition was not met.

Green's first response would be waiver. She can argue that White waived the right to enforce the condition by permitting her to work on the property for more than three months. White can respond that, even if he waived the commencement date, he expressly refused to waive the specified completion date, and Green did not complete the work by August 31.

With respect to the termination date, Green can argue that a court, exercising its discretionary powers, should excuse her failure to satisfy the condition because it would cause a disproportionate forfeiture and because it was not a material part of the agreed exchange. Restatement (Second) of Contracts § 229. Conditions relating to the time of performance are particularly susceptible to an excuse defense. In this case, the forfeiture would be disproportionate because Green worked on White's property for over three months and had completed a substantial part of the demolition work. Moreover, her inability to begin work by the specified commencement date, which impeded her ability to meet the completion date, was caused by circumstances beyond her control. Nothing in the facts indicates that White had a particular need for the work to be performed precisely on the timetable specified in the contract. Therefore, unless he can demonstrate that the contract's timetable was a material term, a court should excuse Green's failure to satisfy the time condition.

If the starting date is construed as a promise, rather than as a condition, Green breached that promise. If the breach was material, White could have terminated the contract, but he did not. Therefore, the breach was non-material or partial.

White is entitled to whatever damages he can show resulted from the breach, which is unclear from the question. Also, as discussed below, Green can argue that her breach should be excused under the doctrine of impracticability or under mutual mistake because of the unusually heavy rains.

B. Incomplete Performance: Effects of Breach

When Green informed White that she would not do the excavation work, she breached the contract by repudiation. This could have been a material breach, allowing White to terminate the contract and to seek damages. Instead, White told Green to continue. Ultimately, White told Green she would not be paid if she did not do all the work. Green then left the site. The parties' rights depend on whether White was justified in refusing to pay or whether, in doing so, he committed the first material breach.

1. Substantial Performance

Green can argue that White committed the first material breach by refusing to pay and that she is entitled to compensation based on the doctrine of substantial performance. The doctrine is designed to prevent the unjust enrichment that would result from permitting a person to enjoy the benefits of another's services with no obligation to pay. To qualify for compensation under the doctrine, the contract need not have been performed strictly in compliance with the contract's specifications unless the specifications were made of the essence in the contract. However, because the doctrine is equitable, it applies only if the claimant has made a good faith effort to comply with the contract terms and substantially has performed.

In this case, Green spent three months demolishing and removing structures and equipment on the property. She can argue that excavating the old subsurface structures was unnecessary to fulfill the stated purpose of the contract—"to provide a reasonably attractive vacant plot for resale." However, the failure to excavate apparently made the property worth $25,000 less than it would have been worth if she had performed. Moreover, she apparently failed to demolish and remove approximately 20% of the structures and equipment; she did not remove $1,000 worth of the property that had been valued at $5,000 at the time of the contract. Additionally, she performed little of the required excavation. She also did not attempt to complete the contract by August 31. These significant failures to perform should preclude her from relying on the substantial performance doctrine.

Even if a court held that the doctrine applies, Green would not recover any compensation. When the doctrine is applied, the measure of damages is the unpaid contract price, less the costs of completion and of any other damages. Because the cost of completion is much greater than the unpaid contract price in this case, a court would not award Green any damages.

2. *Impracticability*

If Green committed the first material breach, she
is liable to White unless her performance is excused.
She can argue that her failures to meet the commencement and completion dates and to excavate
the subsurface structures are excused by the impracticability doctrine. Pursuant to that doctrine, a
contractual duty may be excused if performance is
impracticable through no fault of the party who is
to perform.

a. *Commencement and Completion Dates*

Pursuant to the impracticability doctrine, Green's
failure to commence work by April 1 did not breach
the contract if her performance was rendered impracticable through no fault of hers, the non-occur-
rence of the frustrating event was a basic assumption on which the contract was made, and the
contract did not impose the risk of that event on
her. Restatement (Second) of Contracts § 261.
Green has a good argument that the heavy rains
made it impracticable for her to begin her work by
April 1. She will argue that she physically could not
perform the work because of the rain. Obviously,
the rain was not her fault. She also will argue that
the commencement and completion dates specified
in the contract necessarily were based on the assumption that the weather would not prevent the
work from being performed and that nothing in the
contract shifted the risk of adverse weather to her.

White will respond that the contract provides that
Green will begin work "no later than April 1,

1996." Because the rains did not begin until March 31, Green could have satisfied the contract by beginning work earlier in March. She should not be excused from timely performance of the contract because she waited until the last minute to begin. Moreover, the facts do not indicate that she could have begun work by April 1 even if it had not rained. Finally, the impracticability defense is unlikely to prevail, because a court probably will find that Green, as a demolition and excavation expert, assumed the risk of inclement conditions.

b. Subsurface Structures

Green also can argue that her obligation to excavate the subsurface structures was excused by impracticability. She will have to prove that her performance was rendered impracticable by a condition of which she had no reason to know, that the absence of the condition was a basic assumption of the contract, and that she did not assume the risk of the condition. Restatement (Second) of Contracts § 266. Green may be able to prove that the contract was based on the assumption that only the current plant had to be excavated and that the contract did not impose on her the risk of additional subsurface structures. However, she may be unable to prove that she had no reason to know of the abandoned subsurface structures. White will argue that, as an excavation expert, Green should have anticipated the existence of abandoned subsurface structures and should have conducted additional tests for them before entering into the contract.

Green also may be unable to satisfy the impracticability of performance requirement. Increased cost alone normally does not render performance impracticable. She could excavate the structures. However, the very substantial cost to do so, especially compared to the contract price and to the limited increase in the property's value, may cause a court to hold that her performance was impracticable.

3. *Mistake*

Green also will argue that a mutual mistake by White and by her concerning the subsurface structures entitled her to void the excavation obligation. To establish a sufficient mutual mistake, Green must prove that the mistake concerned a basic assumption on which the contract was made and had a material effect on the contractual obligations and that she did not bear the risk of the mistake. Restatement (Second) of Contracts § 152. The amount of material to be excavated would constitute a basic assumption of the agreement. Both the contract price and the time needed for performance are very directly related to the amount of work that must be performed. Green also can establish that the additional excavation burden materially affected the contractual obligations: the cost of excavation would have been four times the amount she had estimated.

However, Green may have difficulty establishing that she did not bear the risk of a mistake. As with the impracticability defense, White will argue that Green bore the risk of this mistake because she is an excavation expert. Green will respond that, as the owner and operator of the property, White was in a better position to know about prior uses of the land and should have told her about them. In fact, if White knew about the abandoned subsurface structures, he breached his obligation to perform in good faith by failing to disclose that material fact.

C. Remedies

1. White's Damages

If Green inexcusably breached the contract, the usual measure of damages would be the cost to complete the contract, less the costs saved. A court will not use this measure of damages, however, if the cost is grossly disproportionate to the benefit, measured by the diminution in the property's value. In this case, a court probably would hold that the increase in the land's value—$25,000—would not justify the cost of completion—$50,000–$80,000— especially because the land is intended for commercial use. Instead, Green would be liable to White for the diminution in property value caused by the breach. Therefore, she would be liable for $25,000, which is the difference between the value of the land with the subsurface structures removed and the value without them removed, less the costs saved by White, which were $14,000 (the $15,000 unpaid to Green, less the $1,000 paid to the other contractor).

2. Green's Damages

If a court finds that Green breached the contract but that she had substantially performed her contractual duties, she has a claim for compensation based on the contract. However, because she must compensate White for her breach and because the damage to White is greater than the amount due to her under the contract, she will recover nothing.

Alternatively, if the contract provision concerning the dates of performance is construed to be an enforceable condition or Green otherwise cannot recover under the contract, she would have a claim for restitution for the benefit conferred by her work, less the damages for which she is liable and the value of the property she took from the property. As with the traditional damage recovery, however, this would be a negative number and would result in no award to Green.

CRIMINAL LAW I

(One hour)

"Pops" Sanders runs a hardware and farm supply
store in a small, country town. Over a period of
weeks, he sold several thousand pounds of fertilizer
and some diesel fuel to two men, Vic Townsend and
a man identified only as "Mo." Pops knew that
both men were members of a local "militia" group
that held periodic "training" exercises and advocated armed resistance to all federal authorities. Pops
also knew that some militia group members proposed bombing military bases and other federal
operations and that several mysterious explosions
recently had been heard in the area. Pops was not
a member of the militia, did not share its members'
views, and did not like dealing with them. On one
occasion, when Pops seemed to hesitate to continue
selling to Vic, Vic said: "It would be a shame if
anything were to happen to your store, like a fire or
explosion or something. Some of the guys have a
pretty short fuse, but as long as you're helping us
out, I'll make sure they leave you and your family
alone."

As it turned out, Mo is an undercover agent who
had infiltrated the militia. Based on his information, the FBI got a search warrant, raided Vic's
farm, and legally seized several tons of fertilizer and

diesel fuel. The FBI also seized detailed instructions for making bombs from fertilizer and diesel fuel. As the FBI agents were entering the farm to begin the raid, a large dog attacked and seriously injured one of the agents. Vic admitted that the dog was his, was kept unleashed, and did not like strangers. Vic's property was surrounded by high fences and was posted with numerous "Keep Out," "No Trespassing," and "Beware of the Dog" signs.

Immediately after the raid, FBI agents went to Pops' store. After they had identified themselves and were about to tell Pops that he was under arrest, Pops said: "I'm real glad to see you guys. I've been meaning to call you. Do you know about Vic Townsend? I think he's planning to build some bombs. You should check him out right away. His farm is about five miles north of town."

Vic was charged with assault of the injured FBI agent under a statute that prohibits "recklessly causing bodily injury." Vic also was charged with conspiracy to violate the following federal statute, and both Vic and Pops were charged with attempted violation of the statute:

Bomb-Making. Whoever shall manufacture any bomb or other explosive device capable of causing substantial personal injury or property damage without previously registering such device with [designated authorities] is guilty of a felony and may be punished with up to five years in prison and/or a fine not exceeding $10,000.

You are a law clerk for the Assistant United States Attorney who is preparing to prosecute this case. She has asked you to write a memo that describes the arguments for and against (1) Vic's liability for assaulting the injured FBI agent, (2) Vic's liability for attempt and for conspiracy to violate the bomb-making statute, and (3) Pops' liability for attempt. For purposes of part (3) concerning Pops' liability, assume that Vic is liable for attempt even if you concluded in part (2) that he is not.

Note: This question does not specify the jurisdiction in which the alleged crimes occurred. Therefore, if you have studied the law of more than one jurisdiction, you should analyze the question under each type of law. For example, if you studied majority and minority rules and a model code, you should apply each rule to the facts of the question. Your professor wants to see whether you know the different rules and can apply them. Because this question asks you to present the arguments for and against the parties' guilt, present both sides of the issues objectively and describe their strengths and weaknesses. Do not write as an advocate for either side.

MODEL ANSWER
A. Vic's Alleged Assault

The elements of assault under the statute are recklessness, causation, and bodily injury. Allowing the dog to run loose arguably was "reckless" conduct under the Model Penal Code (MPC) definition: a jury could find Vic was aware of a "substantial and unjustifiable risk" of injury to anyone entering the farm because he knew that the dog did not like strangers and because he had posted warning signs about the dog. Indeed, Vic apparently used the dog as a guard dog. If the jury so found and further found that the dog was guarding an illegal bomb-making operation, Vic's actions clearly would constitute a "gross deviation from the standard of conduct of a law-abiding person" under the MPC, especially "considering the nature and purpose of the actor's conduct." Under the latter standard, any illegal purpose weighs very heavily against the defendant. *See Berry* (marijuana plants guarded by a vicious dog).

The reckless act of posting the guard dog was the "but for" cause of the injury and meets the proximate cause requirements under both the MPC (result was within the risk of which the actor was aware) and applicable case law (result was reasonably foreseeable). Courts are very reluctant to find that the victim's acts broke the causal chain. *See, e.g., Hamilton; see also Berry* (similar liability for a vicious dog). Finally, the agent suffered bodily injury.

Vic might claim that his use of the dog was a legally justified use of force. The facts do not suggest any basis for a self-defense argument, but they do suggest a possible defense of justifiable force to protect property. This defense will fail if the dog was guarding an illegal operation. *Berry.* It also will fail if the use of such a dangerous dog constitutes "deadly force." MPC § 3.11 defines "deadly force" as force that creates a known substantial risk of serious bodily injury. Deadly force generally cannot be used to protect property. Vic also does not have a valid "defense of habitation" argument; the agent was not in or entering Vic's house when the dog attacked. Under MPC § 3.09, the defendant's belief that his action was justified is not a defense if the belief was reckless and if that recklessness suffices for culpability, which it does in this case. Even if Vic reasonably thought the agents were burglars, using the dog is like setting a spring gun, which the courts (*Ceballos*) and MPC have rejected because it is too likely to injure innocent people. Although the owner, if present, often could distinguish between possible burglars and various non-threatening persons, such as children and postal carriers, a dog or spring gun cannot.

B. Vic's Alleged Violation of the Bomb–Making Statute

1. *Attempt*

Attempt requires acts beyond "mere preparation" and intent (or "purpose" under the MPC) to complete the crime. Whether Vic's acts progressed far enough to constitute attempt is a close question. A person is not guilty of attempt for merely entertaining "bad thoughts" or for pure intent without any accompanying acts. *Proctor*. A person also is not guilty for committing only very preliminary acts in furtherance of that intent. Vic clearly did not go far enough under the "last act" test. However, he may have done so under the "dangerous proximity" test; the more serious the crime and the more irreparable the potential injury, the "earlier" the law can intervene. He also may have gone far enough under the MPC's "substantial step" test, but only if the preparatory acts are "strongly corroborative" of the actor's criminal purpose. Of the MPC's list of acts that present at least a jury issue of attempt, category (f)—possession of materials to be employed and serving no lawful purpose at the place contemplated for the crime—probably is the most applicable to this case.

To prove intent in this case, you will have to prove intent to build a bomb and not register it. Specific intent is required even if the completed crime would require a lesser mens rea, which this one may. *See Lyerla*. Intent to build a bomb can be shown by the bomb plans, the presence of the needed materials, and Vic's general criminal tendencies, as evidenced by his threatening Pops and perhaps by the militia's views.

The strict mens rea requirements of attempt liability also suggest that you will have to prove specific intent not to register the bomb before its completion. This second element of intent, if required, is a much closer question. Perhaps it can be inferred from the militia's views and from evidence of previous "mysterious explosions" in the area without the explosive devices being registered. You also could attempt to prove that Vic had no apparent lawful use for explosives on his farm. Of course, intent would be much easier to prove if Mo talked with Vic or with other militia members about a bomb-making project.

Vic will argue that the bomb ingredients—fertilizer and diesel fuel—clearly have lawful uses on a farm. He also can argue that these materials, even with the plans, do not strongly corroborate an intent not to register a bomb. However, the bomb plans and Vic's militia views suggest unlawful purposes, and such purposes in turn suggest an intent not to register. Therefore, enough evidence probably exists to raise a jury issue of attempt. Vic's best chance of acquittal would be to introduce evidence suggesting specific intended lawful uses of high explosives on his farm.

2. *Conspiracy*

Conspiracy also requires specific intent (or "purpose" under the MPC). However, it is easier to prove as far as actus reus, because it only requires an "overt act" by any conspirator in furtherance of the conspiratorial plan. Moreover, in some states (and under the MPC for very serious crimes), no overt act is required.

The defense will argue that there was no real "agreement" by Mo or by Pops, who was not even charged with conspiracy. Thus, no "meeting of the minds" or "bilateral" conspiracy occurred. However, the MPC and some states require only that Vic intended to agree with the others ("unilateral" conspiracy theory). The defense can argue that the court should reject the "unilateral" conspiracy theory because the crime of conspiracy is directed at criminal groups and their more efficient division of labor, mutual emboldening, long-term criminal operations, and risk of "diversification" to new types of crime. In this case, the named parties were not a criminal group. The prosecution can argue that other militia members shared Vic's purpose and that they might have helped him carry it out. The defense will respond that, until specific others are charged, this is a "solo" conspiracy, which is not sufficiently dangerous to be punishable for acts that the defense will argue had not gone far enough to constitute attempt.

In most states, Vic could be guilty of conspiracy and of attempt, *Verive*, and could receive consecutive sentences for them. The MPC would merge the offenses unless the conspiracy had broader objectives than the specific crime attempted. The facts are unclear whether Vic had broader objectives.

C. Pops' Alleged Attempt to Violate the Bomb–Making Statute

If Vic is guilty of attempt, is Pops guilty as an accomplice? Pop's sale of the bomb-making ingredients constitutes the actus reus of complicity—aid or encouragement of Vic's attempt. But accomplice liability, like attempt, normally requires intent (or "purpose" under the MPC) to assist or to encourage commission of the crime. *Beeman*. Such a very high mens rea requirement compensates for the limited actus reus of complicity. An accomplice often will have committed fewer acts than the principal party or parties or acts remote from the crime's completion. Both circumstances suggest reduced culpability or greater doubt as to the accomplice's intent. If Pops knew that bombs could be made from fertilizer and diesel fuel, his statements to the officers may show that he knew he was aiding Vic's bomb-making. Moreover, Vic's militia activities might be enough to show that Pops knew Vic would not register the bombs. The *Lauria* decision suggests that purpose can be inferred from knowledge in certain situations, two of which might apply here: (1) the large volume of sales relative to any legitimate use and relative to Pops' total business and (2) knowing aid of a serious felony.

Pops might claim a defense of abandonment of his complicity. Pursuant to MPC § 2.06, Pops will have to show that he either (1) "wholly deprived" his prior complicity of its effectiveness, which was probably impossible after he sold the fertilizer and fuel, or (2) gave "timely warning" or otherwise tried to prevent the crime before its commission. Similarly, the MPC attempt provision, § 5.01(4), requires a "complete and voluntary renunciation" of the criminal purpose unprompted by increased difficulty or by risk of apprehension. If Pops knew that the FBI was aware of his involvement, his statements against Vic would be neither timely nor voluntary. Moreover, they were not "prior" to the "commission" of Vic's attempt.

Pops also might claim a defense of duress if he reasonably feared serious physical harm to his family or to himself. MPC § 2.09 relaxes the traditional strict requirements of duress as to "imminence" and extreme severity of threatened harm. Instead, it uses the "person of reasonable firmness" standard. However, the MPC still excludes threats to one's property. If Vic's statements are viewed as implied physical threats, the defense can argue that a person of reasonable firmness who is subjected to such threats might agree to sell bomb-making materials, citing *Contento-Pachon*. The prosecution will argue that the threats in that case, although not particularly imminent, were much more explicit and severe (death of defendant and his family). Also, the crime excused in that case was not as dangerous as bombing. The defense will reply that the charge in the present case is not bombing but possession of an unregistered explosive device. Under the MPC, Pops probably at least would get his duress defense to the jury. Under more traditional standards, however, he would not have a duress defense because he could not show a threat of imminent death or great bodily harm.

CRIMINAL LAW II

(Forty-five minutes)

Your client, George Jackson, is an auto worker. He has been charged with committing aggravated assault ("intentionally causing great bodily harm") against his assembly-plant foreman, Bill Ward. The essential facts surrounding the incident are undisputed. George came to work late and with alcohol on his breath. Bill confronted him and told him to go home. According to several reliable witnesses, Bill said: "You're a disgrace to yourself and to your co-workers. You've really let us down. Get out of here." George did not respond or start to leave, so Bill and another supervisor approached him and began to lead him to the door. As they did, George suddenly seemed to "explode" with rage and attacked Bill with his fists and with a chair. Bill suffered severe head injuries as a result of the attack.

Your investigation of George's background reveals that he is a Vietnam veteran, who appears to be suffering from a form of Post–Traumatic Stress Disorder (PTSD). Since 1980, the American Psychiatric Association (APA) has recognized PTSD as a "behavioral disorder," and it is described in the APA's Diagnostic and Statistical Manual (DSM). Also known as "delayed stress syndrome," PTSD affects not only many Vietnam veterans, but also survivors of atomic attacks, concentration camps, natural disasters, car or plane accidents, rapes, and other traumatic events. The diagnostic criteria listed in the DSM include:

1. Experiencing a recognizable stress-producing event "that would evoke significant symptoms of distress in almost everyone;"

2. Re-experiencing the trauma by recurrent and intrusive recollections, dreams, or flashbacks ("suddenly acting or feeling as if the traumatic event were re-occurring because of an association with an environmental stimulus");

3. Numbing of responsiveness to or reduced involvement with the external world or other persons; and

4. Two or more of the following symptoms that were not present before the trauma: exaggerated startle response, sleep disturbance, guilt about surviving when others have not, impairment of memory or of concentration ability, avoidance of activities that arouse memories of the trauma, or intensification of symptoms by exposure to events that symbolize or resemble the trauma.

Your investigation reveals that George has exhibited many of these symptoms since returning from Vietnam and that the confrontation with Bill may have triggered a flashback to a very traumatic experience George had during the war: his company was ambushed by the enemy, and George was the sole survivor. George often has discussed these problems with his wife and friends but has not sought professional treatment or counseling.

Write a memorandum to the office file concerning the possible relevance of George's PTSD to any issues in the pending assault charge and the prosecution's likely responses.

Note: This question raises several specific issues of criminal liability. The most obvious defense is insanity, but do not discuss just the most obvious issue. This question invites you to be creative in determining other defenses for which expert testimony concerning mental impairment may be relevant. In addressing each defense, you must raise and apply broad policy arguments. Such arguments most often are raised in connection with the insanity defense, but they are also quite relevant to other defenses involving mental impairment.

MODEL ANSWER

George's PTSD may be relevant to at least three issues in his prosecution for aggravated assault: (1) an insanity defense, (2) a diminished capacity defense, and (3) a claim of self-defense.

A. Insanity Defense

George might present an insanity defense. He has some type of "mental disease or defect," so he would not have to claim "social adversity" or some other overly broad, difficult-to-litigate excuse. He also arguably meets each impairment standard of the competing insanity formulations. To satisfy

these standards, the defense will have to prove that
(1) under *Durham*, the assault was the "product" of
his mental disease; (2) he had an "irresistible im-
pulse;" (3) under the Model Penal Code (MPC), he
lacked "substantial capacity" either to appreciate
the wrongfulness of his conduct, such as thinking
he was back in Vietnam, or to conform his conduct
to the law, which assumes conscious, but uncontrol-
lable, impulsive behavior; or (4) under the
M'Naghten standard, he did not know the "nature
and quality of his act" or that it was "wrong"
because he was experiencing a flashback.

Under each of these standards, the defense will
argue that George does not merit criminal condem-
nation and punishment. Just like persons suffering
from severe schizophrenia or other clearly excusing
mental illness, George is not sufficiently blamewor-
thy to justify application of criminal sanctions; he
is as much a victim as the person he injured. Nor
are persons like George likely to be deterred by the
fear of punishment or to learn any useful deterrent
lesson from the experience of punishment. To the
extent that people like George are dangerous and
require confinement and treatment, they may be
dealt with via civil commitment procedures.

The prosecution will argue that, like alcoholism
and drug addiction, PTSD is too broad and diffuse a
category to support an insanity defense; PTSD
should not be deemed a qualifying "mental disease
or defect" for the insanity defense. The skepticism
about psychiatry that recently has caused courts
and legislatures to retreat from the broader MPC

insanity formulation also should prevent expanding the types of newly-discovered mental problems that qualify for this defense, especially when the problem is likely to involve claims of volitional impairment and is fairly widespread and, therefore, likely to be frequently invoked as an excuse. This expansion of the insanity defense could create the problems of proof, circularity of definition, and the confusing, time-consuming "battle of the experts" that has characterized the MPC formulation.

The prosecution further will argue that, in our current state of knowledge, erring on the side of under-coverage and keeping the insanity defense extremely narrow is preferable. The public will not stand for a broad defense, as the *Hinckley* case shows. Indeed, this defense probably would be raised in cases involving the most violent crimes, for which public protection is a paramount concern. The mental health system cannot be relied on to insure public safety even with the loose not-guilty-by-reason-of-insanity commitment standards allowed under *Jones v. United States*. Finally, like the epileptic defendant in *Decina* and the addict defendant in *Lyons*, George apparently knew he had this dangerous condition but did not take proper precautions to manage and to treat it. Similar concerns may have caused the Supreme Court to reject the chronic alcoholic's claim in *Powell v. Texas*; even if some alcoholics are powerless to stop drinking to excess, they are not powerless to take steps to obtain treatment.

B. Diminished Capacity Defense

George also might present a diminished capacity defense by claiming that his PTSD attack prevented him from having the mental state ("intentionally") required for this offense. This defense is supported by the line of California cases illustrated by *Wetmore* and by due process and compulsory process arguments that criminal defendants must be allowed to introduce evidence relevant to the crucial mens rea issue.

The prosecution will argue against recognition of such a "partial" insanity defense and will cite cases that have rejected it, such as *Wilcox* and *Bouwman*. As with the insanity defense itself, we should avoid doctrines that create difficulties, such as formidable problems of proof and battles of the experts. Also, the absence of automatic commitment statutes for persons who are found not guilty by reason of diminished capacity and the possible absence of any lesser offense that would allow substantial imprisonment mean that a dangerous person will be neither treated nor restrained. Finally, many states and the federal system recently have moved to put the burden of proof of insanity on the defendant for reasons such as problems of proof, lack of public confidence, and safety. In light of this development, it would be unwise to adopt a diminished capacity defense that places the burden of proof on the prosecution for many of the same mental illness issues.

A variant of the diminished capacity defense is the defense of automatism or unconsciousness (or, under the MPC, absence of a "voluntary act"). In addition to the above arguments, the prosecution will argue that George's case is more like *Decina* (epileptic's foreseeable risk of loss of self-control) than *Newton* (unconsciousness caused by gunshot wound). The defense can argue, however, that part of the PTSD syndrome is "numbing," withdrawal, and refusal to face the problem. Also, going to work arguably is not as risky as driving, as in *Decina*.

C. Self–Defense

Finally, George's PTSD may be relevant to a self-defense claim. Any fear George had of being attacked and the degree of force he used in defense seem clearly unreasonable under the prevailing objective standard, *Simon,* especially because Bill and the other supervisor probably were justified in using moderate force to remove George from the premises. However, some states employ a more subjective set of standards, such as "subjective reasonableness," *Leidholm* ("reasonable from defendant's point of view"), or even "pure subjective." *Wanrow*.

The prosecution will make many of the arguments described above. It will argue that mental conditions are too difficult to litigate and should be confined narrowly to the insanity defense itself. It also will argue that, like the choice-of-evils defense, the essence of self-defense is justification, which generally only exonerates people who do the right thing under the circumstances. We can respond that the law allows people to act on reasonable appearances even if they, in fact, do the wrong thing. However, individuals at least should be held to the higher standards of objective reasonableness and should take whatever precautions or preventive measures are necessary to meet that standard.

Even if the court applies purely objective standards of fear and defensive force, George's PTSD may be admissible on other self-defense issues. If this jurisdiction requires retreat, which is a purely subjective standard, the PTSD evidence might help to show that George did not know that he had a safe means of avoiding the confrontation. If this jurisdiction recognizes imperfect self-defense, as in *Shuck*, the PTSD could have caused George to believe, albeit unreasonably, that he was under attack and needed the force he used. The prosecution would counter that *Shuck* only involved mitigation of murder to manslaughter; application of that doctrine here might allow George to escape criminal liability completely, unless a lesser, included offense exists analogous to the manslaughter charge in *Shuck*. However, if this state has a simple assault statute like the one discussed in *Hood* (requiring only "general intent"), George could be found guilty of that lesser offense.

PROPERTY I

(Ninety minutes)

Yi Cheng, a widower, died testate. His will devised his home, which he had owned in fee simple absolute, "to my only child, Won, for life, with remainder over to the heirs of the body of Won, and in the event of Won's death without heirs of his body, then the land shall go to the Society for the Elimination of Law School Exams (SELSE)."

Who owns what interests in the property?

Note: In addition to testing your knowledge of estates in land and future interests, this question is designed to test whether you can spot not only the relevant facts that are in the problem, but also those that are not. The question does not specify, for example, whether Won is still alive, whether he had issue, and whether his issue survived him if he is dead. The problem also raises legal issues about which American jurisdictions are divided, such as the treatment of fee tails and the Rule in Shelley's Case. Finally, the language of the devise is ambiguous in some respects. For this type of problem, you should answer the question for each possible fact pattern, legal rule, and interpretation. Organizing your answer before beginning to write is crucial for this type of question. Otherwise, you quickly will become entangled in all the possible alternatives.

MODEL ANSWER

The answer to this question depends on whether (1) Won is alive, (2) Won had issue, (3) Won's issue, if any, survived him if he is dead, and (4) his surviving issue are still alive. The answer also depends on the jurisdiction's laws concerning fee tails and concerning the Rule in Shelley's Case. Because this information is unavailable, I will interpret the will language for each possible set of circumstances.

A. If the Jurisdiction does not Follow the Rule in Shelley's Case

1. *If Won is Alive*

a. *Won*

A court could interpret Won's interest as a life estate or as a fee tail. The will specifies that Won owns the property "for life" and provides for a remainder to the heirs of his body. This language indicates that the testator intended to devise a life estate.

The language also could be interpreted to devise a fee tail, if the jurisdiction recognizes the fee tail. The will provides that Won will have the property during his life and that it then will go to the heirs of his body, which is the essence of a fee tail. The will uses the term "heirs of the body," which is traditional language for creating a fee tail.

On the other hand, the will does not use the exact language required by the common law: "to A and the heirs of his body." The will also devises an interest in the land to SELSE that will become possessory if Won dies without issue. By specifying a particular time for determining whether Won has issue, the language may indicate a definite, rather than an indefinite, failure of issue. A fee tail is created only if the conveyance specifies an indefinite failure of issue.

However, courts generally are more flexible when construing wills than other types of conveyances. If the evidence establishes that the testator intended to devise a fee tail, the court may hold that the language is sufficient for that purpose. It then would be necessary to determine how this jurisdiction treats the fee tail:

i. Some jurisdictions recognize the fee tail. In these jurisdictions, Won would have a fee tail.

ii. Some jurisdictions statutorily provide that the first taker acquires a fee simple absolute. In this type of jurisdiction, Won would have fee simple absolute title.

iii. Some jurisdictions recognize the fee tail but provide a means for it to be disentailed. In this type of jurisdiction, it would be necessary to investigate whether Won exercised the right to disentail. If so, he acquired a fee simple absolute unless the testator's intent would be served better by preserving SELSE's interest. In that case, Won would have a fee simple subject to executory interest.

iv. Some jurisdictions do not recognize the fee tail. In these jurisdictions, Won would have acquired a fee simple absolute, unless the testator's intent would be served better by giving Won only a life estate or a fee simple subject to executory interest.

v. Some jurisdictions would construe the language to create a life estate in Won and a remainder in fee simple absolute.

vi. Some jurisdictions give the first taker a fee tail and the next takers a fee simple absolute. In these jurisdictions, Won would have a fee tail.

vii. Some jurisdictions would construe the language as creating a fee simple conditional. In that type of jurisdiction, Won could convey fee simple absolute if and when he had a child.

b. Heirs of Won's Body

If the heirs of Won's body have an interest while Won is alive, it is a contingent remainder in fee simple absolute or in fee tail.

i. Will Devised Life Estate to Won

The heirs of Won's body have an alternative contingent remainder in fee simple absolute. It is a remainder because it (1) is an interest that was conveyed to a grantee, rather than retained by the grantor, (2) will not divest a prior possessory estate because it will vest, if ever, at the natural termination of Won's interest, and (3) is capable of becoming immediately possessory upon the termination of Won's interest. The remainder is contingent because the taker is unascertainable; the living have no heirs. It is alternative because the same condition determines whether the heirs of Won's body or SELSE will get the property at Won's death. The remainder is in fee simple absolute because of the modern presumption in favor of fee simple absolute and because the requirement for the common law language "and his heirs" has been abolished in virtually every (if not every) jurisdiction.

ii. *Will Devised Fee Tail to Won*

If the jurisdiction recognizes the fee tail, the heirs of Won's body would have a contingent remainder in fee tail; it is a contingent remainder for the same reasons given above. If the jurisdiction treats Won as acquiring a fee simple absolute, the heirs of his body have no interest. If the jurisdiction converts a fee tail into a fee simple absolute at the death of the first taker, the heirs of Won's body have a contingent remainder in fee simple absolute.

c. *SELSE*

If SELSE has an interest in the property while Won is alive, it is an alternative contingent remainder or a shifting executory interest in fee simple absolute.

i. *Will Devised Life Estate to Won*

SELSE's interest is an alternative contingent remainder in fee simple absolute. It is a remainder because it (1) is an interest that was conveyed to a grantee, rather than retained by the grantor, (2) will not divest a prior possessory estate because it will vest, if ever, at the natural termination of Won's interest, and (3) is capable of becoming immediately possessory upon the termination of Won's interest. It is a contingent remainder because it is subject to the precondition of Won dying without heirs of his body. It is an alternative contingent remainder and in fee simple absolute for the same reasons as for the heirs of Won's body.

ii. *Will Devised Fee Tail to Won*

If the jurisdiction recognizes the fee tail, SELSE would have a contingent remainder in fee simple absolute for the same reasons as described above. If the jurisdiction treats Won as acquiring the fee simple absolute, SELSE has no interest. If the jurisdiction does not recognize the fee tail or permits Won to disentail, SELSE could have a shifting executory interest in fee simple absolute if that construction is more consistent with the testator's intent than treating Won as acquiring fee simple absolute. It would be an executory interest because it would divest Won's fee estate; Won would have acquired fee simple subject to executory interest. It is a shifting interest because possession would shift from one grantee of Cheng (Won) to another grantee (SELSE). It is in fee simple absolute for the reasons given above.

d. Cheng's Estate

The will created a reversion in the home in three ways: (1) following the alternative contingent remainders, (2) following the possible fee tail if Won dies with heirs of his body (otherwise, SELSE would get the property), and (3) in case Won renounces his life estate, because the heirs of his body would be unascertainable and because it could not be determined whether Won will be survived by heirs of his body. If the will contained a residuary clause or a clause expressly devising the reversion, the reversion was devised according to the terms of the clause. If the will did not include a residuary clause or an express devise, the reversion probably passed by intestate succession to Won.

2. If Won Died Without Heirs of his Body

If Won had a life estate or fee tail, SELSE now has fee simple absolute. If Won had fee simple absolute as a result of the jurisdiction's treatment of the fee tail, his title passed by devise to his devisees or by intestate succession to his heirs.

3. If Won Died with Heirs of his Body

If Won had a life estate, the heirs of his body have fee simple absolute. If Won had a fee tail, the heirs of his body have a fee tail unless the jurisdiction converts it into fee simple absolute. If Won had fee simple absolute title, it passed by devise or by intestate succession. If Won died with more than one heir of his body, they hold the property as tenants in common.

B. If the Jurisdiction Follows the Rule in Shelley's Case

If Won acquired a fee simple absolute because of the jurisdiction's treatment of the fee tail, the Rule in Shelley's Case is irrelevant. However, if Won acquired a life estate or fee tail, the Rule may be applicable.

1. Does this Devise Satisfy the Elements of the Rule?

For the Rule in Shelley's Case to apply, the following elements must be satisfied:

a. Does Won have a freehold estate? Yes, either a life estate or fee tail.

b. Do the heirs of his body have a remainder? Yes.

c. Are the grants to Won and to the heirs of his body in the same instrument? Yes.

d. Are the grants to Won and to his heirs both either legal or equitable? Yes, both are legal.

e. Does the devise of the future interest use language of indefinite succession? Although the will specifies that the remainder is held by "the heirs of the body of Won," which is language of indefinite succession, that language is followed by the provision, "in the event of Won's death without heirs of his body, then the land shall go to...." By specifying a particular time for determining whether Won has heirs of the body, the language may indicate definite, rather than indefinite, succession.

Courts generally are hostile to the Rule in Shelley's Case because it can defeat the testator's intent. Therefore, because the will's language is ambiguous, a court may hold that this element is not satisfied and that the Rule does not apply. If a court does hold that the Rule applies, the ownership of the property would be as follows.

2. *If the Rule Applies*

If the Rule applies, the remainder to the heirs of Won's body vested in him and merged with his other interest in the property.

a. *If Won is Alive*

If the express devise to Won is a life estate, it merged with the contingent remainder in the heirs of his body to form a fee simple subject to executory interest. SELSE has a shifting executory interest in fee simple absolute. It is an executory interest because SELSE's interest would become possessory by divesting Won of his fee estate. It is a shifting interest because possession passes from one grantee to another.

If the express devise to Won was a fee tail, it remains a fee tail after application of the Rule in Shelley's Case. SELSE still has a contingent remainder because it will get possession of the property only if Won dies without heirs of his body.

Cheng's estate retained a reversion in the event that Won died survived by heirs of his body; the reversion will become possessory when the fee tail expires. The reversion was transferred by devise or by intestate succession.

b. *If Won Died Without Heirs of his Body*

SELSE has fee simple absolute.

c. *If Won Died with Heirs of his Body*

If the express devise to Won is a life estate, fee simple absolute title passed by devise or by intestate succession. If the express devise was a fee tail, the heirs of Won's body have the fee tail, and Cheng's heir or devisee has the reversion following it.

PROPERTY II

(One hour)

Arthur owned fee simple absolute title to Shady Acres. He conveyed Shady Acres by deed "to Betsy, Carlos, and Daphne in fee simple." Betsy borrowed money from First National Bank (FNB) and gave FNB a mortgage on her interest in Shady Acres. Betsy did not repay the loan, so FNB foreclosed the mortgage. Eddie purchased the property at the foreclosure sale. Carlos then died intestate, survived by his parents and a sister. Daphne then conveyed her interest in Shady Acres by deed "to Fred and Gloria, husband and wife." Fred then executed and delivered a deed of his interest to Harry. Fred then died and was survived by Gloria.

A. Describe the ownership interests that would have existed under the original common law.

B. Describe the ownership interests that exist under current law.

Note: Property law exams often include a question like this one. The question describes a series of title transfers and asks you to give the current state of title. Your professor has included each type of transfer to test your knowledge concerning it. Therefore, you should approach the problem by discussing each transfer in chronological order.

This is the method lawyers use to determine a property title, and it will help you get full credit for the question. Simply belly flopping onto the facts makes untangling the title virtually impossible. Therefore, begin your answer by describing the state of title after the conveyance from Arthur. Then discuss the effects of Betsy's mortgage and of the mortgage foreclosure. Next discuss Carlos' death, and continue in this manner through the subsequent transfers.

MODEL ANSWER

To determine the current state of title to Shady Acres, each event that affected the title must be considered in chronological order. Therefore, I will begin with Arthur's deed to Betsy, Carlos, and Daphne.

A. Original Common Law

1. Arthur's Deed

Under the original common law, Arthur's deed conveyed only a life estate to Betsy, Carlos, and Daphne despite the words "in fee simple." To convey a fee simple, the deed must have included the words "to Betsy, Carlos, and Daphne *and their heirs*."

The life estate would have been held in joint tenancy because of the common law presumption in favor of joint tenancies. The four unities required for a joint tenancy—interest, title, time, and possession—are satisfied; each joint tenant has an equal undivided share (interest), acquired their interests in the same deed (title) and at the same time (time), and has a right to possess all of Shady Acres (possession).

To most closely effectuate Arthur's apparent intent to convey an estate of potentially infinite duration ("in fee simple"), the life estate should be measured by all three grantees' lives, rather than by the life of the first to die. This construction is consistent with the creation of a joint tenancy because the right of survivorship is an integral part of a joint tenancy. That right would be meaningless if the joint tenancy were construed to terminate when the first joint tenant died.

Because Arthur conveyed only a life estate, he retained a reversion in fee simple absolute.

2. *FNB Mortgage and Foreclosure*

In some jurisdictions, Betsy's interest in the joint tenancy would have been severed when she mortgaged it. As a result of the severance, Betsy would have held her undivided one-third interest as a tenant in common, and Carlos and Daphne continued to hold an undivided two-thirds interest as joint tenants.

Even if the common law would not have treated the mortgage as severing Betsy's interest, the foreclosure sale certainly did. Therefore, after the sale, Eddie owned an undivided one-third interest in the life estate as a tenant in common with Carlos and Daphne's joint tenancy. Eddie was a tenant in common because his interest did not satisfy the requisite unities of time and title for a joint tenancy.

3. *Carlos' Death*

When Carlos died, Daphne acquired his interest by right of survivorship. She then owned an undivided two-thirds interest in the life estate as a tenant in common with Eddie.

4. *Daphne's Deed*

Under the original common law, Daphne's conveyance to Fred and Gloria created a tenancy by the entirety, because a conveyance to a married couple automatically created that type of cotenancy. Fred and Gloria's tenancy by the entirety held its undivided two-thirds interest in tenancy in common with Eddie's undivided one-third interest.

5. *Fred's Deed*

Fred's deed conveyed no interest to Harry. In a tenancy by the entirety, neither spouse owns an individual undivided interest. Therefore, neither spouse can sever the estate without the other spouse's consent. The facts do not indicate that Gloria agreed to the severance.

6. *Fred's Death*

When Fred died, Gloria acquired the entire undivided two-thirds interest that had been held in tenancy by the entirety based on the right of survivorship.

7. *Conclusion*

Gloria owns an undivided two-thirds interest as a tenant in common with Eddie's undivided one-third interest in a life estate pur autre vie. Arthur owns a reversion in fee simple absolute.

B. Current Law

1. *Arthur's Deed*

In virtually every state today, the deed would be construed as conveying a fee simple absolute despite the absence of the words "and their heirs." In the absence of a clearly expressed intent to convey a lesser estate, the modern presumption is that fee simple absolute title has been conveyed. The language "in fee simple" in Arthur's deed certainly supports the modern presumption in this case. However, if the state where Shady Acres is located still requires use of the words "and their heirs" to convey a fee simple absolute, Arthur's deed conveyed only a life estate, and he retained a reversion. The life estate would be measured by all three grantees' lives to most closely effectuate Arthur's apparent intent.

Betsy, Carlos, and Daphne owned their interests as tenants in common. Although the original common law presumption was in favor of a joint tenancy, the modern presumption in every state is in favor of a tenancy in common. Nothing in the deed indicates a contrary intent.

2. *FNB Mortgage and Foreclosure*

When Betsy mortgaged her interest in the property, the tenancy in common was unaffected. When FNB foreclosed the mortgage, however, Eddie acquired Betsy's undivided one-third interest, which he held as a tenant in common with Carlos and Daphne.

3. *Carlos' Death*

When Carlos died, his interest in Shady Acres passed pursuant to the terms of the state's intestate succession statute. Under a typical intestate succession statute, Carlos' parents and sister each would receive an equal share of Carlos' property. Therefore, Carlos' parents and sister each acquired an undivided one-ninth interest in the property, which is a one-third interest in Carlos' one-third interest. They held Carlos' one-third interest as tenants in common and held that interest as tenants in common with Daphne and Eddie.

4. *Daphne's Deed*

Daphne's deed to Fred and Gloria created either a tenancy by the entirety or a tenancy in common. Approximately twenty states still permit creation of a tenancy by the entirety. However, courts in those states normally construe a conveyance to a married couple as a tenancy in common unless the intent to create a tenancy by the entirety is clearly expressed. Although Daphne's deed conveyed the property to Fred and Gloria as "husband and wife," the deed did not expressly refer to a tenancy by the entirety or to a right of survivorship, which is a distinctive feature of the tenancy by the entirety. Therefore, a court probably would construe the deed as having created a tenancy in common. If Shady Acres is in a state that does not recognize the tenancy by the entirety, Fred and Gloria acquired Daphne's interest as tenants in common and held it as tenants in common with Eddie and Carlos' heirs.

5. *Fred's Deed*

If Daphne's deed created a tenancy in common, Fred's deed conveyed his undivided one-sixth interest to Harry. Harry holds his interest as a tenant in common with the other co-tenants. On the other hand, if Daphne's deed created a tenancy by the entirety, the deed to Harry conveyed no interest.

6. *Fred's Death*

If Daphne's deed created a tenancy in common, Fred did not own an interest in Shady Acres when he died because he already had conveyed it to Harry. However, if Daphne's deed created a tenancy by the entirety with its attendant right of survivorship, Gloria now owns the entire one-third interest that the deed conveyed. Gloria owns that interest as a tenant in common with Eddie and Carlos' heirs.

7. *Conclusion*

If Daphne's deed created a tenancy in common, Eddie owns an undivided one-third interest, Gloria and Harry each owns an undivided one-sixth interest, and Carlos' parents and sister each owns an undivided one-ninth interest, all as tenants in common in fee simple absolute. If Daphne's deed conveyed a tenancy by the entirety, Eddie and Gloria each owns an undivided one-third interest and Carlos' parents and sister each owns an undivided one-ninth interest, all as tenants in common in fee simple absolute.

TORTS I

(Four hours)

You are an associate in a law firm located in North Butte, the capital of the State of Ravinia. The senior litigation partner sent you the following memorandum and asked you to prepare a responsive memorandum. Assume that the law of Ravinia applies to the case. The Ravinia courts follow all majority common law rules. They are willing to extend or to change rules that do not reflect the trend of decisions or when compelling reasons of equity, policy, or justice warrant doing so.

MEMORANDUM

To: Associate
From: Partner
Re: *Tom and Ellen Harris, and as guardians ad litem for Baby Girl Harris, v. Ravinia & Butte Railroad Company*

We represent Tom, Ellen, and Baby Girl Harris in a tort suit against the Ravinia & Butte Railroad Company (R & B) for personal injuries and wrongful death. On March 29, Tom and Ellen were riding on the Silver Streak luxury train operated by R & B. The train derailed when a bridge over the Eel Pout River near North Butte Bay collapsed.

Ellen, who was pregnant, was injured and suffered a miscarriage. Although Tom escaped physical injury during the wreck, he was injured immediately afterwards. The Harrises seek substantial damages. We have settled our suits with all the potential defendants, except R & B.

The plaintiffs and defendant have completed presentation of their cases. The defendant has moved for directed verdicts. The court has scheduled the hearing on the defendant's motions for next week. Please prepare a memorandum that describes the arguments defendant's counsel can make to support its motions and the arguments I can make. Because the parties have rested and the record is closed, do not add to or modify the facts described below.

The following Ravinia statutes may be applicable to this case:

1. Contributory negligence shall not bar recovery in an action by any person or his legal representative to recover damages for negligence resulting in death or injury to person or to property, but any damages allowed shall be diminished in proportion to the amount of negligence attributable to the person recovering. When two or more persons are jointly liable, contributions to awards shall be in proportion to the percentage of negligence attributable to each.

Ravinia Stat. § 300.41;

2. The amount of damages recoverable by civil action for the death of a person caused by the wrongful act, neglect, or fault of another may include recovery for the loss of society and companionship of the deceased.

Ravinia Stat. § 600.2922;

3. It is a misdemeanor for a person to drive or to move, or for the owner to cause or knowingly permit to be driven or moved, a railroad car of a size or weight exceeding the limitations of this section. . . .

No railroad car shall be operated where the total gross weight on any group of two or more consecutive axles exceeds that given in the following table:

. . .

Four consecutive axles of a four-axle car: 56,000 pounds.

Ravinia Stat. § 169.80;

4. Subject to the limitations on axle loads prescribed in this chapter, the gross weight of any vehicle or combination of vehicles driven onto or over a bridge on any railroad right of way shall not exceed the safe capacity of the bridge, as may be indicated by warnings posted on the bridge or on the approaches thereto.

Ravinia Stat. § 169.84; and

5. Where no special hazard exists, the following speeds shall be lawful:

...

(2) 70 miles per hour in other locations.

Ravinia Stat. § 169.14, subd. 2.

In the controversial decision *Chavez v. Southern Rail Transp. Co.*, 418 R.2d 1203 (1994), the Ravinia Supreme Court held:

> No compelling reason in equity or in policy justifies maintaining archaic doctrines from the Middle Ages that impose strict liability or a higher standard for negligence liability on common carriers than on other modes of conveyance. Henceforth, ordinary principles of negligence shall be used to determine the liability of a common carrier.

TRIAL EVIDENCE

Mike Barger testified that he is the pilot of the barge Loaded Duck, which carries freight in North Butte Bay. Barger has piloted barges in the Bay for nearly fifteen years and "knows the Bay like the back of my hand." At about 8:00 p.m. on March 29, he attempted to pilot the barge across the wide Bay and up the Butte River to pick up a load of grain at a storage elevator several miles upstream. Because it was dark and a heavy fog reduced visibility to less than 100 feet, he became disoriented. Although he thought he had entered the mouth of the Butte River, he had entered another large nearby tributary, Eel Pout River.

Proceeding slowly upstream at five to seven miles per hour for nearly one mile, Barger looked for familiar landmarks but could see nothing because heavy fog limited visibility. Suddenly, heavy timber pilings of a bridge appeared dimly through the fog in a place where he knew a bridge should not be located. He immediately reversed the barge's engine and turned the wheel sharply, but the momentum of the barge carried it into one of the structural supports. There was a shuddering sound as the side of the barge obliquely struck and then slid along the heavy wooden piling. The glancing impact caused a shallow, six-inch depression in the plate-steel side of the barge as it lurched sideways. Barger heard various items in the pilot's cabin crash around him as they were dislodged by the impact. Objects, including a railroad tie, also fell onto the deck of the barge from the railroad bridge that passed about thirty feet overhead.

Barger backed the Duck away from the bridge and headed back downstream. Ten minutes later, when he safely navigated the Duck back into the Bay, he attempted to notify the Ravinia Port Authority of the incident. He then discovered that the barge's radio had been damaged by the impact and was inoperable. He proceeded up the Butte River to the grain elevator and telephoned the Ravinia Port Authority when he arrived, which was about 9:00 p.m.

Raymond Bell was the duty officer at the Ravinia Port Authority on March 29. At 9:02 p.m., he received a telephone call from Mike Barger. Barger told him that the Loaded Duck may have struck a glancing blow to the pilings that support the Eel

Pout River bridge. Bell checked the train schedules and determined that the Silver Streak would cross the bridge in about fifteen minutes. He called the Silver Streak and warned the engineer, Joe Webster, that the bridge over the Eel Pout River may have been damaged and that he should take the Craigville track, an alternate secondary route that intersected the main track about eight miles south of the Eel Pout River bridge. Webster replied that he was running a little ahead of schedule and had passed that secondary track about five minutes earlier. Bell cautioned him that the bridge may have been weakened and to proceed with caution if the Streak was heavily loaded.

Joe Webster testified that he has worked for R & B for more than twenty years and that he was the engineer of the Silver Streak on the night of March 29. The Silver Streak typically carries passengers and containerized freight. Containerized freight consists of goods sealed in large containers that are made to be transferred between ship and train efficiently and securely. Although the containers are bulky, they are not necessarily heavy because they often contain items such as videocassette tapes, tennis shoes, or toys. However, nine cars behind the engine was a large four-axle flat-bed car carrying a 34–ton generator for the Ravinia Power and Light (RP & L) plant. Webster admitted that the axle weight for that car "probably exceeded" the single car load limits. He asserted, however, that this was the fourth of the four huge generators that R & B had hauled across the same Eel Pout

River bridge to the RP & L power plant without any previous mishap. The last four cars of the 32–car train were deluxe passenger cars, a gourmet dining car, and the caboose.

The posted speed limit for the tracks on which the Streak ran was 70 miles per hour, but Webster had run the Streak at its top speed of 79 miles per hour since it left the Deer Lake station more than 100 miles back. Because no oncoming traffic was scheduled and there are no stations between Deer Lake and North Butte, Webster liked to run the Streak "full throttle" over this stretch of track. As a result, the Streak was about nine minutes ahead of schedule.

The Streak proceeded down the long shallow incline to the Eel Pout River bridge. Webster normally coasted the Streak down the quarter-mile incline from its top speed until he crossed the Eel Pout River and then gradually slowed the train to 45 miles per hour for its final twenty-mile approach to the North Butte railroad station, where he would arrive on time. At 9:07 p.m., as the Streak began its descent, he received an emergency radio notification from Raymond Bell at the Ravinia Port Authority. Bell advised him that the Eel Pout River bridge had been struck by a barge and may have been damaged. Bell also told him to take the Craigville alternate route.

Webster applied the train's emergency brakes immediately, but the momentum of the half-mile long train traveling at over 65 miles per hour required a stopping distance of nearly 4,300 feet. As the train's momentum carried it forward, there was a loud shriek of metal and a sharp lurch caused by the braking. Although the bridge seemed to "shift or sway different than usual" as the engine and the first few cars safely reached the other side of the bridge, Webster felt that the bridge was undamaged and that the train safely would cross over it, so he gradually released the emergency brake. As the engine began its ascent, he testified: "There was a deep, loud rumbling. It was similar to an earthquake. It seemed like it lasted so long."

The engine violently jerked to a complete stop, and Webster was thrown forcefully against the front of the engine. When he recovered, he was dazed and staggered down the track to examine the train behind him. A section of the bridge partially had collapsed by one of the supporting pilings, and the flat-bed car carrying the generator lay nearly in the water. As he approached the bridge, Webster could see through the fog that "some of the cars were on top of each other; some were sticking straight up in the air." In the distance, he could hear cries and moans.

He returned to the engine and called for emergency assistance. He told the Ravinia Port Authority: "We have a disaster on our hands." During his testimony, Webster admitted that if the Streak had not been running ahead of schedule, he probably would have had time to take the Craigville bypass and avoid the Eel Pout River bridge when he received the warning from Bell.

Stan Troman testified that, on March 29, he was a brakeman for the R & B on the Silver Streak and was riding in the caboose immediately behind the dining car when the train derailed. Troman is a certified emergency medical technician. After the train stopped moving, he retrieved a first-aid kit, climbed out of the caboose, and immediately encountered Tom Harris, who was running along the track from the dining car. Troman stated that Harris was yelling and screaming. Harris ordered him to bring the first-aid kit to save his wife and baby. Troman told him that a lot of people were injured and that he would help Tom's wife and baby as soon as he could.

Troman then walked carefully from the caboose toward the dining car, which was perched precariously on the edge of the bridge. As Troman approached the dining car, Harris attempted to wrest the first-aid kit from his hands. Troman pulled back on the bag with his left hand and extended his right hand to protect himself and the bag from the obviously hysterical Harris. As Troman pulled the bag, Harris, who was holding onto it, lurched against Troman's hand, lost his footing, staggered back several steps, and fell off the bridge. Troman heard him strike something on the bridge as he fell into the river.

Troman testified that he then had to abandon his efforts to aid other passengers to climb down the river bank to rescue Harris. Troman said that he resented Harris' attempt to tell him how to proceed with his relief efforts and that Harris' fall was a "self-inflicted injury." Troman felt, however, that he had a responsibility to try to retrieve Harris though Troman then had to ignore "more deserving passengers who needed my assistance." Troman found Harris at the edge of the river, pulled him out of the water by his arms, hoisted him into a fire-fighter's carry, and clambered up the bank. Harris screamed as Troman pulled his arms and moaned as he carried him and deposited him beside the caboose. Harris was among the first passengers to be helicopter-evacuated to North Butte Hospital.

Ellen Harris testified that she has been happily married to Tom Harris for seven years, lives in Pine Island, is thirty-two years old, and works as a research chemist. She was more than eight months pregnant with their first child when the accident occurred. Tom and she were riding the Silver Streak from Pine Island to North Butte for a last "romantic weekend" together before their child was born and they had to settle down to the responsibilities of parenthood.

They were seated at a table in the Streak dining car around 9:00 p.m., discussing plans for their weekend in North Butte. Ellen faced the front of the train, and Tom sat across from her. Ellen told Tom that their baby probably would be a dancer because of the way the baby was kicking her ribs. Suddenly, there was a loud screeching sound, and the train abruptly began to slow down. Tom was thrown over backwards out of his chair. Ellen was thrown forward and struck her abdomen against the edge of the table, which was bolted to the floor.

As she struck the edge of the table, "I felt a sharp pain, like somebody was cutting me open. I felt like I was going to pass out from pain."

Within about fifteen seconds, the squealing noise stopped, and the train briefly seemed to resume its speed. Ellen pushed herself back from the table and began to do the breathing exercises she had learned in her childbirth classes to regain her breath and to control the intense abdominal pain. Just as Tom rose from the floor and started toward her, the train stopped violently, and Ellen was propelled against the edge of the table even more forcefully than the first time. The last thing she remembered was a searing pain in her abdomen.

She awoke on March 31 in the North Butte Hospital. Her attending physician, Dr. Marlene Dillon, told her that despite all efforts to save her baby daughter, the infant had not survived the injuries she received in the train wreck. Dr. Dillon also had performed an emergency hysterectomy, which involved removal of Ellen's ovaries and uterus. As a result, Ellen will be unable to bear children.

Tom Harris testified that he has been married to Ellen Harris for seven years, lives in Pine Island, is thirty-four years old, and works as an accountant. Ellen and he were riding the Silver Streak from Pine Island to North Butte for a "romantic weekend" together. They were very much looking forward to the birth of their first child, especially because they had difficulty conceiving. Indeed, they regarded their baby as a "miracle child" because the Pine Island fertility clinic where they sought medical assistance had been very discouraging about their prospects to conceive.

As they sat in the Streak dining car around 9:00 p.m., there was a loud screech of metal against metal, the train abruptly began to slow down, and Ellen was thrown forward against the table while Tom was propelled backwards out of his chair. As Tom regained his feet, he saw Ellen clutching her abdomen and moaning. "Nothing can ever erase the sight of her face, deathly white and twisted in pain," Tom stated. Almost immediately afterward, there was a second, more violent jolt, and Tom again was thrown backwards to the floor as chairs and dishes fell around him. "I could hear a series of loud crashing sounds, like a chain reaction. I realized later that it was each car in the train crashing into and through the ones in front of it."

In the darkness and smoke, Tom's only thoughts were for Ellen, who was sprawled unconscious across the table. After checking her, he immediately sought assistance. Leaving the dining car, Tom encountered Stan Troman, who was descending from the caboose. Tom pleaded with Troman to bring a first-aid kit to save his wife and baby. Tom said that Troman told him that a lot of people were injured and that he would help the Harrises as soon as he could. Fearing that his wife and baby were dying, Tom repeatedly urged Troman to assist them. As they reached the dining car, Troman called Tom "a pushy, yuppie jerk" and told him that he was the last person Troman would help.

In frustration and grief, Tom tried to move past Troman to re-enter the dining car and to attend to Ellen. Troman shoved Tom backwards, and he fell off the bridge. His left shoulder struck something projecting from the bridge as he fell. As he lay in pain in the freezing water, Tom's only thoughts were of his wife and child in the wrecked car on the bridge above him.

Shortly after Tom fell, Troman approached him and began to pull him from the river. Tom screamed: "Haven't you done enough damage for one night?" Tom said that Troman pulled him violently from the water, wrenched Tom's shoulder socket, threw him over his back, and "dumped me on the ground like a sack of potatoes" when they reached the train. Tom passed out from pain and awoke in the North Butte Hospital with his left arm and upper body in a cast. As a result of his injuries, he has virtually no use of his left arm.

Dr. Marlene Dillon testified that she was Tom and Ellen Harris' attending physician. Ellen and Tom were among the most seriously injured people at the train derailment and were evacuated by emergency helicopter to North Butte Hospital. Ellen's primary injury was a ruptured uterus, which was caused by the massive trauma she received in the accident. Within minutes of Ellen's arrival at the hospital, Dr. Dillon performed an emergency

Caesarian section operation on her to try to save her fetus.

Dr. Dillon testified that, in the case of uterine rupture, the fetus might have died immediately from the initial trauma that caused the rupture. However, if the umbilical cord had remained intact and the placenta was attached to an uninjured portion of the uterus, the blood and oxygen supply could have been maintained, and the fetus could have survived in the perforated uterine environment for a short time. Even when fetal monitors fail to indicate any heartbeat or other signs of fetal life, physicians successfully have resuscitated fetuses who were removed within three to four minutes. Because of the extreme emergency, there was no time to attach a fetal monitor.

During the Caesarian procedure, Dr. Dillon removed a viable, nearly full-term baby girl. The baby was limp, motionless, and blue in color. Resuscitation efforts were unsuccessful. Despite a subsequent autopsy, Dr. Dillon could not determine whether the fetus died from the initial trauma to the womb, from subsequent intra-uterine asphyxia, or sometime during the emergency delivery. Dr. Dillon admitted: "The baby probably was not alive when I removed her if you just think of these things technically in terms of brain activity. But it was just a matter of minutes from the initial injury to the emergency delivery." Because of the trauma to and multiple perforations of Ellen's uterus, Dr. Dillon performed an emergency hysterectomy. As a result, Ellen cannot have children.

Dr. Dillon also attended to Tom Harris. His left shoulder was separated either from trauma or from a twisting or torquing action. A rupture of the left shoulder rotator cuff and severe nerve damage have disabled the arm permanently.

Michelle Albala testified that she is an investigator with the National Transportation Safety Board (NTSB) and that she investigated the March 29 train derailment. She explained that determining the specific cause of the accident was very difficult. Like airplanes, trains carry black box recording devices that monitor engine performance and conversations in the engine compartment for post-accident investigations. The black box recorded Webster's conversation with Bell and registered the immediate application of the emergency brakes and their release just before the derailment. However, because black boxes are located in the engine and are designed to measure front-end impacts, they cannot measure the cause of an accident at the rear of a train, as apparently happened in this case.

Although the bridge collapse caused the derailment, the derailment destroyed the bridge and prevented the NTSB from determining the cause of the collapse. Albala speculated that, if a vertical piling is somewhat out of alignment when weight is applied from above, the vertical force may transfer into horizontal movement, which causes shearing. However, even if the piling alignment is proper, a grossly excessive vertical load may cause horizontal movement because the footings supporting the piling can shift. Moreover, while one grossly excessive load can cause horizontal shifting, excess load-factors also can cumulate so that a series of marginally excessive loads eventually can cause horizontal movement.

Albala acknowledged that wood-piling Class IV bridges, such as the fifty year old structure spanning the Eel Pout River, can deteriorate over time and are being replaced by steel and concrete bridges. She testified that the posted single-car single-axle gross weight limit on the Class IV Eel Pout River bridge was 15,000 pounds, which would allow a single four-axle car to carry a 60,000 pound load without adverse consequences. She also testified that railroad bridges usually are "over-engineered" and are designed to support weight loads well in excess of their rated capacity.

Note: This question is an example of a single-question exam. Organizing your answer before beginning to write it is essential for such a lengthy question. In addition to making your answer more comprehensible, organizing your answer will make it more comprehensive. You are less likely to omit a necessary part of the answer if you outline it before writing. Be sure to address the procedural, as well as substantive, issues raised by the question.

This question also illustrates the importance of following instructions. The question is limited to the causes of action against the railroad company and the motion for directed verdict. You would not receive credit for discussing any other causes of action or procedures. Additionally, the exam directs you to respond in memorandum form. Therefore, your answer should provide a neutral evaluation of the strong and weak points of your clients' case. A memorandum should not advocate a particular position unless you are directed to do so.

MODEL ANSWER

MEMORANDUM

To: Partner

From: Associate

Re: *Tom and Ellen Harris, and as guardians ad litem for Baby Girl Harris, v. Ravinia & Butte Railroad Company*

Based on the information you gave me, R & B is potentially liable to the Harrises for the injuries they suffered because of R & B's overloading the train with the 34–ton generator, Webster's speeding, and Troman's contacts with Tom Harris on the bridge and on the river bank. The weight overload and Webster's speeding each provides the grounds for actions for negligence and for negligent infliction of emotional distress. Tom and Ellen Harris also can bring a wrongful death claim on behalf of their stillborn daughter. Finally, Tom has intentional tort claims for Troman's possible batteries and for intentional infliction of emotional distress. Each of these causes of action must be evaluated in light of R & B's motions for directed verdict.

A. Procedural Posture

To succeed on a motion for directed verdict, R & B will have to show either that (1) the plaintiffs failed to establish each element of each cause of action or, in other words, failed to satisfy their burden of production or (2) R & B has established each element of an adequate defense. In reviewing R & B's motions, the court will view the evidence in the light most favorable to the non-moving parties, the plaintiffs. The court will grant a motion for a directed verdict only if a contrary verdict clearly would be against the evidence or the relevant law, so that no reasonable jury could find for the plaintiffs.

B. Respondeat Superior

Because the pending lawsuit is against R & B, the first issue is whether it is vicariously liable for Webster's and Troman's actions. Webster and Troman clearly are both R & B employees; Webster was the Silver Streak's engineer, and Troman was the brakeman. Next, it must be determined whether Webster and Troman were acting within the scope of their employment when the accident occurred. We should have no difficulty satisfying either the control or the enterprise theories of vicarious liability.

With respect to the control theory, both Webster and Troman were working for R & B when the accident occurred, were using R & B equipment, were operating in accordance with R & B's schedule, and otherwise were working at R & B's direction. Similarly, under the broader enterprise theory, R & B operated the enterprise and was benefited by Webster's and Troman's performance of their duties. Therefore, R & B should bear the costs of the enterprise's operations, especially because it is in the best position to spread costs.

R & B might argue that it cannot be held vicariously liable for any intentional torts committed by Troman because he was acting outside the scope of his employment when he committed them. We can respond that, although courts in earlier cases declined to impose vicarious liability for an employee's intentional torts, the modern trend is to hold the employer liable if the tort was committed in the scope of employment and to assist the employer's enterprise. R & B might argue that Troman was not acting within the scope of his employment because, when he pulled the first-aid kit from Tom or pushed him, Troman was acting as a medical technician and not as a brakeman.

This argument is extremely weak, particularly if the record supports the assertion that Troman's responsibilities included tending to injured passengers. Even if it was not an express duty, assisting injured passengers certainly could be treated as an implied duty. Therefore, protecting the first-aid kit was in furtherance of R & B's interests. Pulling Tom from the river also comes within the scope of the duty to aid injured passengers. Therefore, even if Troman committed an intentional tort in performing this duty, R & B should be vicariously liable except in the unlikely case that R & B can establish that Troman was acting solely to satisfy a personal whim. This may be impossible because Troman testified that he was trying to get away from Tom to tend to other passengers.

R & B also might argue that it is not vicariously liable for the injuries resulting from Webster's speeding because he was violating Ravinia law. R & B would argue that, when speeding, Webster was not under R & B's practical control and was not acting in furtherance of R & B's interests. This argument, too, will be unsuccessful because an employer is vicariously liable for its employee's negligence when performing an assigned duty. Webster clearly was performing an assigned duty.

In the unlikely case that the court holds that R & B is not vicariously liable for Webster's and Troman's actions, we can argue that we have a direct cause of action against R & B. If the actual cause of the collapse was the weight overload on the train, this is more a matter of R & B policy than of Webster's and Troman's actions and may constitute a direct cause of action against R & B, rather than one founded on respondeat superior. Even if Webster, as the engineer, was responsible for ensuring that the train was loaded properly, we can sue R & B directly based on a claim of negligent supervision.

C. Negligence—Weight Overload

Our first cause of action against R & B is for negligence for overloading the train. To hold R & B liable for negligence, the court must find (1) a duty, (2) a breach of duty, (3) cause in fact, (4) proximate cause, and (5) damages.

1. *Duty*

The first and crucial issue is whether R & B owed the plaintiffs any duty that was breached. The existence of a duty can be established by applying Judge Hand's formula for the common law reasonable person standard—B<PG: a duty exists if the burden of preventing a harm is less than the probability of harm times the gravity of the potential harm. The burden of preventing this accident was minimal—not overloading the train. On the other hand, the probability that harm will occur when an overloaded train crosses a bridge is significant, and the gravity of the potential harm to persons and to property is great, as demonstrated by the accident in this case. Therefore, because the burden on R & B to prevent the harm was substantially less than the product of the probability of harm and the gravity of the potential harm, R & B had a duty to the plaintiffs.

The next issue is the scope of the duty. Unless we can convince the court that a special standard of care should be applied, it will analyze the case as a regular negligence action. We have three arguments for application of a special standard of care. First, although the Ravinia Supreme Court held in *Chavez v. Southern Rail Transp. Co.* that no special common carrier rule creates a higher standard of care for railroads, we can make several policy arguments that the court should reconsider and should reverse that controversial decision.

Other jurisdictions have held common carriers to a higher standard of care because passengers are completely within the carrier's control; they have virtually no ability to control the way in which the carrier is operated. Passengers also often have few, if any, alternatives to using a common carrier. Imposing a more stringent standard of care will increase common carriers' incentives to hire responsible employees and to implement and to enforce adequate safety standards. Moreover, common carriers are best able to spread the cost of injuries. In fact, this case strongly illustrates why common carriers should bear a special responsibility.

Second, we can argue for a heightened standard of care based on the professional engineer standard. On the facts of this case, the court should apply a higher professional standard because Webster had twenty years of experience as an engineer. From the trial testimony you provided, however, no evidence was introduced at trial concerning what the higher standard would require. The issue of the professional engineer standard also does not affect the basic issue of whether the defendant owed a duty to the plaintiffs.

Our final argument for a higher standard of care is based on Webster's knowledge of the potential danger. When Bell notified Webster that the bridge may have been damaged, R & B, through its agent, was on notice that a greater risk of harm existed and that the situation required additional precautions. R & B will respond that, when Bell notified Webster about the risk, the accident could not be avoided. However, the bridge did not collapse until after Webster released the emergency brake and permitted the car with the generator to start across the bridge.

2. *Breach of Duty*

We have two main arguments that the defendant breached its duty to the plaintiffs: (1) the statutory violations and (2) res ipsa loquitur.

a. *Statutory Violations*

Our first argument that R & B breached its duty is based on the Ravinia statutes. We can argue that the statutes established the applicable standard of care in this case and that, by violating the statutes, the duty to the plaintiffs was breached. Two statutes in particular are helpful to us—Ravinia Stat. §§ 169.80 and 169.84. Section 169.80 provides that a four-axle car, such as the car carrying the generator, should not exceed 56,000 pounds. In this case, the car carrying the generator had a load of at least 34 tons (68,000 pounds). Section 169.84 incorporates the weight limit in § 169.80 and further prohibits exceeding posted bridge weight limits. In this case, the posted single-car single-axle gross weight limit for the bridge was 15,000 pounds. Therefore, the maximum permitted weight for a four-axle car on the bridge was 60,000 pounds. The car with the generator obviously violated this posted weight limit, as well as the 56,000 pound limit incorporated from § 169.80.

Even though R & B violated the statutes, a court will adopt a statute as the standard of care only if the statute, in fact, creates a standard of care. We can argue that, unlike a licensing statute, these statutes establish a standard of conduct for the operation of a train. They expressly prohibit overloading railroad cars. This argument is particularly strong with respect to the posted bridge weight limit.

Even if the court holds that the statutes created a standard of care, the court has discretion whether to adopt that standard. It will do so only if we can show that the plaintiffs are in the class of persons intended to be protected by the statutes and that the harms they suffered are of the kind the statutes were intended to prevent. The relevant Ravinia statutes do not indicate their underlying legislative intents, so the court will have to speculate concerning them.

R & B will argue that the legislative intent underlying § 169.80 was to reduce wear and tear on tracks and bridges by requiring that load weights be distributed in accordance with the statutory standards. Presumably, if the railroad cars in this case had more than four axles, they could have carried heavier loads, which negates an inference of a legislative intent to prevent bridge collapses and the resulting personal injuries. We can respond that § 169.84, which is in the same chapter, incorporates the weight limits in § 169.80 and applies them to bridge traffic. This statute creates a stronger inference that the weight limit is intended, at least in part, to prevent bridge collapses and the related personal injuries.

In addition to persuading a court concerning the legislative intent, we must prove a causal connection between the statutory violations and the plaintiffs' injuries. The arguments set forth below concerning causation for the negligence action apply with equal force to the statutory violations. We will argue that the bridge would not have collapsed and the plaintiffs would not have been injured if the railroad car had not exceeded the statutory weight limits. Proving that the statutory violations caused the injuries, however, may be difficult because of the possible damage by the barge. The bridge may have collapsed even if the car had not been overloaded.

If we convince the court to adopt the statutes as the applicable standard of care, the court, like a majority of state courts, probably will treat the violations as constituting negligence per se. The defendant's negligence will have been established conclusively unless it has a valid defense. If the court does not treat the statutory violations as constituting negligence per se because, for example, it holds that the plaintiffs are not within the scope of protected people, the court may hold that the violations create a rebuttable presumption of negligence, and R & B would have to rebut the presumption. If this approach also fails, we can argue that the statutory violations are at least evidence of negligence under the reasonable person standard. In any event, proof of the statutory violations should be sufficient to withstand the defendant's motions for directed verdict.

The defendant might defend its practice of overloading cars based on industry custom and usage. R & B could argue that an industry custom exists of driving overloaded cars across the bridge and that the absence of previous accidents rebuts any inference of negligence and supports its contention that it behaved reasonably. In fact, Webster testified that the train was pulling the fourth of four overweight generators. Even if a practice is prevalent in an industry, however, it does not necessarily meet the reasonable person standard.

b. *Res Ipsa Loquitur*

The doctrine of res ipsa loquitur provides an alternative theory for proving R & B's breach of duty. Res ipsa loquitur allows the trier of fact to infer negligence, thereby satisfying our burden of production and possibly also our burden of proof. Therefore, this inference of negligence can be enough to defeat the defendant's motions for directed verdict.

For the doctrine to apply, we must show that (1) the accident would not have occurred in the absence of negligence, (2) the defendant was in exclusive control of the instrumentality that caused the accident, and (3) the plaintiffs did not contribute to the accident. We should be able to prove these elements. First, bridges normally do not collapse unless someone has been negligent.

Second, the defendant was in exclusive control of the overloaded train. The defendant will argue, however, that it was not in exclusive control of the bridge and that the bridge collapsed because of structural damage caused by the barge. Some courts have applied res ipsa loquitur against common carriers even when other defendants may have contributed to the accident. Because these decisions are based on a higher standard of care for common carriers, however, this precedent will help us only if we can persuade the court to overturn the *Chavez* decision.

If we are unsuccessful in doing so, *Ybarra v. Spangard* provides an alternative theory to satisfy this second element of the doctrine. We can argue that, because the accident could have been caused only by one or both of two causes, assigning liability to both actors is appropriate. This result would serve an underlying purpose of res ipsa loquitur, which is to assist a plaintiff who has no direct way of establishing the cause of an accident. Here, the bridge was destroyed when it collapsed, and discovering the cause of the collapse is impossible.

Finally, we can satisfy the third element for res ipsa loquitur because the plaintiffs clearly did not contribute to the bridge collapse. Therefore, the doctrine of res ipsa loquitur should prevent a directed verdict on our negligence action.

3. *Cause in Fact*

Assuming that R & B breached a duty that it owed to the plaintiffs, we next must show that the breach caused the plaintiffs' injuries. In determining factual cause, the question often is phrased: "But for the defendant's act, would the injuries have occurred?" R & B will argue that running the overloaded car over the bridge did not cause the plaintiffs' injuries. Rather, the barge colliding with the bridge caused the collapse and injuries. The defendant also will argue that the previous running of overloaded cars over the bridge demonstrates that the bridge could have supported the train if the barge had not struck the pilings.

We will argue that this case is analytically analogous to *Reynolds v. Texas R.R.*, in which a person fell down an unlit flight of stairs. The court found in that case that, although the event may have occurred even in the absence of negligence, the negligence greatly multiplied the probability that the accident would occur. We also can point to Albala's testimony that overweight loads can cause cumulative damage and that a series of marginally excessive loads eventually can cause horizontal movement of the bridge supports. Therefore, the bridge may have collapsed even if the barge had not struck it. However, that argument requires speculation concerning causation.

Our strongest causation argument is that, even if we cannot demonstrate conclusively that the bridge would not have collapsed but for the train's excess weight, the overload was a substantial factor.

When two or more causes concur to produce damage, showing that the defendant's negligence was a substantial factor is sufficient. Although R & B's and the barge's relative contributions to the accident affect the amount of comparative damages, they do not affect the issue of liability. We also could argue that, because R & B and the barge operator both were negligent and because their negligence made proving causation impossible, the burden should be shifted to them to establish which is primarily responsible. In any event, a sufficient question concerning causation exists to avoid a directed verdict.

4. *Proximate Cause*

The next element of the negligence action is proximate cause. This element raises the *Palsgraf, Polemis*, and *Wagon Mound I & II* issues concerning direct versus proximate causation. If the court adopts the reasoning of Judge Andrews' dissent in *Palsgraf*, we will have no difficulty establishing proximate cause. Judge Andrews reasoned that a defendant is liable if its negligent acts are linked to the plaintiff's injuries in a close, direct, and immediate way. In this case, the plaintiffs' injuries directly were linked to the bridge collapse and, therefore, satisfy Judge Andrews' standard.

The defendant may argue that the court should adopt the more restrictive reasoning of Judge Cardozo's majority opinion in *Palsgraf*. Judge Cardozo limited the concept of proximate cause to foreseeable plaintiffs who suffered foreseeable injuries. R & B may argue that, with respect to running an

overweight railroad car over a bridge, our clients
were unforeseeable plaintiffs who suffered unforeseeable harms. However, a close analysis of what is
foreseeable, as in *Wagon Mound II*, should demonstrate that an overloaded train creates a foreseeable
risk of passengers suffering injuries from a bridge
collapse. If the court determines that the defendant's dangerous conduct created a foreseeable hazard, even a low probability hazard, the plaintiffs
should prevail. The issue of foreseeability is a
sufficiently close fact question to create a jury issue
and to withstand a motion for directed verdict.

5. *Damages*

The plaintiffs suffered direct injuries from the
derailment. Ellen's miscarriage clearly is compensable. The Caesarian section and hysterectomy
also are compensable because they were performed
as a result of the injuries caused by the defendant.
The inability to have children in the future also
should be a compensable injury, although R & B
may argue that the Harrises' history of fertility
problems makes the nature of the loss too speculative. Finally, the loss of consortium is compensable.

R & B may attempt to avoid liability by arguing
that Ellen was injured when Webster initially put
on the emergency brakes and not when the train
subsequently derailed. R & B can argue that Webster did not act negligently when he initially applied
the train's emergency brakes in response to the
warning about the bridge; Webster was responding
as a professional engineer to an emergency. R & B

also will argue that Ellen's uterus ruptured the first time she hit the table. Ellen's testimony that she "felt a sharp pain, like somebody cutting [her] open" the first time she hit the table supports this contention. This argument will be difficult for us to rebut because we have no medical proof that the second impact, rather than the first, caused the rupture. Ellen did testify, however, that she hit the table more forcefully the second time and that she passed out from the "searing pain." Webster also testified that he was thrown down and dazed only when the train derailed. This creates a sufficient question of fact to avoid a directed verdict.

D. Negligence—Webster's Speeding

In addition to the negligence action based on the overweight car, we may have a negligence action based on Webster's speeding. Webster violated Ravinia Stat. § 169.4, subd. 2, which limits trains to 70 miles per hour. We can argue that this violation constitutes negligence per se or at least a rebuttable presumption or evidence of negligence. We also can argue that Webster's speeding caused the accident because he lost the opportunity to take the Craigville cut-off, thereby avoiding the bridge. R & B will argue that no cause in fact exists because the speeding did not cause the bridge to collapse and because the train was not speeding when the collapse occurred.

R & B also will argue that proximate cause does not exist. While being unable to stop quickly and injuring people are foreseeable risks of speeding, arriving too soon at a bridge that is going to collapse is not. Although the speeding contributed to the train's early approach to the bridge, liability for this type of earlier negligent action normally is cut off. Therefore, the court may grant the motion for a directed verdict for this cause of action.

E. R & B's Affirmative Defenses

1. Contributory Negligence

R & B may argue that, even if the bridge collapse breached R & B's duty to Tom, he had a duty to protect himself and to avoid aggravating his injuries. His failure to do so caused the injury to his left arm or at least constituted contributory negligence. To support its argument, R & B will cite Troman's testimony that Tom was "obviously hysterical."

We can respond that, in evaluating the reasonableness of Tom's behavior, the circumstances must be considered. Even if Tom was upset, he behaved as a reasonable person under emergency circumstances. Moreover, R & B and its employees negligently caused the emergency. Whether Tom's actions proximately caused his injury is a question for the trier of fact and should not be decided on a motion for directed verdict. Besides, Ravinia is a comparative negligence state in which contributory negligence reduces the amount of recovery but does not bar it. The question of apportioning liability among the plaintiffs and defendants is an issue for the trier of fact and would be inappropriate for a directed verdict.

2. *Assumption of the Risk*

R & B could not argue successfully that Tom assumed the risk of his injury. To assume a risk, a person subjectively must be aware of what the risk entails and voluntarily must agree to accept it. R & B created the risk to which Tom involuntarily was exposed. Moreover, given the emergency circumstances, Tom would not have perceived even the risks that would be apparent to a reasonably prudent person, and he could not have agreed to accept them.

F. Negligent Infliction of Emotional Distress

In addition to suing to recover for their physical injuries, Tom and Ellen may have causes of action for negligent infliction of emotional distress. This theory of liability is based on the contention that R & B negligently created a situation in which third parties were likely to suffer severe emotional distress. Tom has a cause of action arising from observing Ellen's injuries, and Tom and Ellen each has a cause of action arising from their unborn daughter's death. To establish this cause of action, we must prove that the plaintiff (1) suffered severe emotional distress, (2) was subjected to a physical impact or was in the zone of danger, (3) physically manifested distress, and (4) proximate cause.

1. *Ellen's Injuries*

Tom's cause of action arising from Ellen's injuries should be sufficient to withstand the motion for directed verdict.

a. *Severe Emotional Distress*

We should have no trouble showing severe emotional distress. Tom gave powerful testimony at the trial concerning his distress and fear that his wife and baby were dying. Moreover, his marital relationship assures the genuineness of his distress over his wife's injuries. Finally, Tom was at risk of immediate injury, which further establishes that he suffered genuine distress.

b. *Impact or Zone of Danger*

The impact requirement resulted from early courts' reluctance to award damages for emotional distress unless the plaintiff also was injured physically. Today, most courts have so relaxed the requirement that only a slight physical impact is required, and the impact need not cause significant or even any physical harm. Some courts have gone even further and require only that the plaintiff have been in the "zone of danger" that was created by the defendant's negligence, as long as the plaintiff reasonably feared injury from that danger.

We should be able to satisfy this element because Tom both suffered an impact and was in the zone of danger. Both times the train stopped, Tom was thrown to the floor, thereby satisfying the impact requirement. As a passenger on the derailed train, he was at risk of immediate injury and, therefore, was in the zone of danger. He also undoubtedly feared injury from that danger.

c. *Physical Manifestation*

In some jurisdictions, a plaintiff can recover damages for negligent infliction of emotional distress only if the distress causes a physical manifestation, such as illness or aggravation of a pre-existing condition. The purpose for this requirement is to reduce the number of false claims by requiring observable evidence of distress. In this case, R & B might argue that Tom's injuries were not directly caused by his emotional distress. Apart from his initial and immediate emotional distress, R & B can argue that no other evidence supports the emotional distress claim and that this is the kind of vague, unsubstantiated, and uncorroborated complaint that the law should not compensate. Moreover, if R & B is liable for negligence, Tom will recover for more direct injuries to himself, including for his own pain and suffering.

We will respond that, in this case, little reason exists to believe that Tom's claim is false. Tom's relationship with Ellen and the severity of her injuries strongly support Tom's claim. We also should argue that, as a matter of policy, the court should eliminate this element of the cause of action, at least in cases such as this in which little danger exists of false or imagined mental distress.

d. *Proximate Cause*

We should argue that Ellen's injury was foreseeable and that the presence of a closely related person who would witness her injury also was foreseeable. The defendant may respond that, even if it had a duty to Tom with respect to his physical injuries, his emotional distress was an unforeseeable injury like that in *Palsgraf*. This argument is unpersuasive in light of the risks R & B created for its passengers.

2. Baby Girl's Death

Tom and Ellen also can claim negligent infliction of emotional distress based on Baby Girl's death. The analysis for this claim is similar to that for Tom's claim with respect to Ellen's injuries.

a. Severe Emotional Distress

Tom and Ellen obviously suffered severe emotional distress at the loss of their baby, perhaps particularly because of their conception difficulties ("miracle baby") and their inability to conceive another child. Some case law raises an issue, however, concerning whether legally cognizable emotional distress can be suffered with respect to an unborn child.

b. Impact or Zone of Danger

Tom and Ellen both suffered an impact and were in the zone of danger.

c. Physical Manifestation

In *St. Elizabeth Hospital v. Garrard*, the court overturned the physical manifestation requirement for an emotional distress claim with respect to a stillborn child. Although the Garrards' claim arguably was based on a mishandling of the child's corpse, the court characterized the case more broadly with respect to the emotional distress claim. Therefore, we can argue that the Ravinia court also should reject the physical manifestation requirement in this case.

d. Proximate Cause

Proximate cause exists because Baby Girl's death was foreseeable, as was her parents' emotional distress.

G. Baby Girl Harris' Wrongful Death Claim

On behalf of Baby Girl Harris, Tom and Ellen have a cause of action for wrongful death. The primary legal issue with respect to this claim is whether a viable fetus who is stillborn as a result of injuries to her mother is a "person" within the meaning of the wrongful death statute. In *Endresz v. Friedberg*, the court articulated the different policies that apply with respect to compensation for a fetus who is injured but is born alive and for a fetus who is stillborn as a result of the injuries. In part, allowing recovery for a stillborn who never suffers monetary damages raises the issue whether the damage award constitutes compensation or punishment.

The defendant will argue that damages for wrongful death would be a windfall to Tom and Ellen, especially because Ellen can recover for her miscarriage. The defendant also may argue that the amount of damages would be speculative because an issue exists concerning the damages Baby Girl actually suffered, apart from deprivation of life. Finally, the defendant can argue that the statutory term "person" does not include the unborn.

We can argue that allowing recovery to a fetus who is born alive but not to a stillborn fetus is inconsistent. The medical testimony established that the accident caused the unborn child's fatal injuries. The child was viable when the accident occurred because she was kicking just beforehand. In fact, the attending physician testified that the baby may have been alive when the Caesarian section was performed. Therefore, recovery should not depend on the fortuity of whether the baby died during the medical procedure or several minutes earlier in the train accident.

Tom and Ellen also may be able to recover damages pursuant to Ravinia Stat. § 600.2922, which provides for damages for the loss of the society and companionship of a deceased "person." Whether Tom and Ellen can recover under this statute raises the same legal issue as the wrongful death statute: was the unborn child a "person" within the meaning of the statute. If the court holds that a wrongful death action exists, it first must hold that an unborn child is a "person." If it does so, Tom and Ellen also should be able to recover for loss of society and companionship under § 600.2922.

H. Battery

Tom may have battery claims based on Troman's allegedly pushing Tom off the bridge and pulling

Tom from the river by his arms. A battery is an intentional harmful or offensive contact. Therefore, both claims raise the issue whether Troman's purpose when he pushed or pulled Tom was to cause harmful or offensive contact or whether Troman knew to a substantial certainty that such contact would occur. Tom's testimony that Troman called him "a pushy, yuppie jerk" and said that he was the last person Troman would help supports an inference that he purposely caused harmful or offensive contact. Moreover, pushing Tom on the edge of a bridge and pulling him by the arms from the river support an inference that Troman knew to a substantial certainty that such contact would occur.

Troman, of course, characterized Tom's injury as being "self-inflicted." He described Tom's fall from the bridge as the result of his losing his footing while grabbing at the first-aid kit. Troman described Tom's shoulder injuries as part of the rescue process. The trier of fact will determine whether Tom's or Troman's testimony is more credible. Because both versions of the facts are plausible, a factual dispute exists that a court cannot resolve on a motion for directed verdict.

R & B may argue that, even if Troman intended to cause harmful or offensive contact or even if he knew to a substantial certainty that such contact would occur, his actions were privileged because he was acting in self-defense. Tom's pulling on the first-aid kit arguably was a battery on Troman, *Fisher v. Carousel*, and he was privileged in defending himself. R & B also can argue that Troman's actions were privileged because he was defending the other passengers' interests. Troman had a responsibility to all the passengers. While R & B might claim that a public necessity existed to rescue the other passengers, that claim normally applies only to damages to property and not to persons.

R & B also will argue that Troman's actions were privileged when he pulled Tom from the river. Because the rescue occurred under emergency conditions, R & B will argue that Troman's privilege extended to conduct that otherwise would be somewhat negligent. We can respond that Troman had a duty to rescue Tom because Troman placed him in a position of danger. And even if no initial duty of rescue existed, Troman was required to act reasonably when he voluntarily undertook the rescue. The determination of reasonableness, however, may be qualified by "Good Samaritan" policies that insulate rescuers from liability unless they act recklessly.

I. Intentional Infliction of Emotional Distress

Tom also may have a cause of action for intentional infliction of emotional distress based on Troman's conduct. To establish this cause of action, Tom will have to show that Troman's conduct was outrageous, caused Tom severe emotional distress, and intentionally inflicted distress. When Tom approached Troman, Tom urgently told him about Ellen and the baby. In such circumstances, if

Tom's testimony is believed, telling him that his family would be the last to be helped and calling him "a pushy, yuppie jerk" was outrageous conduct. Troman must have known to a substantial certainty that his conduct would cause severe emotional distress, which it in fact did. Tom testified that, even when lying injured in the freezing water, Ellen and the baby were all he could think about.

As with the action for battery, the trier of fact will have to determine whether Tom's or Troman's testimony is more credible. This factual dispute should prevent the court from granting the defendant's motion for directed verdict.

TORTS II

(Forty-five minutes)

George is in the business of supplying bucking broncos to rodeos. He is always on the lookout for horses that cannot be trained to overcome their instinctive fear of humans. He keeps a herd of these horses at his ranch. One night, a large and apparently healthy tree fell and destroyed part of the fence on George's ranch. His most unruly stallion escaped. In its frenzy, it ran through a nearby campground and awoke Kurst who was lying in a sleeping bag. Kurst ran away in fear, but the stallion pursued him and inflicted severe injuries on him. The stallion then ran out onto the highway. Rod, who was driving a motorcycle on the highway, unsuccessfully tried to avoid colliding with the animal. Both Rod and the stallion were injured. The animal continued its rampage until George roped it some hours later. George then called a veterinarian, and she came to treat the stallion. When the veterinarian approached the wounded animal, it bit her.

George has retained your services as a lawyer. Advise him concerning the legal significance of these events.

Note: When answering this question, you should consider each potential cause of action separately.

Although more than one action will be based on strict liability, each action presents different issues. Often, professors include more than one potential plaintiff or defendant in an exam question to determine whether you can recognize the analytic differences among them. Therefore, to get full credit for a question, you should discuss each action separately unless you are certain that they are analytically indistinguishable.

MODEL ANSWER

As a result of these events, George may be liable to the campground owner, Kurst, Rod, and the veterinarian. George may have a cause of action against Rod.

A. Campground Owner

The campground owner can sue George for the damages caused by the horse's trespass. The campground owner will argue that George is strictly liable for any damage caused by his trespassing domestic livestock, which includes a trespassing horse. Under this theory of strict liability, George is liable even if he was without fault. Therefore, he could not defend the action by showing that the tree that destroyed the fence was apparently healthy.

However, many American jurisdictions do not follow this old English rule of strict liability. In some jurisdictions, livestock legally can range at large as a matter of common law; if a landowner wishes to prevent the livestock from trespassing, they must be fenced out. Other jurisdictions have enacted an express fence-out statute that imposes liability on a livestock owner only if an animal breaches a fence. On the other hand, other jurisdictions have a fence-in statute, which imposes strict liability on a livestock owner who does not fence in livestock. In many states, each county is authorized to adopt its own rule, so that the legal rule applied by a court varies from county to county. Therefore, I will have to research the law of the relevant jurisdiction to determine which liability rule a court would apply to George.

In addition to the campground owner, George may be liable for the horse's trespass on other properties. We do not know whether the horse caused damage on other property. Therefore, I will not discuss that possibility further.

B. Kurst

Kurst also has a strict liability cause of action against George. Unlike the campground owner, Kurst will not sue based on the trespass theory. Instead, he will argue that the owner of a dangerous animal is strictly liable for the harm that it causes. Although this rule of strict liability usually does not apply to domestic animals, it does apply if the animal's owner knows that it poses an abnormal risk to the community. In this case, George kept the horse precisely because it was especially dangerous. Therefore, the strict liability rule will apply in this case.

The reasons for imposing strict liability on a dangerous animal's owner are similar to those for imposing strict liability for abnormally dangerous activities, such as blasting. Strict liability allocates the losses that are likely to result from the dangerous activity, makes businesses pay the full cost of their enterprise, and encourages the development of better safety measures. Imposing strict liability in this case will serve all three purposes; George is in the business of supplying bucking broncos and consciously chooses especially dangerous creatures. By keeping the horses on his ranch, he is subjecting the surrounding community to an abnormal risk.

Because George is strictly liable, any contributory negligence by Kurst is irrelevant. Therefore, even if we could show that running away from the horse or some other action was negligent, it would not be a defense to strict liability. Although assumption of the risk is a defense to strict liability, no facts indicate that Kurst knew he was assuming the risk of injury by a bucking bronco when he chose to camp at the campground. He may have assumed the risk of injury from an animal in the wild but not from dangerous livestock.

C. Rod

Unlike the campground owner and Kurst, Rod does not have a good strict liability action against George. Strict liability extends only to the types of risks that the strict liability rule was intended to address. The risk of keeping a dangerous animal is that it will attack people or other animals. Just as mink-cannibalism is not a hazard that makes blasting dangerous, traffic accidents are not the kind of hazard that makes aggressive horses dangerous. In fact, courts have held that the owner of an escaped animal is not strictly liable for injuries that it causes on a highway.

Even if George is not strictly liable, Rod might argue that George is liable for negligence. This action should be unsuccessful, however, because the fence was breached by an unanticipated accident. The tree appeared to be healthy, and no facts indicate that the fence was substandard or that George otherwise acted in a negligent manner.

In fact, we should investigate whether Rod was negligent in hitting and injuring the stallion. If so, he may be liable to George for the stallion's injuries. To determine whether Rod was negligent, however, I will have to investigate how the accident occurred.

D. Veterinarian

The veterinarian also will sue on the theory of strict liability. We can defend that action on the basis of assumption of the risk. Our defense will succeed if George told the vet that the horse had not been trained to overcome its fear of humans. Even if George did not warn the vet, we can argue that she knew of the danger and appreciated its magnitude if she knew George's business or could tell based on her training that the wounded horse was dangerous. Because veterinarians generally assume the risk with respect to the animals they treat, we should prevail on this argument.

*

INDEX

References are to Pages

CONTRACT LAW
Course content, 58–59
Sample exam questions and answers

COURSE OUTLINES
See Outlines

COURSE SELECTION
See Curriculum

COURTS
Court of equity, 20–21
See also Chancery
Modern relevance, 21
Courts of law, 19–20
Decision-making, 18–20
Federal court system
Article III courts, 25
Circuit courts of appeal, 26–28
District courts, 25–26
Specialized courts, 28
Supreme Court, 28–29
History
American, 21–23
English, 19–21
Merger of courts of law and equity, 21
State court systems, 29–30

CRIMINAL LAW
Course content, 59–60
Sample exam questions and answers, 276–284

CRIMINAL PROCEDURE
Course content, 60–61

CURRICULUM
First-year courses, 53–66
Civil Procedure, 55–57
Constitutional Law, 57–58
Contracts, 58–59
Criminal Law, 59–60
Criminal Procedure, 60–61
Legal Research and Legal Writing, 61–62
Legislation, 61–62
Property, 62–64
Torts, 64
Upperclass

†